Living Our Language

NATIVE ✢ VOICES

Native peoples telling their stories, writing their history

Living Our Language

Ojibwe Tales & Oral Histories

Edited by
ANTON TREUER

MINNESOTA HISTORICAL SOCIETY PRESS

ST. PAUL

Native Voices

Native peoples telling their stories,
writing their history

*To embody the principles set forth by the series, all
Native Voices books are emblazoned with a bird
glyph adapted from the Jeffers Petroglyph
site in southern Minnesota. The rock art there
represents one of the first recorded voices
of Native Americans in the Upper Midwest.
This symbol stands as a reminder of the enduring
presence of Native Voices on the American
landscape.*

Publication of Native Voices
is supported in part by a grant
from The St. Paul Companies.

www.mnhs.org/mhspress

Manufactured in the
United States of America

10 9 8 7 6 5 4 3 2 1

♾ The paper used in this publication meets
the minimum requirements of the American National Standard for Information
Sciences—Permanence for Printed Library
materials, ANSI Z39.48-1984

International Standard Book Number
0-87351-403-3 (cloth)
0-87351-404-1 (paper)

*Library of Congress
Cataloging-in-Publication Data*

Living our Language : Ojibwe tales and oral
histories / edited by Anton Treuer.
   p. cm. — (Native voices)
ISBN 0-87351-403-3 (cloth : alk. paper) —
ISBN 0-87351-404-1 (pbk. : alk. paper)
   1. Ojibwa Indians—History.
   2. Ojibwa Indians—Folklore.
   3. Ojibwa Indians—Social life and cus-
      toms.
   4. Ojibwa language—Texts.
   I. Treuer, Anton.
   II. Series.

E99.C6 L535 2001
977'.004973—dc21
                          00-067562

Picture credits
Archie Mosay (1991) and Anton Treuer
(2000), photos © Greg Gent; Jim Clark
(2001) and Melvin Eagle (2001), photos by
Anton Treuer; Joe Auginaush (1974), photo
courtesy of Gertrude Auginaush; Collins
Oakgrove (1996), photo by Minnie Oakgrove; Emma Fisher (1992), Scott Headbird
(1992), and Porky White (2000), photos by
Aaron Fairbanks; Susan Jackson (2000),
photo by Beth Collins, courtesy of Leech
Lake Heritage Sites; Hartley White (1985),
photo by Terri LaDuke, courtesy of *Di-Bah-
Ji-Mon Newspaper*

Living Our Language

Living Our Language

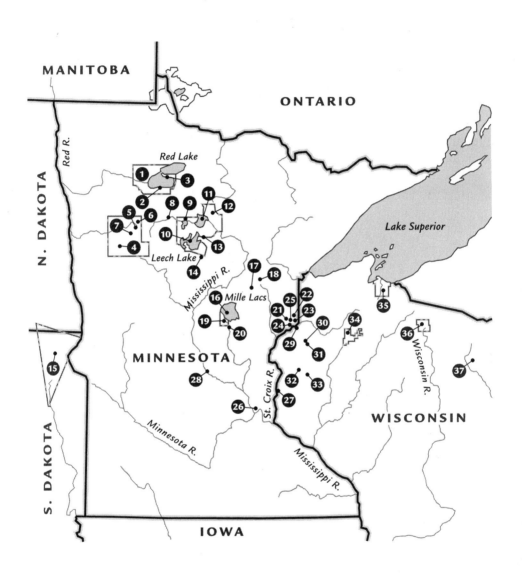

MANITOBA

ONTARIO

N. DAKOTA

Red R.

Red Lake

① ③
② ⑧ ⑨ ⑪
⑤ ⑥ ⑫
⑦ ⑩
④ ⑬
Leech Lake
⑭

Lake Superior

Mississippi R.

⑰
⑱

⑯ Mille Lacs

⑮

MINNESOTA

⑲
⑳

⑤
②②
②⑤
②①
②③
②④
③⓪
②⑨
③①

③④

③⑤

③⑥

Wisconsin R.

③⑦

②⑧

③②
③③

②⑥
②⑦

St. Croix R.

WISCONSIN

Minnesota R.

Mississippi R.

S. DAKOTA

IOWA

LEGEND

We're Not Losing Our Language

"WE'RE NOT LOSING OUR LANGUAGE, OUR LANGUAGE IS LOSING US," says White Earth elder Joe Auginaush. I have been both haunted and driven by that thought for many years now. The current peril faced by the Ojibwe (Chippewa) language is a matter of a declining number of speakers and a people who have lost their way, rather than a language that is lost or dying. The Ojibwe language, spoken by as many as 60,000 Anishinaabe people in Michigan, Wisconsin, Minnesota, North Dakota, Quebec, Ontario, Manitoba, and Saskatchewan, is alive.[1] The grammar, syntax, and structure of the language are complete. The oral tradition and history of the Ojibwe are still with us. Yet in many areas fluency rates have plummeted to unprecedented and unsustainable levels. Especially in the United States, most speakers are more than forty-five years of age.[2] In some places, the fluency rate is as low as one percent.[3] As the population of fluent speakers ages and eventually leaves, there is no doubt that the Ojibwe language will lose its carriers. We are not losing our language. Our language is losing us.

A battle now rages to keep Ojibwe alive. At stake is the future of not only the language, but the knowledge contained within the language, the unique Ojibwe worldview and way of thinking, the Anishinaabe connection to the past, to the earth, and to the future. In recent years, educational initiatives have been implemented at every level of the curriculum. Elders, such as those whose stories are collected in this book, have made extra efforts to teach and to be heard. Young Anishinaabe people have been making extra efforts to listen and to learn. It is the hope and prayer of all those involved in creating this book that these recent efforts will not be too little, too late. "We are not losing our language" is a statement of fact. "We are not losing our language" is a battle cry. "We are not losing our language" is a promise to all who care about the Ojibwe language, a promise that it will not die. Culture and language are inextricably linked, and all of the stories in this volume echo this belief in one way or another. It is my hope that this collection of bilingual Ojibwe stories can help to turn the tide of that battle as well as educate readers about Ojibwe history, culture, and humor.

Over the past several years, I recorded numerous Ojibwe elders from my home community of Leech Lake and the neighboring reservations of White Earth, Red Lake, and Mille Lacs. I also came under the cultural tutelage of Archie Mosay, an elder from the St. Croix Reservation of Wisconsin, and recorded some of his stories as well. I never recorded any sacred legends, which are strictly taught through oral instruction only. However, the narrations of childhood memories and Ojibwe lifeways tell a great deal about how Ojibwe people lived, thought, and persevered during the tumultuous twentieth century.

This anthology is rich and varied. Not only do the assorted speakers have different ways of speaking Ojibwe, they also have very different experiences and philosophies about *anishinaabe-izhichigewin*—the Indian culture—and *anishinaabemowin*—the Ojibwe language. The stories are vividly detailed, and often the speakers paint a verbal canvas of Ojibwe living: maple sugar camps, ricing, spearing fish, and religious ceremonies. A picture of early-twentieth-century life comes alive in the tellings of these gifted orators—whether it is Susan Jackson's explanations of rabbit snaring at Inger on the Leech Lake Reservation or Archie Mosay's description of the tall pine forests of the 1910s, where lack of undergrowth left a silent carpet upon which he could approach whitetailed deer. The history revealed in these stories is of great importance as well, and historical narrations about everything from Ojibwe-Dakota warfare to boarding schools and military experience during the Second World War abound. Indeed, when Porky White remembers his namesake, a Civil War veteran, it becomes strikingly clear just how much has changed in a very short time for the Ojibwe.

The serious narratives about culture and history are great fun to read, as they are interwoven with a thread of humor. Examples of comic recollections include the image of Archie Mosay, a full-grown man and father, fearfully running off the footpath and hiding in the brush the first time he saw an automobile, as well as his stories about the first time he saw a black man and the devilish tricks he played on people while hunting. Other speakers describe their misbehavior as children with enthusiasm and detail, whether is it Emma Fisher siccing her dogs on her uncle or Porky White explaining that he was nicknamed "Porky" because he followed around an elder man who looked like a porcupine. And, at times, the stories presented have the sole purpose of entertainment, whether it is Scott Headbird telling about two Red Lake Indians who got a mouse inebriated or Joe Auginaush describing Wenabozho playing baseball at Rice Lake. The narrations contain a breadth of character and detail that covers every experience, from the fun and folly of youth to the wisdom and deep-thinking philosophy of old age.

The Ojibwe of Minnesota

From their original homelands on the Atlantic Coast of the United States, the Ojibwe and other Algonquian tribes had been migrating westward for centuries before European contact. The spiritual and economic rationales for this radical change in demographics are still well documented in the oral tradition of the Ojibwe people.[4] By the time French explorers first penetrated the central Great Lakes in the middle of the seventeenth century, the Ojibwe had already established numerous villages west of Sault Ste. Marie.

The fur trade was to change Ojibwe life forever. As Dutch and then British empires sparred with the French for control of the beaver trade and first rights to colonization, their actions sparked both declines in the populations of fur-bearing animals due to over-trapping and the Iroquois Wars that dominated the latter half of the seventeenth century.[5] The French-supported Ojibwe and their allies, the Ottawa and the Potowatomi, eventually emerged victorious in their conflict with the British-allied Iroquois Confederacy. However, European diseases, particularly smallpox, had a devastating effect on native populations in the Great Lakes during this period, claiming over ninety percent of the Indian lives in some villages.

The Ojibwe did rebound from the debilitating effects of the Iroquois Wars and European diseases, and, contrary to conventional thought, they expanded their territorial domain and population over the next one hundred years. The Ojibwe displaced many of their western Indian neighbors, the Dakota and the Nakota.[6] However, the western Lakota had been expanding westward through this period as well, displacing other Indian groups on the plains. Standard models for studying Indian history do not adequately describe the process of Ojibwe and Lakota expansion in the eighteenth century. Both groups were being *pulled* to the west far more than they were being *pushed* from the east.[7] By 1800, the Ojibwe had exclusive control over the northern half of Minnesota. The Red Lake and Pembina Bands of Ojibwe continued to push on to the Great Plains over the next fifty years, eventually establishing new communities, with their new allies the Cree and the Assiniboin, at Turtle Mountain, North Dakota, and Rocky Boy, Montana.

Tensions between the Ojibwe and the Dakota in Minnesota eased some in the early nineteenth century. There were numerous battles, but the scale of the conflict had greatly diminished and significant territorial changes were now a thing of the past. Both groups had to contend with a new aggressor: the United States of America.

The Minnesota Ojibwe's eventual dispossession of their land was piecemeal, as treaties were negotiated in 1837, 1847, 1854, 1855, 1863, 1864, 1866, and 1867. After treaty-making in the United States came to a close, the Nelson Act of 1889 established the Red Lake Reservation, including large land cessions from Red Lake and White Earth. Additional land cessions were made at Red Lake in 1904.

The remaining Indian reservation landholdings in Minnesota came under assault through the policy of allotment, established by the General Allotment Act of 1887, also known as the Dawes Act. Two years later, the Nelson Act of 1889 implemented allotment for all Minnesota Ojibwe except for those at Red Lake.[8] Allotment was utilized to break up reservations. Through this policy, tribal governments would no longer own land (except at Red Lake) and each individual Indian would receive a parcel in private ownership. In spite of a twenty-five-year trust period prohibiting the sale of Indian allotments, many allotments were illegally sold or stolen. Timber and land speculators preyed on Indian allottees, with devastating effects. Some reservations, such as White Earth, emerged with less than ten percent of their reservation in Indian hands. Government officials found ways to circumvent protections in the Dawes or Nelson Acts with riders to appropriation bills and amendments to the trust period for mixed blood and "competent" Indians.[9] Allotment was not implemented at Mille Lacs until 1926 in order to encourage Indians there to relocate and take allotments at White Earth. By the time allotment was implemented at Mille Lacs, however, there were only 284 Ojibwe left and the remaining land base for allotment was very small.[10]

The Indian Reorganization Act (IRA) of 1934 opened the door to stronger tribal sovereignty for the Minnesota Ojibwe, as reservation governments organized and displaced the unwelcome Bureau of Indian Affairs, which had managed the day-to-day affairs on reservations. There were problems with the IRA, as it lumped together the previously separate Ojibwe communities of Sandy Lake, East Lake, Lake Lena, Isle, and Mille Lacs under the rubric of one reservation, leaving many Indians from the district of East Lake in particular feeling disempowered and not properly represented.[11] The IRA also included in the Minnesota Chippewa Tribe all Ojibwe reservations except for Red Lake. This joint governing and funding authority increased communication between reservations and coordinated many programs but made constitutional reforms and major changes in political structure nearly impossible, hampering efforts at constitutional reform by Leech Lake and White Earth residents even today.

From the late nineteenth century until the close of World War II, numerous Ojibwe children were taken from their homes and sent to government boarding schools, where they were often beaten for speaking the Ojibwe language. The effects of this forced assimilation were particularly damaging to long-term language retention for Ojibwe communities, creating a permanent break in language instruction for many families. Those who regained the language after boarding school often did not teach the language to their children. As a result, most Minnesota Ojibwe communities today have fluency rates of ten percent or less, with the vast majority of speakers being forty-five or more years of age.[12]

In spite of the devastating effects of dispossession and assimilation policies, the Ojibwe still maintain a vibrant culture and a strong, unbroken religious tradition. The base of speakers was surely in decline, but the Big Drum Ceremonials and Medicine Dance have continued to be practiced. Today, those ceremonies are experiencing revitalization as numerous young Ojibwe people attempt to regain contact with ancient history and culture. In many ways Ojibwe tradition lives on, although fluency in Ojibwe is a requirement for anyone telling funeral legends or conducting a Medicine Dance. Ojibwe culture is intact, but it is affixed by very thin threads.

The waxing power of tribal governments and the upsurge of interest in traditional culture has sparked new hope for the language in recent years. Casinos provide a much-needed income stream for Ojibwe communities, and many tribes have put the money to good use, building Big Drum dance halls and funding language programs. Among these communities there is hope for a revitalization of Ojibwe language and culture. Without doubt, it is in the spirit of revitalization that the speakers represented here have chosen to share their knowledge.

The Journey: From Meeting Speakers to Pursuing Publication

When I first began recording Ojibwe speakers and transcribing their stories, I didn't think about publishing them. I simply wanted to preserve the language of some of my family members and community elders for myself. I was interested in working with people close to me who spoke the same dialect of Ojibwe. Thus, my first contacts were primarily Leech

Lake elders—Scott Headbird, Emma Fisher, and Walter "Porky" White. A few years later, I also recorded Leech Lake elders Hartley White and Susan Jackson.

As I continued to collect language material, I came to understand more and more how precious that material was and how useful it would be for anyone interested in Ojibwe language and culture. Earl Otchingwanigan (formerly Nyholm) and Kent Smith, both of whom worked at Bemidji State University, encouraged me to assume the position of editor for the *Oshkaabewis Native Journal*, an Ojibwe language publication produced by Bemidji State University Indian Studies. In speaking with the elders I had been recording, I decided that it wouldn't be fair for me to keep their stories to myself. Many of the elders recorded stories for the expressed purpose of sharing them with me and with anyone else who would listen. To further their goal, I began to publish some of those stories in monolingual Ojibwe transcription and, later, with English translation as well. As the journal's circulation grew, I began to record other Ojibwe elders, including several from communities with significantly different dialects. I eventually worked with people from all of the major Minnesotan Ojibwe dialects, including a number of people from the Red Lake community of Ponemah, Mille Lacs and communities along the St. Croix border region, and especially the late Archie Mosay of Balsam Lake, Wisconsin. I also visited with several elders from White Earth and established a good friendship with Joe Auginaush through those visits. There aren't enough speakers in this book to represent each Ojibwe community in Minnesota, but most dialects of Southwestern Ojibwe are well represented. The stories in this book are organized by speaker, with an introduction detailing the life and background of each teller preceding his or her stories.

From Oral Tradition to Written Text: Recording, Transcribing, and Translating

Oral tradition is meant to be handed down through the spoken word. Maintaining strong oral traditions is a top priority for the survival of Ojibwe language and culture. This book is not intended to substitute written stories for oral tradition or spoken language. Rather, it is a tool that language students and teachers can use to augment their spoken instruction and recorded tapes. Textualizing the language is a necessary step to developing an Ojibwe language literature, allowing us both to preserve the language and to teach it. Furthermore, in producing books like this one, the contributing elders can reach Ojibwe people in urban areas and other communities they would not otherwise be able to reach. The written text before you is meant to assist in the preservation of spoken Ojibwe and the oral tradition. It never could nor should replace any part of the vocalized word or its usage.

Over the past several years, I have visited numerous Ojibwe elders from Minnesota and Wisconsin as a part of my efforts to learn more about Ojibwe language and culture, as well as for the simple joys of visiting. Eventually, I recorded some of those elders on cassette. Usually, we would sit at their kitchen tables, or sometimes in their living rooms. I only recorded elders when they were both willing to participate and comfortable with the idea. Sometimes I recorded stories at language camps or other events, but for the most part recordings took place in the speakers' homes.

After recording the stories, I brought the tapes to my home near Cass Lake, Minnesota, and went to work transcribing them. Some of the transcriptions were completed while I was traveling or working in Milwaukee. It sometimes took me weeks to transcribe a story. When transcriptions were ready, I translated the stories. When there were words I didn't know or parts of the original recording I didn't fully understand, I noted the places for my next visit. When transcription and translation for a story or set of stories were complete, I would then visit the elder again and clarify any questions I had in transcription or translation. I then read stories back to the speakers for proofing. Although there were often minor changes, the written versions correspond very closely to those recorded on the cassette tapes.

Many of the stories collected here were published in the *Oshkaabewis Native Journal* with the original cassette. *The Oshkaabewis Native Journal* (*ONJ*) is the only academic journal of the Ojibwe language. It includes numerous stories and articles about linguistics and language acquisition. Many of the stories published in *ONJ* were also proofread by Earl Otchingwanigan.

I decided to present these stories in the double vowel orthography for a number of reasons. The double vowel system was developed in the early 1950s by C.E. Fiero and, over the past thirty years especially, has come to be the most frequently used system for writing Ojibwe in the United States. It is important to maintain orthographic consistency throughout the primary and secondary school systems, as having to learn different writing systems every time a student transfers can be frustrating and intimidating, not to mention stifling to the learning process.

The double vowel system is the most widely used orthography, but certainly not the only one. Some speakers use "folk phonetics," meaning that they write romanized spellings of Ojibwe words based on "how they sound," with very little consistency or thought given to the nature of the writing system. Other speakers, especially those in Canada, use a system called "syllabics," which has had a unique application in Algonquian languages and was developed almost one hundred years before the double vowel system.[13] The problem with the syllabic orthography is that the symbols it uses are not found in any roman alphabet, forcing second language learners to study a separate set of symbols as well as a new language, pronunciation, and grammar system. The double vowel system is well designed, easy to use, consistent, and accessible to all students of the language.[14] For a detailed description of the system, see John Nichols and Earl Otchingwanigan (Nyholm), *A Concise Dictionary of Minnesota Ojibwe*.[15]

The editing process is quite long and technical, and I have elected not to include editorial or textual notes in this book. Such editorial apparatus takes up a good deal of space and is not consulted frequently. However, all handwritten transcription notes, editorial notes, drafts, and original Ojibwe recordings have been archived at the Minnesota Historical Society. They are available for public use by those interested in the transcription and editorial process and by those interested in listening to and using the cassette tapes. Many of the recordings have been published through the *Oshkaabewis Native Journal* and are still in print.[16]

Acknowledgments

This work and the process of creating it were fundamentally shaped by many people. This book was created by and is owned by the speakers who tell its stories. I am personally indebted to each one of them for their generosity and kindness in opening up to me and allowing their stories to be recorded. *Miigwech* Archie Mosay, Jim Clark, Melvin Eagle, Joe Auginaush, Collins Oakgrove, Emma Fisher, Scott Headbird, Susan Jackson, Hartley White, and Porky White.

Many people assisted with my transcription and editing work. Several stories were proofread by Earl Otchingwanigan and John Nichols. *Miigwech* for your assistance and invaluable contributions. Thanks to

Dick Barber, Connie Rivard, Betsy Schultz, and Dora Ammann for help in glossing certain words and place names. *Miigwech* also to Louise Erdrich, who recorded many of Jim Clark's stories, and to Paul DeMain, who recorded one of Archie Mosay's stories. Your efforts and concern for the Ojibwe language have done much to bring this work to fruition. Many thanks to Shannon Pennefeather, Greg Britton, Ann Regan, and the editorial staff at MHS for your faith in and attention to this work. At times the laughter of many people can be heard on the tapes. I hope these written transcriptions can do the tellings justice. Thanks to Susie Headbird, Dora Ammann, Brooke Ammann, Veronica Hvezda, Henry Flocken, David Treuer, Madeline Treuer, Sean Fahrlander, Keller Paap, and Sheila LaFriniere for sharing in the fun.

I received three grants to buy recording equipment and to travel to record the stories in this book. *Miigwech* to the Leech Lake Reservation Tribal Council, the Committee on Institutional Cooperation, and the Minnesota Historical Society for their support of this endeavor.

The process of recording, transcribing, and translating these stories has been paralleled by a personal spiritual journey for me. I was profoundly moved, motivated, and guided by many people. I especially want to thank Archie Mosay, Tom Stillday, and Earl Otchingwanigan, who devoted so much of their precious time and boundless wisdom to my endeavors. *Miigwech* for your patience, wisdom, and support. Thanks also to my parents Robert Treuer and Margaret Treuer, my siblings Megan, Micah, and David, my daughter Madeline, my ex-wife Sheila LaFriniere, and my dear friends James Hardy, Adrian Liberty, Henry Flocken, Sean Fahrlander, Mike Montano, Jay Saros, Dan and Dennis Jones, Isadore Toulouse, Keller Paap, Lisa LaRange, and Shannon White for supporting me and my endeavors without question. Without their guidance and faith, this project and my personal journey would not have come nearly so far.

Notes

1. As cited in census data taken from http://www.dickshovel.com and John Nichols, "Ojibwa Language," in Frederick Hoxie, *Encyclopedia of North American Indians* (Boston: Houghton Mifflin, 1996), 440–41.

2. Mary Losure, "Saving Ojibwe." National Public Radio: December 26, 1996.

3. Sweetgrass First Nations Language Council, "Sample of Fluent Native Speakers in Southern Ontario," *Aboriginal Languages Development in Southern Ontario: Interim Report*, October 1994; Joe Chosa, interview, 1997.

4. There have been some attempts to textualize oral versions of Ojibwe migration. See William Warren, *History of the Ojibway People* (St. Paul: Minnesota Histori-

cal Society Press, 1985) and Edward Benton, *The Mishoomis Book* (Hayward: Indian Country Communications, 1988).

5. For a good overview of the Iroquois Wars, see Helen Tanner, *Atlas of Great Lakes Indian History* (Norman: University of Oklahoma Press, 1987).

6. The Dakota, Nakota, and Lakota have often been collectively called the Sioux. They are very closely related in terms of language and culture, although they did not function as one group or political entity during this period. The word "Sioux" is a corruption of the Ojibwe word *naadowesiwag*, meaning "snakes," in reference to them as an enemy.

7. Anton Treuer, "Ojibwe-Dakota Relations: Diplomacy, War and Social Union, 1679–1862" (master's thesis, University of Minnesota, 1994); Richard White, "The Winning of the West: The Expansion of the Western Sioux in the Eighteenth and Nineteenth Centuries," *Journal of American History* 65.2 (1978): 319–43.

8. The Nelson Act mandated that the Ojibwe people consent to allotment. For most Ojibwe communities, treaties had already stripped away most of the primary land base, so they didn't have any leverage with which to bargain. At Red Lake, however, the entire land base was unceded. Commissioners seeking consent for allotment in Minnesota found that asking those at Red Lake to give up their primary land base and have the remainder alloted was simply too much to ask. Thus, commissioners succeeded in securing land cession from Red Lake but not allotment.

9. See the Morris Act of 1902, Clapp Rider of 1904, Clapp Rider of 1906, and Burke Act of 1906 in particular, discussed in Melissa L. Meyer, *The White Earth Tragedy: Ethnicity and Dispossession at a Minnesota Anishinaabe Reservation, 1889–1920* (Lincoln: University of Nebraska Press, 1994).

10. Maude Kegg, *Portage Lake: Memories of an Ojibwe Childhood* (Edmonton: University of Alberta Press, 1991), ix.

11. Although this sentiment is well known, my understanding of this political division at Mille Lacs was developed by several conversations I had with David Aubid of Sandy Lake.

12. Anton Treuer, "The Importance of Language: A Closer Look," *Oshkaabewis Native Journal* (Bemidji State University) 4 (Spring 1997): 3–11.

13. Inuktitut uses a syllabic writing system, although it is different from the one employed for Ojibwe and Cree.

14. Anton Treuer, "New Directions in Ojibwe Language Study," *Oshkaabewis Native Journal* (Bemidji State University) 2 (Spring 1995): 3–6.

15. John Nichols and Earl Otchingwanigan (Nyholm), *A Concise Dictionary of Minnesota Ojibwe* (Minneapolis: University of Minnesota Press, 1995).

16. To order tapes of the available recordings, write to *Oshkaabewis Native Journal*, P.O. Box 1003, Bemidji, MN 56619, or call (218) 755-3977.

Inaandagokaag
Balsam Lake
(St. Croix)

ARCHIE MOSAY

ARCHIE MOSAY (1901-1996), whose Indian name was *Niibaa-giizhig* (Sleeping Sky or Evening Sky), was a man whose influence transcended his many titles.[1] Medicine man, *Midewakiwenzii*, Chief, Boss, Healer, Speaker, Religious Leader, Spiritual Advisor, Grandpa, Dad, Friend: he was all of these things and many more. The 1,200 people who paid their respects at his funeral represent a mere fraction of the lives he touched so deeply.[2]

Archie Mosay's parents did not send him to school after the second grade, choosing instead to keep him home and to instruct him in the art and rituals of traditional Indian religious leadership. This lack of education in the Western tradition enabled him to learn more about Ojibwe culture than most of his peers.

Born in a *wiigiwaam* on August 20, 1901, near Balsam Lake, Wisconsin, Archie was raised in a traditional Indian community.[3] He was known only by his Indian name. The name "Archie" was given to him as a teenager when he went to work as a farm hand. The white wife of his employer was shocked to learn that he had no English name. When he returned to the farmhouse for lunch one day, she told him, "I have a name for you—'Archie.'" *Niibaa-giizhig* liked his new name and carried it with pride throughout the rest of his years.

Life was filled with hardships for Archie's family during his youth. In 1918 a flu epidemic ravaged the Ojibwe communities along the St. Croix River, taking Archie's maternal grandmother and his two siblings in one night. Archie's first wife and first child died of tuberculosis. In spite of these sorrows, Archie rebounded, remarried, and fathered eight more children.

Like his father and grandfather before him, Archie was instructed not only in ancient Ojibwe lifeways, but also in the complicated rituals of ceremonial leadership. At the age of twelve, he became *Oshkaabewis* (Messenger) in the *Midewiwin* (Medicine Lodge). In this position, he began to learn the complicated procedures and detailed legends essential to the ceremonies he would conduct later in his life. A skilled medicine man, Archie knew hundreds of plants and trees used for different types of healing, and he eagerly shared this wisdom with his children. He knew many ancient secrets for hunting and fishing, including the elaborate rituals of bear hunting. He was also well acquainted with the art of making bows and traditional Ojibwe birch-bark canoes.

When Archie's father, Mike Mosay, died in 1971 at the age of 102, the communities of Round Lake and Balsam Lake were in a quandary as to how best to fill the vacuum left by his death. Mike Mosay had been the

Grand Chief of the St. Croix Band and a central spiritual leader of his people. For a few years, the Medicine Dance was not conducted, as the people adjusted to the loss of their ceremonial chief.

In the early 1970s, an Ojibwe man from Round Lake approached Archie, offered him tobacco, and told him that his daughter would die if she could not be initiated into the *Midewiwin*. He begged Archie to help his girl, and eventually Archie acquiesced. Archie healed the man's daughter and revived his father's *Midewiwin*. From that point on, Archie assumed his father's role in presiding over the Medicine Dance and speaking at Big Drum Ceremonies. Initially, John Stone of Lac Courte Oreilles and other Ojibwe spiritual leaders from Wisconsin and Minnesota helped Archie conduct his ceremonies. As time went on and other leaders died, Archie carried on the work alone, and increasing numbers of people traveled from other Ojibwe communities to participate in ceremonies at Round Lake and at Balsam Lake.

Shortly after his father's death, Archie also assumed the honored position of Grand Chief of the St. Croix Ojibwe. The position had been in the family for several generations, and Archie carried the feather war bonnet and 1789 United States peace medallion, which had been passed on through his father, as proud symbols of that title and position.[4]

In all of his spiritual work, Archie used his first language, the only language he knew until a teenager, and, according to him, the only language intended for Ojibwe prayer—*anishinaabemowin*, the Ojibwe language. One day, Archie stepped outside of his ceremonial Medicine Lodge to lecture his helpers, saying, "I can't use English in there. The Spirit doesn't understand me when I use English." This perspective also explains Archie's focus on the importance of keeping the Ojibwe language alive. Without the language, there is no *Midewiwin*, no Big Drum, no *Jiisakaan* (Shake Tent Ceremony). Without the Ojibwe language, there is no Ojibwe culture.

At various times Archie fed his family by hunting and fishing and by working as a groundskeeper at Balsam Lake resorts and as a mason and a rations plant worker during World War II. For the bulk of his working years—thirty-four to be exact—Archie worked for the Polk County Highway Department. However, as often happens with Indian elders, Archie in his retirement was more active than in his working years. His new work included counseling people recovering from alcohol addiction at the *Ain-Dah-Ing* (*Endaayang*) Half Way House in Spooner, Wisconsin. Throughout his ninety-four years on earth, Archie Mosay had never used alcohol, a practice to which he attributed his good health and long life. Traveling frequently to conduct various ceremonies and to speak at pow-wows and conferences, Archie became a true servant of the Spirit—working hard for his people until his last day on earth.

At age ninety-four, Archie was still independent, driving himself and living alone. His children looked after him, bringing food to his house and washing his clothes, but Archie lived his own life every day, never residing in a nursing home. He died in 1996.

Thousands of people approached Archie over the years—from his maternal grandmother's reservation, Lac Courte Oreilles, from his father's place of origin, Mille Lacs, and from many other places as well. Archie gave hundreds of people their Indian names. He initiated over a thousand people into the Medicine Lodge. He spoke at countless pipe ceremonies and Big Drum feasts.

Archie's stories collected here are rich and varied. Archie remembered the first time he saw a car and the first time he saw a black man. He remembered what it was like when his children were born in *wiigiwaams*.[5] He also recalled how Ojibwe people traveled long distances on foot to participate in the Medicine Dance at other communities. Frequently his family walked to Lac Courte Oreilles for this purpose, a one-way journey of three days on foot. His father journeyed by foot from Mille Lacs to Balsam Lake, six days round trip, in order to court Archie's mother. Archie also remembered hunting in the St. Croix River Valley's tall pine forests before logging decimated them—trees so large and canopies so dense that no other plant life grew on the forest floor and one could walk on the pine needles more quietly than on pavement. All these stories as well as several jokes and remembrances are included in this collection.

The stories presented here were usually recorded at the home of Archie Mosay.[6] Sometimes I would arrange special trips to visit Archie for this purpose. More often, we would record a few stories before or after a ceremonial event that had brought me to Balsam Lake, such as the naming ceremony for my daughter, a funeral, a drum ceremony, or a Medicine Dance. The story "Mii Sa Iw" was written down through dictation. All others were recorded and then transcribed. Archie died before the transcription work was complete. For this reason, the titles for all of the stories presented here are of my creation. They are usually derived from lines in the stories themselves, but they are not part of the oral tradition they label. They are used here for ease of reading and differentiating stories. In the process of translating stories and selecting titles, I consulted Archie's friends and family members as well as Ojibwe linguist Earl Otchingwanigan.

Usually, Archie selected the topics for discussion or the stories he wished to tell. Occasionally, one of his daughters or I would encourage him to share a story we had heard him tell before. In all cases, however, Archie, his daughter Dora Ammann, and I were careful to choose topics appropriate for recording and publication. No sacred legends from the *Midewiwin* were ever recorded. Archie always strictly maintained that those stories could only be learned in the Medicine Lodge itself and that they had to be passed on through oral tradition, without the aid of modern technology.

Archie's dialect of Ojibwe differs somewhat from that of most other speakers in this book. Although two of Archie's grandparents were from East Lake, his language was more heavily influenced by his grandmother from Lac Courte Oreilles and his grandfather from Balsam Lake. Thus, Archie uses *zaaga'egan* for "lake" where most speakers of Minnesota Ojibwe use *zaaga'igan*. In addition, *aniw* is used in place of *iniw*. Archie also seemed to prefer using the first to third person conjunct transitive animate verb paradigm *-agig* rather than *-agwaa*: for example, *waabam-agig* (when I see them) rather than *waabamagwaa* (when I see them). These forms are used by many speakers interchangeably, but the patterns of Archie's language usage and pronunciation are noteworthy. Archie and his contemporaries wanted all dialects of the Ojibwe language to survive. Differences are to be celebrated rather than denigrated.

Notes

1. This observation, held by many people, was eloquently written by David Hanners in "Spirit World Now Beckons to Legendary Tribal Leader," *St. Paul Pioneer Press*, August 2, 1996, 1B, 4B.

2. Paul DeMain, "Nebageshig is Laid to Rest," *News From Indian Country*, mid-September 1996, 7A.

3. The exact date of Archie Mosay's birth is not known. Archie and his children accepted the date of August 20, 1901. However, this is only their best guess. His exact place of birth is also unknown—whether in the woods or a *wiigiwaam*—although he was born somewhere in the vicinity of the Indian village of Inaandagokaag near present-day Balsam Lake, Wisconsin.

4. It is not clear if the peace medallion was originally given to Archie's paternal grandfather Shakopee of Mille Lacs or to a chief on his mother's side at St. Croix. The feather war bonnet appears to have come from Mille Lacs. The name "Shakopee" was adopted from the Dakota and was carried by a couple of prominent Ojibwe leaders as well as by Dakota people.

5. Wayne Mosay, his youngest child, was the only one of Archie's offspring to have been born in a hospital.

6. The *dibaajimowin* "Mii Gaa-pi-izhichigewaad Mewinzha" was originally recorded by Paul DeMain during an interview with Archie broadcast on Lac Courte Oreilles tribal radio station WOJB 88.9 FM of Reserve, Wisconsin, on April 10, 1996. He released reproduction rights for the recording with the permission of Archie's family.

Gaa-tazhi-ondaadiziyaang

[1] Akawe niwii-tibaajim o'ow gaa-izhiwebiziyaan o'ow isa gii-oshki-bimaadiziyaan. Gaawiin ingikendanziin aandi gaa-tazhi-ondaadiziyaan—gemaa gaye wiigiwaaming gaa-tazhi-ondaadiziwaanen gemaa gaye nisawa'ogaaning gemaa gaye iwidi ingoji megwekob gemaa gaye. Mii iwidi gaa-tazhi-ondaadiziwaambaanen.

[2] Baanimaa ashi-niiyo-biboonagiziyaan, mii apii waakaa'igaans noosiban gaa-ozhitood. Mii apii gii-ayaayaang. Ishkweyaang, mii apane wiigiwaaming ingii-taamin. Mii dash imaa gaa-tazhi-nitaawigiyaan imaa, imaa sa Inaandagokaag ezhinikaadeg. Mewinzha ingii-tazhi-ondaadiz. Ingitiziimag igaye imaa ginwenzh omaa gii-tanakiiwag, nayenzh igo.

[3] Noosiban, iwidi sa Misi-zaaga'iganiing ezhinikaadeg, mii iwidi gaa-tazhi-ondaadizid a'aw noosiban. Mii dash imaa, miish imaa midaaswi-ashi-zhaangaso-biboonagizid, mii imaa gii-wiidigemaad nimaamaayibanen. Miish omaa gii-ayaad biinish gii-maajaad. Miinawaa onow oniijaanisan gii-shaangachiwan oniijaanisan, ingitiziimag.

Mii Gaa-pi-izhichigewaad Mewinzha

[1] Boozhoo anishinaabedog! Akawe niwii-tibaajim o'ow isa ayindiyaan ishkweyaang gii-oshki-bimaadiziyaan. Gaawiin indaa-gikendanziin dibi gaa-tazhi-ondaadiziwaanen—gemaa gaye wiigiwaaming gemaa gaye nisawa'ogaaning gemaa gaye iwidi ingoji megwekob gemaa gaye. Mii iwidi gaa-tazhi-ondaadiziwaad aanind anishinaabeg ishkweyaang.

[2] Ganabaj gii-ashi-niiyo-biboonagiziyaan, mii bijiinag apii gaa-piindigeyaan ayi'ii waakaa'igaans indedeyiban gaa-ozhitood. Mii eta go wiigiwaaming gii-ayaayaang bebiboon. Miinawaa wa'aw ingitiziimag iwidi Odaawaa-zaaga'eganiing izhinikaadeg, mii iwidi nimaamaayiban gaa-tazhi-ondaadizid. Imaa o'ow, aya'aa Aanakwad ezhinikaazod anishinaabe, iwidi gaa-tanakiiwaad. Miish iwidi ingoji gaa-tazhi-ondaadiziwagobanen a'aw nimaamaayiban aya'aa Neweyaash akiwenzii gii-izhinikaazowan odedeyan. O'ow dash nimaamaa onaabeman gaa-wiidigemaajin ishkweyaang a'aw mindimooyenh gii-izhinikaazod.

Where We Were Born

[1] First of all, I am going to talk about what happened with me when I was young. I don't know where I was born—in a bark lodge, or maybe I was born in a lodge with a peaked roof, or maybe somewhere in the woods. That's where I must have been born.

[2] Later on, when I was fourteen years old, my father made a house. We stayed there at that time. Before that we had always lived in bark lodges. Then I was born there, there at Balsam Lake as it's called. I was born a long time ago. And both of my parents lived here for a long time.

[3] My father, he was born over there at Mille Lacs as it is called. Then, when he was nineteen years old, there he married my mother. Then he stayed here until he left [for the spirit world]. And my parents had nine children.

What They Did Long Ago

[1] Hello Indians! First of all I want to talk about how things were with me in former times when I was young. I can't know where I must have been born—in a bark lodge or a lodge with a peaked roof or somewhere out there in the bush. In former times some Indians were born out there.

[2] Maybe when I was fourteen, that was the first time I went inside a house my father had built. We had only been in bark lodges each winter. And this one of my parents, over there at Lac Courte Oreilles as it is called, my mother was born over there. There with that Indian named *Aanakwad*, they lived over there. Then over there somewhere they must have been born, my mother and the old man *Neweyaash* as her father was called. And my mother's husband she had married long ago, this old woman as she was called.

[3] Mayaajaanid sa onow onaabeman, miish imaa neyaab
Inaandagokaag gaa-pi-izhi-goziwaad. Mii dash imaa
gaa-tanakiiwaad, gaa-tazhi-gonaadizid a'aw nookomisiban,
nimaamaayiban igaye wiiba go gaawiin aapiji mewinzha
gaa-ako-bimaadizid. Miinawaa a'aw isa noosiban, iwidi
Misi-zaaga'eganiing ezhinikaadeg, mii imaa gaa-
tazhi-ondaadizid. Imaa dash Inaandagokaag, imaa
gii-wiidigemaad iniw nimaamaayibanen. Midaaswi-
ashi-zhaangaso-biboonagizid, mii apii imaa gaa-wiidigemaad
nimaamaayibanen.

[4] Mii dash gaye niin imaa gaa-onji-maajiishkaayaan
wendaadiziyaan. Waakaa'igaans ogii-ozhitoon imaa a'aw
noosiban. Mii imaa gii-ayaayaang.

[5] Gaye dash o'ow isa ziigwang, o'ow apiitak, mii apii mewinzha
anishinaabe gii-kozid noopiming izhi-gozi, gii-ozhitood
o'ow, o'ow isa ziinzibaakwad mitigong ininigaadeg
zhiiwaagamizigan. Mii gaa-ozhitoowaad. Mii iwidi gaa-
taawaad, gaawiin waasa—gemaa gaye naano-diba'igan o'ow
apii iwidi ingoji megwaayaak. Mii iwidi gaa-taawaad
iskigamizigewaad.

[6] Mii miinawaa ishkwaa-iskigamizigewaad, miish imaa
jiigibiig zaaga'eganiing Inaandagokaag, mii imaa
gii-kabeshiwaad. Noongom miinawaa imaa gii-kabeshiwag
gii-noojigiigoonyiwewaad waaswaawaad, ashiganan
aajigwaawaad. Mii imaa gaa-tanakiid wa'aw,
gaa-onji-bimaadizid a'aw anishinaabe mewinzha.

[7] Mii miinawaa giiwegoziwaad. Mii dash zhayiigwa
gii-ozhiitaawaad o'ow isa gii-midewid anishinaabe. Akina
ingoji gii-midewi aw anishinaabe—Odaawaa-zaaga'eganiing,
miinawaa a'aw Waaswaaganing, miinawaa Mashkii-ziibiing,
miinawaa iwidi Dewegishigamiing. Namanj ezhinikaadegwen
i'iw, anishinaabewinikaadeg iwidi ishkonigan. Miinawaa go
omaa ayi'iing gaye Wekonamindaawagaansing izhinikaadeg,
miinawaa iwidi Metaawangaag, Bikoganaaganing—mii imaa
gii-midewiwaad iko ingiw anishinaabeg mewinzha.

[8] Mii miinawaa ishkwaa-midewiwaad, mii dash miinawaa
gii-sagaswe'idiwaad o'ow baakibii'ang o'ow zaaga'eganiing;
gii-asemaakewaad onji-naanaagadawenimigoowaad manidoon
imaa wenjishkaawaaniwenijin.

[9] Mii miinawaa ishkwaa-zagaswe'idiwaad, mii dash miinawaa

[3] When her husband left [for the spirit world], then she
moved back there to Balsam Lake. Then they lived there,
my grandmother who had spent her entire life there and
my mother who had come to live there not so very long
ago. And my father, over there at Mille Lacs as it's called,
that's where he was born. And there at Balsam Lake, there
he married my mother. When he was nineteen years old, at
that time he married my mother there.

[4] And that's where my own life began when I was born.
My father built a house there. We were right there.

[5] And in the spring too, in the midst of this season, long
ago the Indian moved then, moving into the deep forest,
he made this here sugar from the trees, as the syrup was
handled in a certain way. That's how they made it. Over
there where they lived, it wasn't far—five miles out in the
woods somewhere. They lived over there when they sugared
off.

[6] Again when they're done sugaring off, then there on the
shore of Balsam Lake, that's where they set up camp. They
set up camp there again, at this time harvesting fish by
shining them, hauling in the largemouth bass. He lived
right there, that's how the Indian lived long ago.

[7] Then again the Indian moved home. Then already they
began preparations for when the Indian participated in
the medicine lodge. The Indian took part in the medicine
lodge everywhere—at Lac Courte Oreilles, again at Lac
du Flambeau, and at Bad River, and again over there at
Dewegishigamiing. I am not sure what it's called, what that
reservation over there is called in Indian. And here too at
Little Sand Lake (Maple Plain) as it's called, and again over
there at Big Sand Lake (Hertel), at Danbury—right there
those Indians customarily did the medicine dance long ago.

[8] And then when they finished the medicine dance, then
again they had a pipe ceremony when the ice went out on
this lake; they made tobacco offerings to the spirit to be
thought of there in what they were up against in their lives.

[9] Then again after they had the pipe ceremony, then again

ayiigwa o'ow isa gii-mawinzowaad onow editeg miinan,
miskominan, godagaagominan, o'ow isa gegoo editenig.
Mii i'iw gaa-mawinzowaad. Mii gaa-onji-bimaadizid a'aw
anishinaabe mewinzha, gaye niin bi-de-gikendamaan.
Mii dash i'iw.

[10] Miinawaa dagwaaginig, mii azhigwa gii-madaabiigoziwaad
o'ow isa gii-manoominikewaad, manoomin gii-bawa'amowaad.
Akawe gii-sagaswe'idiwag waa-manoominikewaad,
asemaakewag o'ow isa zaaga'eganiing gii-kaagiijitoowaad o'ow
isa manoomin wii-pawa'amowaad. Gaawiin awiiya gii-izhi-
boozisiin. Akawe asemaan ogii-pagidinaan nibiikaang.

[11] Miinawaa gii-kiizhitood a'aw anishinaabe manoomin, akawe
asemaan ogii-pagidinamawaan manidoon wii-izhi-miijisig i'iw
manoomin. Mii gaa-miijiwaad. Mii akeyaa gaa-pi-izhi-
waabamagig ingiw anishinaabeg ishkweyaang.

[12] Akina ingoji gii-izhaa gaye aw anishinaabe sa o'ow isa gii-paa-
midewid. Gaye iwidi Odaawaa-zaaga'eganiing izhinikaadeg
imaa Baatawigamaag, mii imaa gaa-tazhi-midewiwaad
mewinzha anishinaabeg. Ingoji gaa-izhi-bimoseyaang gii-o-
midewiyaang gii-nandomaakawaa noosiban o-wiidookaazod
owidi wiidookawaad akiwenziiyan gaa-midewiwinijin. Niso-
giizhigon ingii-tazhi-izhaamin gii-tagoshinaang. Mii akeyaa
gaa-izhichiged a'aw anishinaabe ishkweyaang gii-naazikang
o'ow isa gaa-onji-bimaadizid. Noongom gaawiin izhichigesiin
a'aw anishinaabe bi-naazikang bi-onji-bimaadizid. Gaye o'ow
midewiwin ogii-igoon a'aw manidoon, mii go gaa-ani-izhi-
maamawookang a'aw anishinaabe o'ow isa maanangid, o'ow
isa gii-onji-maajiishkaad mii gaa-ininang manidoo. Mii sa i'iw
gaa-izhichigewaad mewinzha ongow anishinaabeg,
gii-izhaawaad gegoo inakamigizid ingoji anishinaabe.

[13] Mii go gaye a'aw, a'aw isa dewe'igan gaa-pi-bagidinaajin a'aw
meyagwed anishinaabe omaa akeyaa. Iwidi mashkodeng
izhinikaadeg, mii iwidi gaa-onjiid a'aw meyagwed anishinaabe
imaa Neyaashiing Misi-zaaga'eganiing izhinikaadeg. Mii imaa
gii-pi-bagidinaad iniw dewe'iganan gaa-onji-maajiishkaanid
anishinaaben. Mii imaa gaa-pi-onji-bagidinaad. Mii dash
imaa gaa-onji-maajiishkaad aw anishinaabe. Gaye a'aw
meyagwed anishinaabe, o'ow isa gii-aasamigaabawi'aad
onow isa meyagwenijin chimookomaanan ogii-igoon

already they picked berries when they were ripe—the blueberries, the raspberries, the blackberries, whenever they ripened. That's how they harvested berries. That's how the Indian lived long ago, from the extent of what I've come to know of it myself. And that's it.

[10] Again in the fall, now they moved to the shores of the water to pick rice, knocking the rice. First of all they had a pipe ceremony when they wanted to pick rice, making tobacco offerings to this lake, tying up this rice they want to knock. Nobody embarked. First of all he offered tobacco in the waterways.

[11] And when that Indian finished the rice, first of all he offered tobacco to the spirit as he didn't want to eat that rice. Then they ate it. That's how I saw those Indians [do things] in former times.

[12] And all the Indian people went to different places when they participated in this medicine dance. And over there at the Lac Courte Oreilles reservation as it's called, there at Whitefish, right there the Indians held the medicine dance long ago. We walked everywhere to participate in the medicine dance as my father was summoned to go over and help out, assisting those old men who did the medicine dance. It took us three days to get there. That's how the Indian did things in former times when he approached where his life originated. Today the Indian doesn't do this when he goes to where his life comes from. And the spirit told him of this medicine dance, that he was to come to do that which he had been given together, that this was the reason his life started as the spirit handed it down to him. That's how these Indians did things long ago, when they went to where the Indian people did certain things.

[13] And this too, this Drum, was set down here by that strange speaking Indian [Dakota] in this direction. Over there on the prairies as they are called, it's over there that the strange speaking Indian came from to *Neyaashiing* there at Mille Lacs Lake as it's called. It's there that he put that Drum from which the Indian started his life. That's why he put it there. And that's why the Indian started it there. And that strange speaking Indian, as these strange speaking Indians stood before [the onslaught] of the white man, he

wii-chaaginanigod. Manidoo dash gaawiin ogii-
minwaabandanziin. Mii sa ji-gaawi'awiwid aabiding
inwed anishinaabe. Mii dash gaa-onji-niishimaad
manidoo naagaanizid onow dewe'iganan omaa noongom
enawiindamaagenijin.

[14]   Mii akeyaa gaa-izhichiged a'aw anishinaabe ishkweyaang.
O'ow isa gaye niin gii-te-gitenimag gii-waabamagig
gaa-izhichigewaad. Mii gaye niin imaa bangii wenji-
gikendamaan o'ow isa izhi-inaadamawag anishinaabe.
Gii-kikinoo'amawiwaad, mii a'aw Neweyaash akiwenzii
gaa-izhinikaazod nimishoomisiban, mii a'aw gaa-
waawiindamawid i'iw ge-ani-izhichigeyaan naadamawag
anishinaabe gegoo. Gaawiin indaa-inaasiin. Gaawiin
indaa-inaasiin gegoo gagwejimid. Mii eta go wiindamawag
gegoo gaye wii-kikendang.

[15]   Gaye onow izhinikaazowinan, anishinaabe-izhinikaazowinan,
mii o'ow i'iw isa gii-kii'igoshimoyaan mewinzha gii-
kwiiwizensiwiyaan. Mii imaa wendinamaan iniw, iniw isa
anishinaabe-izhinikaazowinan. Noongom gaawiin gwech
anishinaabe-izhinikaazowinan odayaanziinan. Mii i'iw
wanitoowaad i'iw. Akina sa go gegoo owanitoon anishinaabe
mewinzha gaa-pi-izhi-waabamagig.

[16]   Gaye onow wiigiwaaman, gabe-niibin ongow ikwewag gii-
ozhitoowaad onow, onow isa gaa-apishimowaajin anaakaning,
gaa-izhi-wiindamawaajin. Miinawaa onow megwaa abakwang
iniw wiigwaasan, mii apii gaa-mamoowaad gii-ozhitoowaad
iniw, iniw isa wiigwaasi-abakwayan. Miinawaa ingiw aya'aa
apakweshkweyag gii-iniibinaawaad ingoji ayi'ii wiigiwaaming.
Mii imaa gii-aabaji'aawaad iniw agidigamish iniw wiigwaasan
wiigwaasi-abakwayan. Mii akeyaa gaa-ozhitoowaad iniw, iniw
isa gii-abiwaad.

Wenabozho Gaa-kiishkigwebinaad Zhiishiiban

[1]   Wenabozho gii-pimosed bakade; gaa gegoo omiijisiin.
Maajiibadaabiid zaaga'egan owaabamaan zhiishiiban
gii-awi-bakaded omaa jiigibiig. Miish abezhig zhiishiib,
"Zhiishiibidog!" odinaan, "Wenabozho madaabii. Naawij
inaadagaag. Anooj izhiwebizi Wenabozho."

was told he would be used up, destroyed. But the spirit did not look favorably upon this. For once, he was thwarted as the Indian sounded his voice. And that's why the head spirit placed among him these Drums that are spoken of here today.

[14] This is how that Indian did things in former times. I have been impressed with [the Indian people] myself as I have seen them doing these things. That's why I know a little bit myself, which I use to help the Indian. That's how they taught me, that is to say my grandfather, the old man named *Neweyaash*. He is the one who told me what I would come to do in helping the Indian with certain things. I can't dictate to him. I can't just dictate something to him when he asks me. And I only tell him things he wants to know about.

[15] And these names, the Indian names, I fasted for them a long time ago when I was a boy. Out there is where I received them, those Indian names. Today not enough [Indian people] have Indian names. They are losing it. The Indian is losing everything I saw them [do] long ago.

[16] And these bark lodges, every spring these women made them, they laid the beds for them on the mats, the ones that have been talked about. And while the birch bark was being hung, at this time they took it and made them, those birch bark shingles. And they lined up those birch bark roofing rolls in a certain way on the lodges. They used those birch bark coverings there on top of the lodges. That's how they made the places they lived in.

When Wenabozho Decapitated the Ducks

[1] Wenabozho was hungry as he walked along; he hadn't eaten anything. When he started to come to the shore of the lake he sees the ducks, getting hungry here on the beach. Then a certain duck tells them, "My fellow ducks! Wenabozho is coming to the shore. Swim for the middle of the lake. Wenabozho is up to something."

[2]	Wenabozho onoondawaan zhiishiiban. "Gaawiin
nishiimeyidog! Imaa noopiming niwii-niimi'idiimin noongom
onaagoshig." Mii gaa-izhi-gopiid wiigiwaam imaa gaa-ozhitood
waagaashkang. Wiigiwaam imaa badakidenig. Mii
gaa-izhi-onapidood giboodiyegwaazonan, aasaakamig
gaa-kashkapidood omaa o'ow bimoondang.

[3]	Miish i'iw inaad zhiishiiban, "Nishiimenyidog!" Odizhi-
inaan, "Nishiimeyidog! Mii akeyaa bemoondamaan," ikido.
"Nagamonan onow bimoondamaanen. Owidi Mooniyaang
izhinikaadeg, mii iwidi wenjibaayaan. Miish omaa waa-onji-
niimi'idiiyaang noongom noopiming." "Apegish," gii-inendam
wii-nisaad iniw zhiishiiban, wii-amwaad bakaded.

[4]	Gaa-izhi-gopiiwaad iwidi, zhiishiibag o-niimi'idiiwaad,
biindigewaad imaa wiigiwaam. Megwaa oganoonaan,
"Nishiimeyidog! Inga-nagam. Nishiimeyidog,
bazangwaabishimok! Gego inaabikegon," odinaan
iniw zhiishiiban. "Omaa apii azhigwa maajiiyaan
nishiweyaan."

>	*Nishiimeyidogwen, gego inaabikegon*
>	*Giga-mamiskoshkiinzhigwem*
>	*Yo weh heh heh*
>	*Yo weh heh heh*

[5]	Mii aangodinong giishkigwebinaad iniw zhiishiiban, "kwenk,"
inwewan giiwenh. "Haa nishiimeyidog, mii go waa-inweyeg."
Nagamo, giishkigwebinaad. "Wenk."

[6]	Miish a'aw zhingibiz gaa-izhi-dooskaabamaad aaniin
ezhichiged. Awenesh ingiw gaa-kiishkigwebinaawaad
iniw zhiishiiban? Mii gaa-izhi-biibaagimaad zhiishiiban,
"*Hey* zhiishiibidog! Gidishkwamigonaan Wenabozho.
Giga-abwaanigonaan." Aabita-zaagiziba'idiwaad ingiw
zhiishiibag. Mii go giiwenh iniw zhingibizan gaa-waagaawinid
omadaabiiba'igoon ini-daangishkawaad. Miish i'iw gaa-inaad,
"Oon gidizhi-maajiikamigoog. Gaawiin a'aw iwidi, a'aw
anishinaabe, giga-amwigosiin," ogii-inaan zhingibizan.
"Giga-mamiskoshkiinzhigwe gaye," ogii-inaan. Mii wenji-
mamiskoshkiinzhigwed a'aw zhingibiz.

[7]	Mii gaa-izhi-ayaad Wenabozho.

[2] Wenabozho hears the ducks. "No my little brothers! We are going to have a pow-wow this evening there in the forest." Then he went inland, making an arbor there, bending it to shape. The arbor was planted in the ground there. Then he tied a pair of pants in place like this, bundling up some moss here and carrying this off on his back.

[3] Then he tells those ducks this, "My little brothers!" He tells them like so, "My little brothers! I'm carrying it this way," he says. "I'm carrying these on my back for the [give-away] songs. Over here at Montreal as it's called, I'm from over there. That's why we are going to have a pow-wow here in the forest today." "I hope," he thinks, as he wants to kill those ducks, wants to eat them as he's hungry.

[4] As they went inland over there, the ducks went over and danced, entering the arbor there. In the midst of it he talks to them, "My little brothers! I am going to sing. My little brothers, dance with your eyes closed! Don't peek," he tells those ducks. "Here at this time now I am starting the slaughter."

> *My little brothers, don't peek*
> *Your eyes will turn red*
> *Yo weh heh heh*
> *Yo weh heh heh*

[5] From time to time he decapitated those ducks by wringing their necks, and, as the story goes, they called out, "kwenk." "Ha my little brothers, that's how you want to sound." He sings, wringing their heads off, "Wenk."

[6] Then that helldiver opened his eyes to see what he [Wenabozho] was doing. Who had twisted the heads off the ducks? Then he called out to the ducks, "Hey my fellow ducks! Wenabozho is piling up our corpses. He's going to roast us over a fire." Those ducks are halfway out the door. Then, as the story goes, that helldiver is running away from him to the shore as [Wenabozho] kicked him, hunching up his back. Then he told him this, "Oh they'll work on you like this. That one over there, that Indian, he isn't going to eat you," he told that helldiver. "And your eyes will turn red," he told him. That's why that helldiver's eyes turned red.

[7] That's how Wenabozho was.

[8] Mii gaa-maajaad, apii ziibiwan madaabii, bimoomaad
zhiishiiban gaa-kiishkigwebinaajin, iidog iwidi waabandang
wii-abwed iniw zhiishiiban. Imaa naa akawe gii-kiizhiitaad
gii-nibaa aapiji giizizwaad onow zhiishiiban. Mii dash o'ow
gii-nibaad.

[9] Mii dash awedig, ongow akandoowaagwen, "Akawaabin,"
iniw gaa-inaajimaad, "inaabin." Bwaanag ongow boonowag.
"Wiindamawishin awiiya biidaaboonod." Namanj apii
nibaagobanen. Mii wiin waabamaawaad omaa bashkinedenig
bwaanag. "Mii a'aw Wenabozho," ikidowag. "Gegoo omaa
odayaan." Miish iniw miskwaanziganan wewebinamowaad,
mii niigaan wiindamawaasig iniw akandoowaajin, akina
gaa-izhi-mamoonid iniw abwaadang maajaanid.

[10] Omaa apii wiin gaye gweshkozid, a'aw mewinzha iidog igo
minozogoban, onishkaad inaabid Wenabozho bangii
odabwaan gii-mamoonid, mamigod iniw bwaanan. Mii dash
ayi'ii gaa-izhi-nishkaadizid. Mii gaa-izhi-jaagizodizod, omaa
apii maajaad. Mii dash o'ow gii-chaagizod, gizhiibazhed
giiwenh omigiid. Mii dash onow mitigoonsan gaa-ani-
izhi-ayaang.

[11] Mii dash i'iw gaa-ikidod: "Nishiimeyidog," ogii-inaan, "a'aw
anishinaabe omaa ge-ani-bimaadizid. Mii gaye ezhi-wiinineg
apaakozigan, gaa-izhi-miinigoowaawiyeg." Mii gaa-ondinang
anishinaabe gaa-sagaswaadang apaakoziganan. Mii i'iw
Wenabozho gaa-ozhitood i'iw.

[12] Mii inaadizookewaad ongow akiwenziiyag mewinzha.

Wayeshkad Gaa-waabamag Aadamoobii

[1] Wayeshkad, ayaaban a'aw chimookomaan, bimiwinigoojin
a'aw isa aadamoobii gaa-izhi-wiinaawaajin. Miikana
imbima'adoomin bezhig oshki-inini. Aazhaa noondawangid
biidwewebizod, biidweweg gegoo. Mii dash gaawiin,
ingwiiwizensiwimin. Ingii-segizimin dash noondamaang
biidweweg omaa miikanaang.

[2] Gaawiin igo, noongom izhinaagwak onow miikanan,

[8] As he left, [Wenabozho] came to the shore of the rivers, carrying the decapitated ducks, maybe seeing where he would roast those ducks over there. First of all he slept there extensively when he was ready, as he finished cooking those ducks. Then he slept.

[9] Then those people over there, these ones who must have been waiting in ambush, "Wait in watch," they said of him, "peek down there." These were Sioux that floated there. "Tell me if anybody floats up here." I don't know when he must have been sleeping. The Sioux could see him here as the steam rose [from his breath]. "That's Wenabozho," they said, "He's got something here." Then they shook [their] roaches in agreement, as the leader didn't have to say anything to those waiting in ambush, they took all those things [Wenabozho] had roasted and left.

[10] And at this time as he wakes up, that [duck] having been done a long time, Wenabozho gets up glancing a little bit towards his roast that they had stolen, those Sioux having taken it from him. Then he got mad. He burned himself, leaving here at this time. Then he burned up this here, so the story goes, getting itchy skin as he scabbed up. Then these sticks came to be like this.

[11] Then he said this: "My little brothers," he told them, "That Indian shall come to live here. And he'll call you *apaakozigan*, that's how you'll all be called." That's where the Indian gets the *kinnikinnick* he smokes. That's how Wenabozho made that.

[12] That's how these old men told legends long ago.

The First Time I Saw an Automobile

[1] The first time, there was a white man riding in that *aadamoobii* as they called it. A certain young man and I were following the road. We already heard him speeding up there, with some approaching sound. But no, we were boys. And we were scared when we heard the noise coming here on the road.

[2] No, the way the roads look now, they didn't look like that.

gaawiin gii-izhinaagwasinoon. Mii eta go onow;
gitawaakwaa'igaadewan. Mii gaa-izhinaagwak iniw
miikanan mewinzha.

[3] Mii eta bebezhigoganzhiig miinawaa dibidaabaanan
gaa-izhidaabii'iwewaad chimookomaanag. Mii dash imaa
gaye gii-noondawangid a'aw, biidweweg gegoo, mii gaa-izhi-
bakeyaang gaa-kaazootawangid. Nimikigaazomin opime-
miikanaang megwaa omaa go besho baa-ayaad ginwenzh
wa'aw, wa'aw isa aadamoobii bemiwininang noongom.

[4] Ginwenzh wii-adima'wiyangid imaa gaa-waabamiyangid
bimibizod, ingii-segi'igoonaan gii-piidwewed. Mii go
wayeshkad gii-waabamag a'aw, a'aw isa aadamoobii izhi-
wiinaajin anishinaabe mewinzha. Mii dash imaa gaa-onji-
gaazotawangid gii-segi'iyangid.

[5] Mii dash imaa akawe minik waa-kaagiigidoyaan.

Nitamising Gaa-waabamag Makadewiiyaas

[1] Wayeshkad gii-waabamag a'aw isa makadewiiyaas
aazhaa wiindamawaajin anishinaabe omaa oodenaang,
omaa endanakiiyaan, gaye imaa gii-pagaboodegoziwaad
ingiw makadewiiyaasag, oniijaanisan a'aw inini,
wiiwan, gaa-pi-aanjigoziwaad omaa o'ow isa gaa-
paapaagokozhiwewinini, mii i'iw a'aw makadewiiyaas.
Ginwenzh omaa gii-tanakii Inaandakokaag, gii-
paapaagokozhiwewininiiwid wayeshkad gii-waabamag a'aw,
a'aw isa makadewiiyaas ezhi-wiinind.

[2] Imaa wiin gaye weweni ogii-inenimaan anishinaaben. Imaa
gaa-tanakiinijin, gaawiin wiikaa gegoo omaa ayaasiin endaad
inini. Gaye odaa-gii-inaan. Mii eta go anooj gii-inaajimod
igaye aanawi ojibwemo gaye gii-kikinoo'amawangid i'iw
isa ojibwemowin. Mii apii gii-oshki-waabamag a'aw isa
mekadewizid bemaadizid. Iwidi chi-agaamiing akeyaa o'ow
isa bezhig minis, mii iwidi gaa-onjibaad, a'aw makadewiiyaas
ezhi-wiinaajin anishinaabe.

[3] Mii dash akawe imaa minik waa-kaagiigidoyaan.

These were the only kind; they were made of corduroy. That's how those roads looked long ago.

[3] Only horses and carriages, that's how the white men drove. And then when we heard that thing, some sound approaching, we went off to the side, hiding from it. We could be found by the side trail for a long time while this thing was hanging around near here, this automobile that carries us today.

[4] For a long time when he was going to catch up to us, seeing us there as he sped along, we were frightened as he was heard coming. That was the first time I saw that *aadamoobii* as the Indian named it long ago. And that's why we hid from him when he scared us.

[5] And that's all I want to say for now.

The First Time I Saw a Black Man

[1] When I first saw that black man the Indians already talked about here in town, here where I live, those black people floated down [the river] to settle there too, the children of that man, his wife, they moved here, this here barber, that is [to say] that black man. He lived here at Balsam Lake for a long time, the one who was the barber when I first saw him, that *makadewiiyaas* as he was named.

[2] And he thought well of the Indians there. There where they lived, they never told the man that he couldn't be here where he lived. But they could've told him. And he only talked in a certain way in spite of the fact that he spoke Ojibwe as we taught him that Ojibwe language too. At that time I first saw that black person. Over across the ocean towards this certain island, he was from over there, that *makadewiiyaas* as the Indian called him.

[3] And that's all I'm going to say for now.

Nandawaaboozwe Makadewiiyaas

[1]   Aabiding bezhig inini ingii-wiiji'igoonaan baa-
      nandawaaboozweyaang. Waabishkiki imaa ayaamagad,
      mii imaa gii-ayaawaad ingiw waabishki-waaboozoog.
      Miish imaa gaa-inaad, "Mii omaa akandoon," ogii-inaan,
      "Da-bi-naazikawaawag waaboozoog."
[2]   Miish imaa gii-naaniibawid aw makadewiiyaas. Gaawiin
      dash ogii-naazikawaasiiwaawaan ingiw waaboozoog,
      iniw anishinaabe gaa-wiiji'waad. Mii iwidi gii-naganaad gaa-
      pi-izhi-giiwed. Mii wenji-izhiwebizigwen a'aw makadewiiyaas.

Waabooz Gaa-piindashkwaanind

[1]   Aabiding gaye mii go makadewiiyaas, mii go a'aw inini gaa-
      maajiinaad. Mii dash iniw waaboozoon gii-kijiigibinaad, gaa-
      izhi-biindashkwaanaad. Mii dash iwidi waa-izhiwinaagwen,
      mii iwidi gii-wenabi'aad iniw waaboozoon.
[2]   Maajii-giiwewaad idash, bebimosewaad gaa-izhi-gaganoonaad,
      "Waabam awedi waabooz nemadabid," ogii-inaan. Ginwezh
      wiin a'aw waabooz gaa-piindashkwaanind, ezhi-gaabawid
      imaa makadewiiyaas ezhi-baashkizwaad iniw—gaa-
      piindashkwaanaawaanijin waaboozoon.

Gaa-amwaawaad Animoonsan

[1]   Ingoding iwidi Bwaanakiing gii-izhaayaan, gii-niimi'idiiwag
      iwidi anishinaabeg. Mii gaa-izhaayaan gii-waabamangidwaa
      wenaagoshing gii-wiisiniwaad. Mii dash iwidi jiigi-ziibiing,
      gabeshiwin iwidi ayaamagad. Mii i'iw waa-tazhi-wiisiniwaad.
      Mii dash imaa bii'oyaang, bezhig imaa inini gii-pi-wawenabi
      namadabiyaan adoopowining, imaa gaagiigidod, dibaajimod.
      Mii gaa-tibaajimotawid:
[2]   Waakaa'igan imaa ate. Bedosewag endaawaagwen. Ininiwag-sh
      omaa niswi gii-kiiwashkwebiiwag. Agwajiing imaa
      boodawewag, boodawazowag.
[3]   Chimookomaan imaa gii-pimibizo. Animoonsan ogii-ayaawaan
      imaa odoodaabaaning. Miish gaa-inaad anishinaaben, "Awiiya

The Makadewiiyaas *Goes Rabbit Hunting*

[1] Once a certain man came with us when we went about rabbit hunting. There is a swamp out there, and there is where the white rabbits were. And then he told him there, "Right here you lie in wait," he told him, "The rabbits will come [to you]."

[2] Then that black man stood right there. But none of those rabbits approached him, he who the Indian had brought along. He [the Indian] abandoned him out there and went home. That's why that happened to that black man.

The Stuffed Rabbit

[1] And one time it's the black man, that man brought him along. Then he snared that rabbit and stuffed him. Then out there where he must have wanted to bring him, out there he placed that rabbit.

[2] And as they started to go home, walking along he thusly spoke to him, "See that rabbit sitting over there," he told him. That rabbit had been stuffed for a long time, as that black man stood there, shooting—that stuffed rabbit.

When They Ate Puppies

[1] One time when I went over there to the Sioux lands, the Indians were dancing over there. When I went in the evening I saw them eating. Then over there near the river, there was a campsite over there. That's where they were eating. Then as we were waiting there, a certain man came to sit there where I was sitting at the table, talking there, telling stories. This is what he told me:

[2] There's a house there. They were walking slowly from where they must have lived. And three men were drunk here. There outside they made a fire, warming themselves up by the fire.

[3] A white man came driving up there. He had puppies there in his car. Then he told the Indians, "Did anybody there own

na imaa animoonsan ogii-ayaawaan?" Odinaan gaye wiin
ininiwan niswi. "Gaawiin indayaasiiwaanaanig ingiw
animoonsag," odinaan. Mii dash chimookomaan odinaan,
"Inga-naganaag awiiya waa-ayaawaad," gii-izhi-mamaad.
Mii inaad iniw anishinaaben.

[4] Miish imaa gii-naganaad iniw animoonsan, niswi ganabaj
inaajimotaagooyaan. Miish ingiw ininiwag, gaawashkwebiijig,
gemaa gaye gaa-pakadewaagwen. Mii waa-izhi-amwaad bezhig
animoonsan. Imaa dash a'aw inini wii-inendam, bezhig inini.
Miish i'iw waa-panzwaad a'aw bezhig inini animoonsan. Mii
dash ganabaj gaa-izhi-aabizhiishing a'aw animoons. Mii
gaa-izhi-dakwamigod omaa oninjiing. Mii apaginaad iwidi
megwe-mashkosiing. Mii gaa-izhi-maadakizige'iding. Niibowa
gii-chaagide.

[5] Niizh waakaa'iganan ogii-chaagizaanan a'aw waa-
pagamibizowaad ingiw getewininiwag. Bezhig gwiiwizens
imaa babaamibizod oditibiwebishkiganan. Miish a'aw
naagaanizid i'iw baate gaye miinawaa ogagwejimaan
gwiiwizensan, "Aaniish gaye wiin wenji-maadaakideg omaa,"
odinaan ji-izhi-gagwejimaad. "Namanj iidog," ikido. "Gaawiin
ingikendanziin," ikido. "Mii eta go ingiwedig ininiwag,
nemadabijig," ikido. "Animoonsan imaa owii-panzwaawaan.
Megwe-mashkosiwishiing owii-apaginaan. Mii imaa gaa-onji-
maadaakideg," odinaan iniw chimookomaanan. "Oon chi-
baakizigewaad i'iw. Niizh waakaa'iganan ojaagizaanaawaan."

Gaa-pazhiba'wid Niijanishinaabe

[1] Oodenaang-sh ingii-izhaa maajaayaan. Omaa apii aabita
inagakeyaa anishinaabeg endaawaad, ikwe imaa zaagizibatoo
waakaa'igaansing. "Inini omaa omiigaanaan ninaabeman.
Ogii-pazhiba'waan mookomaanens," indig.

[2] Ingii-ashi-naano-biboonagiz i'iw apii. Namanj iidog
izhichigewaanen. "Gaa indaa-bazhiba'wigosiig waa-
ani-miigaanaajin," indinendam. Imaa anooj igo inendamaan,
ingii-o-biindige. Imaa dash dazhiikodaadiwaad imaa
michisag, debibidowag i'iw onik da-bagijwebinang i'iw
mookomaanens. Mii imaa apiichiikawag o'ow, aanawi
maakabiwag mookomaanens gaa-izhi-bazhiba'odamaan
nindinimaanganaang.

[these] puppies?" He tells those three men too. "We don't own those puppies," [one] tells him. Then the white man tells him, as he picked them up, "I'm going to leave them with someone who wants to have them." That's what he told the Indians.

[4]   Then he left those puppies, perhaps three of them as it was told to me. Then those men, the drunks, they must have been hungry. They wanted to eat a certain puppy. And that was this one man's intention, that one guy. Then that one man wanted to singe the puppies. Maybe then that puppy came to, coming back to life. [That man] got bit here on his hand. He throws him over there among the grass. It burst into flames. Everything burned up.

[5]   That [guy] burned down two houses when those old men were going to drive up. A certain boy was cruising by there on his bicycle. The air was parched and then that leader asks the boy, "And why did the fire start here," he tells him in order to ask him this. "I wonder how," he says. "I don't know," he says. "Only those men over there, the ones sitting," he says. "They wanted to singe puppies there. He was going to throw one among that old grass. That's why the fire started there," he tells that white man. "Oh they really got everything consumed in flames. They burned down two houses."

When I Was Stabbed by My Fellow Indian

[1]   I was going to town when I left. At this time halfway here towards where the Indians lived, a woman came running out of the house there. "A man is fighting my husband here. He stabbed him with a knife," she tells me.

[2]   I was fifteen years old at that time. I don't know what I must have been doing. "Those who want to fight shouldn't stab me," I think. As I thought about all kinds of things there, I went over and entered. And there as they were involved with one another there on the floor, they grappled over his arm so he would release that knife. Right there I was controlling him to a certain extent, but anyway they were wounding [each other] with the knife as I was stabbed in the shoulder.

[3] Miinawaa omaa ninikaang gaye omaa ingii-inizhwig. Miinawaa indiy ingii-pazhiba'wig niizhing. Imbeshizhwig o'ow nininjiining. Mii gii-gwayako-giishkizhwid o'ow mashkijiitad a'aw. Oon aanawi giishkizhaa omaa apii. Mii dash gaa-inizhang. Mii go omaa o'ow ezhinaagwak. Mii gaawiin dash ogii-kiishkizhanziin. Mii i'iw akeyaa gaa-inaapinazhid a'aw inini.

[4] Miish gaa-azhegiiweyaan endaayaan, biindigeyaan imaa endaawaad, nimaamaayiban, "Aaniish ezhiwebiziyan miskwiiwiyan," ikido. "Oon," wiindamawag, "Ezhi-bimaaji'ag a'aw inini imaa, ininiwan omiigaanaan owii-pazhiba'waan dash indaa-inaaginaan," indinaa. Miish a'aw noosiban gaa-izhi-mamood obaashkizigan, wii-o-baashkizwaad; gaye wiin imaa akawe nimaamaayiban gaa-izhi-gagwe-makamangid i'iw baashkizigan o-baashkizwaasigwaa.

Apane Anishinaabe Ogaganoonaan Manidoon

[1] Miinawaa o'ow isa anooj izhichiged anishinaabe ganoonaad manidoon, niigaan bezhig apegish inenimiyangid manidoo. Mii gaa-izhichigewaad o'ow midewiwin. Mii i'iw gaa-tazhiikang anishinaabe, gii-onji-maajiishkaad, gii-onji-bimaadizid. Mii gaa-onji-tazhiikang.

[2] Miinawaa wa'aw noongom dewe'igan omaa ayaabaji'aajin anishinaabe, imaa Misi-zaaga'eganiing izhinikaadeg, mii imaa gii-pagidinaad a'aw sa meyagwed anishinaabe ji-onji-maajiishkaanid anishinaaben neyaab imaa ji-onji-bagidinamawaad. Mii dash imaa gaa-onji-maajiishkaad a'aw dewe'igan. Akina anooj omaa wendaabang akeyaa; mii imaa gii-pimibaagid gii-inindwaa dewe'iganag. Geyaabi noongom aanind a'aw anishinaabe ominjimendaan i'iw isa gaa-miinigod manidoon ji-onji-bimaadizid, ji-onji-maajiishkaad. Mii gaa-onji-miinigod.

[3] Miinawaa o'ow isa abwezod anishinaabe, mii gaye bezhig gaa-miinind a'aw anishinaabe daa-izhichiged. Gaye o'ow megwaa wii-aabawakamigak, mii i'iw apii gaa-inind anishinaabe ji-abwezod. Miinawaa zhayiigwa dagwagig wii-biibooninig, mii gaye i'iw apii gii-inind anishinaabe ji-abwezod. Ayi'ii o'ow isa wesidaagishkaagod anishinaabe akina ingoji, mii i'iw gaa-onji-izhi'ind a'aw anishinaabe ji-izhichiged.

[3] And here in my arm, here too he cut me. And he stabbed me twice in the butt. He cut me in my finger. That guy cut me straight through in this tendon. Oh anyway, it's cut through at this time. And he cut it like this. That's how this looks here. And he didn't cut it [this way]. That's how that man sliced me up.

[4] Then when I returned to my home, going inside there where they lived, my mom says, "What happened to you that you're so bloody." "Oh," I tell her, "When I was saving the life of that man there, another man was fighting him and was going to stab him and I had to intervene," I tell her. Then my dad picked up his gun, wanting to go over and shoot him; and right away my mother and I had to try to take that gun away from him by force so he wouldn't go over and shoot him.

The Indian Always Talks to the Spirit

[1] And the Indian does this when he talks to the spirit, when he wants the head spirit to think of us. That's what they did in the medicine dance. That's why the Indian participated in it, why he started [his life], why he lived. That's why he was involved.

[2] And this Drum the Indian uses here today, it was placed among the Indian people there at Mille Lacs as it is called, placed there for him so that the Indian could start [his life] as it was before. That's why that Drum started there. They all went out there toward the east; they were told this of the Drums. Today the Indian still keeps this in mind, how the spirit gave him this to start [his life]. That's why it was given to him.

[3] And when the Indian sweats, a certain [person] was given this so that the Indian could do so. And while it will be the warm season, at that time the Indian was told to sweat. And when it's fall already or when it's winter, the Indian was told to sweat at that time too. When the Indian was afflicted with something, that's when the Indian was told to do this.

[4] Mii dash gaa-izhichiged mewinzha a'aw anishinaabe gii-
abwezod miinawaa gii-kii'igoshimod gaye oshki-bimaadizid—
gwiiwizensag, ikwezensag. Gii-kii'igoshimowag mewinzha imaa
noongom manidoon gii-inandawenimaawaad ji-
naanaagadawenimigoowaad. Mii gaa-onji-izhichigewaad.
Mii gaye imaa gaa-onji-gikendamowaad o'ow isa anishinaabe
gaye izhinikaazowinan ji-miinind anishinaabe. Mii imaa
gaa-onji-gikendamowaad, gikenimaawaad onow awesiinyan
miinawaa binesiwan.

[5] Akina sa go awiiya onow omaa akiing bebaamibatood
awesiinyag, mii iniw gaa-shawenimigoowaajin wenjida a'aw
isa makwa ezhinikaazod, miinawaa wa'aw, a'aw isa migizi.
Mii gaye a'aw wenjida gaa-shawenimaawaad anishinaaben,
gii-miinaawaad i'iw isa ge-ani-izhi-ayaanid giigidonid ge-ani-
izhi-gaagiikimaanid anishinaaben. Mii gaa-onji-miinigod
manidoon.

[6] O'ow gaye ikwezensag, mii go gaye wiinawaa gaa-izhi-
gaganoonigoowaad mindimooyenyan, gii-wiindamaagoowaad
o'ow isa gaa-pi-izhi-bimaadizinid ishkweyaang. Mii dash i'iw
gaa-onji-gikendang anishinaabe gaa-ani-izhichiged, gii-
kaganoonigoowaad ogitiziimiwaan. Apegish ani-gikendang
i'iw isa gaa-pi-izhi-bimaadiziyaan niin, mii inendang.

[7] Miinawaa o'ow isa mewinzha go anishinaabeg gii-kiiyosewaad
gaye, wa'aw oshki-inini oshki-nisaad awesiinyan, awegwen
igo awesiinyan weshki-nisaajin, mii iniw ogii-sagaswe'aan
manidoon. Asemaan ogii-pagidinaawaan o'ow isa gii-
oshki-nisaad onow awesiinyan. Miinawaa asemaan ogii-
pagidinamawaan manidoon wii-izhi-miijid i'iw isa, o'ow
isa gaa-nisaajin. Akawe manidoon ogii-wiindamawaan.

[8] O'ow gaye manoomin, mii gaye aw anishinaabe gaawiin
ogii-izhi-miijisiin gii-kiizhitood. Baanimaa asemaan
obagidinamawaawaan manidoon, mii i'iw apii gaa-miijid i'iw
manoomin. Ayiigwa gaye wii-pawa'iganaandang, mii gaye i'iw
apii manidoon gii-kanoonaad, bagidinamawaad asemaan o'ow
isa wii-mamood o'ow isa nibiikaang gaa-pagidinang manidoon
ji-inanjiged anishinaabe.

[9] Miinawaa yo'ow isa mashkiki gaa-miininang manidoo
ji-aabajitooyang, akawe asemaan obagidinaan wii-mamood
anishinaabe i'iw. Mii sa mashkiki gaa-aabajitood mewinzha

[4]   And that is what the Indian did long ago when he sweated
      and again when he fasted in his youth—boys, girls. Now long
      ago they fasted so the spirits would want them to be
      considered [for pity]. That is why they did that. And that is
      why the Indian came to know names there to be given to the
      Indian people. That is why they knew them there, knowing
      the animals and the birds.

[5]   And every one of the animals running about here on earth,
      they were blessed for a reason—the bear as he is called, and
      also the bald eagle. And they pitied the Indian for a reason,
      giving him things to improve his condition, appeasing the
      Indian when he talked. That is why the spirit gave things to
      him.

[6]   And the girls, they were spoken to by the old ladies and told
      how the Indian lived before. When they were talked to by
      their parents, that is how the Indian knew what to do. I
      hope he will come to know this by the way I lived myself,
      when he thinks about it.

[7]   And when the Indians went hunting long ago as well, when
      a young man first killed an animal, whatever kind of animal
      was first killed, he smoked to the spirit. He offered tobacco
      for killing this animal first. Again tobacco was offered to the
      spirit when he ate that which he killed. He talked to the
      spirit first.

[8]   And this here rice, the Indian could not eat it when he
      finished making it. After they offer tobacco to the spirit,
      at that time they ate the rice. And now already when he
      knocks it, at that time too he speaks to the spirit, offering
      him tobacco when he will take this from the waterways
      so that the spirit gives permission for the Indian to have
      a traditional diet.

[9]   And this here medicine the spirit gave us to use, when the
      Indian wants to pick it, he offers tobacco first. That is how
      the Indian used medicine long ago. Thus he could not use

anishinaabe. Gaawiin ogii-izhi-aabajitoosiin, ogii-igoon manidoon, akawe asemaan ji-bagidinaad wii-mamood mashkiki o'ow isa ayiigwa wii-pakaaninakamigisidood manidoo o'ow akiing. Mii gaa-igod iniw manidoon.

[10] O'ow gaye, o'ow isa nibiikaang endanakiid giigoonh, mii gaye iniw akawe awiiya ogii-izhinawaan. Akawe manidoon ogii-pagidinamawaan asemaan wii-amwaad iniw isa giigoonyan.

[11] Mii akeyaa gaa-izhi-bagidinind anishininaabe mewinzha. O'ow isa gii-pi-noondawagig akiwenziiyag gaa-pi-gaagiigidojig. Miish i'iw noongom ezhi-gaganoonag anishinaabe naadamawag gegoo waanzod.

[12] Mii dash akawe imaa minik waa-kaagiigidoyaan. Baanimaa apii miinawaa inga-gaagiigid. Mii i'iw.

Mii Sa Iw

[1] Aabiding gii-ayaa mooska'osi nandawaabamaad omakakiin imaa sa waabashkikiing. Mii gaa-izhi-wiisinid aw mooska'osi, gii-pagamise zhashagi, noonde-wiisinid gaye wiin. Ogii-kagwe-maajinizhikawaan iniw mooska'osiwan.

[2] Mii nawaj sa mindidod zhashagi awashime iniginid mooska'osi. Gaawiin idash gii-segizisiin a'aw mooska'osi. Gaawiin wii-maajaasiin mooska'osi. Gaawiin igaye owii-gii-maada'ookiisiin iw wiisiniwin. Giizhiitaa da-miigaazod.

[3] Enigok ogii-mawinanaan iniw zhashagiwan. Geget igo gii-pakite'odiwag, aabajitoowaad oningwiiganiwaan, bapawaangeniwaad, dakwamidiwaad igaye. Waasa gii-noondaagwad omiigazowiniwaa.

[4] Baanimaa go bijiinag a'aw mooska'osi ogii-pakinawaan iniw zhashagiwan. Gegaa gii-niiwana'aagoo a'aw zhashagi. Mii dash ezhi-ikidod a'aw mooska'osi, "Mii sa iw. Mii sa iw."

it, the spirit told him, tobacco was to be put down first when he wanted to pick medicine or already the spirit will change its condition on this earth. That is what he was told by the spirit.

[10] This too, this water where the fish live, for them too one thinks of them respectfully first of all. He offered the spirit tobacco first when he wanted to eat those fish.

[11] In this way the Indian was put [here] long ago. This [is] what I heard the old men that gave the lectures say. Now that is what I tell my fellow Indian when I help someone getting a name or something.

[12] And for starters, that is all I want to say. At a later time I will talk again. That is it.

That's It

[1] Once there was a shitepoke* looking for frogs there in the swamp. As that shitepoke was eating, a great blue heron showed up, having a big appetite himself. He tried to chase off that shitepoke.

[2] The great blue heron is larger than the size of a shitepoke. But that shitepoke wasn't scared. The shitepoke wasn't going to leave. And he didn't want to share that food. He was ready to fight.

[3] He attacked that great blue heron ferociously. They were really hitting each other, using their wings, shaking their wings, and biting one another. Their fight was heard from a long way off.

[4] Later on after a while that shitepoke defeated that great blue heron. That great blue heron was almost beaten to death. Then that shitepoke says like this, "That's it. That's it."

---

* A small relative of the great blue heron, the shitepoke is also known as the swamp pump or American bittern.

45

Misi-zaaga'igan
Mille Lacs

JIM CLARK

JIM CLARK (b. 1918), whose Anishinaabe name is *Naawi-giizis* (Center of the Sun), answered one of my most perplexing questions about the Mille Lacs Indian Reservation. I often wondered how the communities there could be so successful in maintaining their language and culture. They've fared far better than most of their neighbors in this regard, despite the fact that they are located a little over one hundred miles from Minneapolis and have a small population surrounded by a sea of white resorts, hotels, and summer homes. In particular, they've managed to preserve Big Drum culture in the face of consistent efforts to remove them from their homeland, including the burning of their homes in 1901 and the withholding of allotments until 1926 for all who did not relocate to White Earth.

As I became more and more familiar with Big Drum culture, the answers to that question became manifest. The power of the Drums themselves did much to protect the people of Neyaashiing and its cousins to the east in Sandy Lake and Lake Lena. The unbending faith of the Drum Keepers did much to protect the Drums and everything associated with them as well. It was the strength of traditional Ojibwe religion and the tenacity of traditional Ojibwe people that enabled the communities of Mille Lacs to retain so much in spite of the enormous pressures to relinquish all they had.

As I got to know some of the elders from Mille Lacs and heard them tell the history of their physical and cultural survival, I came to appreciate more and more the importance of strong leadership. And I realized that strong leadership is an acquired skill much more than a natural gift. The people of Mille Lacs have maintained regional Big Drum culture for all Ojibwe people through the strength of their teaching and the strength of their learning. Good students make good teachers, and the legacy of strong leadership at Mille Lacs is one that has been handed down for generations in the families of that community. The process of keeping cultural knowledge depends upon a large web of knowledgeable family and community members with an unshaken faith in the power of the Drum.

Jim Clark has certainly exemplified that development. His parents and grandparents taught by example rather than by command, and Jim grew up immersed in his language, culture, and religion. The success of his Anishinaabe education has proven to be remarkable indeed. His advice and prayers are frequently sought at the Big Drum ceremonials in Mille Lacs and with every other sort of spiritual endeavor that the Ojibwe maintain today.

Most of Jim's childhood was spent at Nenaandago-ziibiing, a small village on the Tamarack River near the present day Mille Lacs Reservation community of Lake Lena. He moved several times in his life, serving as a medic in the United States Army during World War II and then taking various jobs in Minneapolis and elsewhere to support his growing family. He currently resides in the Mille Lacs community of Neyaashiing (Onamia, Minnesota).

Jim Clark recorded many of the stories in this book himself. Others were recorded by Louise Erdrich. At her request and with Jim's permission, I worked on the transcriptions and translations. The material here is very rich. Some of the stories about Jim's childhood include numerous Ojibwe place names that only a small handful of Anishinaabe people still know. The inclusion of nursery rhymes and jokes also demonstrates the importance of Ojibwe in all types of communication and reinforces Jim's hope that the language and the culture it contains will survive.

Dibaakonigewinini Miinawaa Anishinaabe

[1] Namanj igo ingoding ingii-tazhi-nitaawiz, mii iwidi akeyaa
biinish igo gii-kichi-miigaading, *World War II* gii-izhinikaadeg.
Mii apii ganabaj gaa-maajaayaan. Name-ayi'ii gii-izhaayaan
dibishkoo go ingii-paa-nanda-bami'idiz. Mewinzha-sh igo iwidi
jibwaa-nisidotamowaad aapiji ingiw anishinaabeg i'iw
chimookomaanimowin. Gii-ayaawag iwidi. Gaawiin igo gegoo
ogii-kwayakotanziinaawaa gegoo inindwaa.

[2] Miish i'iw apane, mii gaye i'iw apii, ganabaj gemaa gaye *1937*,
1938, geget gii-minikweshkiwag aanind ingiw anishinaabeg,
gii-kiiwashkwebiiwaad. Aaningodinong-sh gii-tebibinaawag
miigaadiwaad gaa-izhi-gibaakwa'indwaa. Mii i'iw miigaazong
miinawaa go awiiya babakite'waawaad. Miish a'aw bezhig inini
gaa-izhi-maajiinind. Gii-nitaa-miigaazo geget a'aw gaa-izhi-
maajiinind Wiigaziibiigiing. Mii iko iwidi gaa-izhiwinindwaa
gii-kibaakwa'indwaa. Namanj iwidi gaa-izhiwinind, mii
a'aw inini. Gaawiin go aapiji ogii-nisidotanziin. Baamaa
go gaye zhaaganaashiimo. Miish iwidi azhigwa gii-
izhiwinind imaa wii-tibaakwanind. Niibawid imaa
agindaamagad dibaakonigewininiwan. Awegonen
wenji-gibaakwa'ind ginwenzh gii-wiindamaagod. Odigoon
iniw dibaakonigewininiwan. *"You're charged with assault and
battery,"* inaa giiwenh.

[3] Ani-ganawaabamaad iniw dibaakonigewininiwind, "Oonh
wenh, gaawiin sa niin wiikaa zhiiwitaagan gemaa gaye
waasamoo-makakoons igaye ingimoodisiin," odinaan giiwenh.
Mii i'iw gaa-initang. Mii gaa-izhi-noondamaan iwidi gaa-o-
bizindaagwak ayi'ii, mii dibaakwa'ind.

Mawinzowin

[1] Anooj igo indinaajim, dadibaajimoyaan aaningodinong.
A'aw-sh nookomisiban iniw indedeyiban omaamaayan, mii i'iw
nookomis, mii a'aw apane gaa-wiiji-ayaawangid, besho endaad
apane gii-ayaayaang. Aanishinange ingii-saagi'aanaan sa go.
Gii-indanitaawaadizooke a'aw mindimooyenh.

[2] Miish ingoding iko awiiya gaa-kagwejimid aaniin gaa-
izhichiged a'aw anishinaabe gegoo gii-atamaazod ge-miijid

The Judge and the Indian

[1] I was raised over there until the time of the big war, World War II as it was called. That was probably the time when I left. When I went away from there, it was like I was going around in search of ways to support myself. This was a long time before those Indians had a good understanding of that American language. They were over there. They didn't hear things right when something was said to them.

[2] It was always the case at that point in time, maybe around 1937, 1938, that some Indians were truly chronic drinkers, getting drunk. And once in a while they got caught fighting one another and were thus imprisoned. And that's how fighting was when they boxed someone. Then that one man was taken away. He was really a good fighter, the one taken away to Grantsburg. They were usually brought there when they were locked up. He must have been brought over there, that man. He did not understand very well. Later he would speak English. Now he was brought there when he would be indicted. As he stood there it was read by the judge. He was told at length what the reason for his imprisonment was. He was informed by the judge, "You're charged with assault and battery," he said, so the story goes.

[3] As he looked at that judge, "Oh baloney, I never stole any salt or battery," he told him, so the story goes. That's how he understood [the charge]. That's how I heard it over there, listening about how he was indicted.

Berry Picking

[1] I speak about all sorts of things, telling stories from time to time. That grandmother of mine, my father's mother, that was my grandma, the one we always accompanied as we were always at her house. We really loved her. That old lady told stories there.

[2] Then one time someone asked me about how the Indian people did things, how he stored away things he wanted to

JIM CLARK

ishkwaa-ayaamagak, aaniish gaye iniw anooj editeg—
asasaweminan, miinan igaye. Miish iniw gagwejimigooyaan
iko aaniin gaa-izhitoowaad. Miish a'aw, dibaajimagwaa,
anooj inaajimowin nimaamaanaaban, gemaa gaye gii-
mawinzoyaang gaye niinawind dibi sa gaa-ondinamogwen
iniw miinan. Ingoding igo aazhaa gaa-izhi-anoozhiyangid
zhingaatesidooyaang omaa wagidigamig. Daa-bazakiteniwan
endaawaad. Oshtiwagidigamig gii-iningaatesidooyaang
iniw. Mii miinawaa gii-kanawaabamangidwaa ingiw
gii-koshko'angidwaa bineshiinyag ji-miijisigwaa.
Omaa apiish igo gii-paatewan iniw miinan,
wawiiziigiminagoon. Mii gii-paateg. Ishkwaa-izhi-mamood,
ganabaj mashkimodensing, apagiwayaanimashkimodensing
ogii-atoonan. Mii gaye agoodeg apane.

[3]   Baamaash ingoding ingiw, gemaa gaye gaa-piboonogwen, omaa
apii gaa-izhi-mookinang iniw miinan gaa-paatenigin a'aw
mindimooyenh. Nibiing gii-agwanjitood gemaa gaye gegoo
omaa, gemaa gaye gegoo mashkikiwan. Mii sa omaa
mayaajiiging gaa-tago-atoogwen, gii-agwanjitood iniw miinan.
Gomaa apii gii-siigobiigin imaa gii-agwanjitood. Gomaa
godandamaang indagonaa geget oshki-miinan iniw. Oshki-
ayi'iin igo miinan gaa-izhinaagwak. Migwandagoon gaye
wenda-minopogwadoon igo gaye.

[4]   Mii gemaa gaye aanawi gikinoo'amawiyangid gegoo.
Aanishinange ingii-kagiibaadizimin. Mii gaa-onji-
gikendanziwaang gaye niinawind awegonen imaa gaa-atood,
gegoo aano-gikinoo'amawiyangid a'aw mindimooyenh,
mindimooyenyiban.

Ayaabadak Ishkode

[1]   Mii go geyaabi wiin nenda-dibaadodamaan gegoo noongom
ezhi-aagonwetang awiiya. Gaa-izhi-bimaadizid a'aw
anishinaabe mewinzha, imaa gaye anooj aapiji gichi-mewinzha
ogii-kikendaanaawaa gegoo waa-aabajitoowaad. Miish aya'aag,
gichi-aya'aag, ingii-mawidisaanaanig indedeyiban iwidi
endaawaad. Gii-tagwaagin igo omaa. Niinawind ingii-taamin
Gaakaabikaang.Wiinawaash iwidi ishkonigan Misi-
zaaga'iganiing gii-ayaawag indedeyiban iwidi gaa-taawaad.

54

eat after [harvest], such as the variety of things that ripen—
chokecherries and blueberries. These are the things I was
asked about, how they customarily prepared things. Then
I spoke about them, different stories of my grandmother,
maybe about when we went berry picking ourselves and the
different places she got blueberries. One time she had
already told us to spread them out in the sun on the top of
the house here. Their houses were built low to the ground
so we spread them out on top of the roof. And whenever
we saw those little birds, we startled them away so they
wouldn't eat them. The blueberries were dried here at that
time, wrinkled [like raisins]. They were dried. After they
were retrieved she put them in a small bag, maybe a little
cloth bag. And it was always hung up.

[3] And sometime later, perhaps when it might be winter,
at this time here that old lady brought out those dried
blueberries. She submersed them in water here, kind of like
some medicines. So they started to rehydrate as she added
them in here, soaking those blueberries. Liquid was poured
in for some time there when she soaked them. When we
tasted them they were just like fresh new blueberries. They
looked like [fresh-picked] blueberries. And it was like they
were still growing and they tasted just good.

[4] So in any event, that's how she taught us things. We really
were foolish. That's why we don't know what all the different things were that she put in there, as that old lady
taught us to no avail.

The Use of Fire

[1] Today I still search for ways to tell about these things which
people find unbelievable. This is how the Indian lived long
ago, because a very long time ago they had knowledge of the
many things that they wanted to use. My father and I visited
some of them, the elders over there at their houses. It was
fall here. We lived in Minneapolis. But they were over there
at the Mille Lacs reservation, over there where my father and
the [others] lived. Then as we went over [there] visiting one

Miish o-mawidisangidwaa ingoding endazhindamowaad gegoo. Mii o'ow niwiiji'aawaagan gegoo ani-gagwedwed.

[2] Miish i'iw gii-tibaajimod indedeyiban i'iw. Mii go omaa wiigwaasing gaa-tazhi-onzamowaad iko gaye gegoo gii-chiibaakwaadamowaad, inaajimo. Maagizhaa gaawiin gaye aapiji, gaye aapiji indebwetanziimin. Inashke sa wiin, inashke jaagide wiigwaas ingoji ishkodeng. Miish iwidi, nimoonenimaazawaanaan onow. Akiwenzii, indedeyiban gii-ani-zaaga'amogwen. Namanj igo madwe-ganoozhiyangid iwidi.

[3] Agwajiing imaa gii-poodawegwen. Miish agwajiing iko gii-poodawewaad, mii igo anishinaabeg. Mii i'iw gii-poodawegwen imaa agaasishkodeyaa ishkode. Owii-takonaan i'iw makakoons. Biskitenaanganing igo izhinaagwad i'iw wiigwaasimakakoons. Mii i'iw nibi atenig. Gegaa go imaa gaye ingodoninj eko-biigwen i'iw makakoons. Gaawiin igo gii-michaasinoon. Gemaa gaye niiyoninj, niiyoninjiiskaayaa. Inigokwadeyaagwen. Ingodwaasoninj gii-akwaa. Miinawaa gemaa gaye nishwaasoninj gaa-apiitadogwen, apiitoonigod. Miish igo nibi atemagak. Miish imaa ishkode. Gaawiin gaye gichi-zakwanesinoon. Gaawiin gaye gichi-michaamagasinoon ishkode. Mii imaa ayagwanang i'iw wiigwaasimakakoons nibi atenig. Ingoding gegoo imaa ji-ganawaabandamaang, geget imaa gii-tazhi-ondemagad i'iw nibi.

[4] Miish waabanda'iyangid i'iw wiigwaasing iko gegoo gii-tazhi-giizizamowaad mewinzha ingiw anishinaabeg. Gaawiin gii-chaagidesinoon i'iw wiigwaas megwaa nibi ateg biinjayi'ii. Gaye, mii gaye wiinawaa gii-kikinoo'amawiyangid gegoo gaa-ani-izhichigewaad ingiw anishinaabeg gaa-ani-izhi-bimaadiziwaad.

Inday

[1] Gaawiin niin ingezikwenimaasiin a'aw nimishoomisinaaban, iniw indedeyiban gaa-oosijin. Mii eta go a'aw nimaamaanaaban ginwenzh gii-pimaadizi. Mii iniw indedeyiban omaamaayan. Miish a'aw benaadiziwobanen a'aw nimishoomisinaaban, a'aw indedeyiban odedeyan. Nibogobanen a'aw akiwenzii. Inashke gaawiin ingezikwenimaasiin gemaa gaye gaa-niizhobiboonagiziwaanen benaadizid. Ginwenzh idash

time, they were talking about something. This is what my partner came to ask about.

[2] Then my father told a story about it. They used to boil [water] in birch bark here and cook things with it, he says. Maybe we didn't really believe it, not entirely. You see birch bark just burns up anywhere in a fire. We were unable to sense what he was doing. The old man, my father must have gone outside. He was heard talking to us out there.

[3] Outside there he must have built a fire. The Indians customarily built fires outside then. The fire was a small fire where he must have kindled it there. He grasped that basket. It looked like a birch bark sap-collecting bucket inside. Water had been put in there. There must have been about an inch of liquid in that basket. It wasn't big. It was four inches across, approximately four inches. It was that wide. It was six inches long. And it must have been about eight inches in height, made to that size. Then there was water inside. It was there on the fire. And it did not burst into flames. The fire wasn't especially large. But that birch bark basket was resting level there with water inside. We looked inside there then, and that water in there was really boiling.

[4] That's when he showed us how birch bark was customarily used by those Indians long ago when they cooked things. That birch bark did not burn while water was put inside. And that's how they taught us something about what those Indian people did and the way they lived their lives.

My Horse

[1] I don't vividly remember my grandfather, my dad's father. It was only my grandmother that lived a long time. That was my father's mother. My grandfather passed away then, my dad's dad. The old man has since died. You see I don't have a clear memory of him, as I must have been about two years old when he passed away. And my grandmother had been single for a long time, my grandma. That's what we always

gii-pizhishigozi a'aw nimaamaanaaban, nookomisiban. Mii go i'iw apane gaa-izhinikaanangid "maamaanaan." Miinawaa, mii ezhinikaanangidwaa niinawind ingiw ganoonangidwaa ingiw nookomisinaanig. Mii azhigwa ginwenzh gii-pizhishigozid.

[2] Mii ingoding gaa-izhi-mikawaad, mii iniw ge-bami'igojin akiwenziiyan. Ayi'iin, ganabaj imaa akeyaa agamiing gii-onjibaa a'aw akiwenzii. Gii-panaadiziwan gaye wiin iniw gaa-wiiwijin. Agaawaa go ingezikwenimaa a'aw. Gii-izhaayaang imaa gii-ani-inind a'aw mindimooyenh, mii iniw a'aw dibaajimag akiwenzii. Gaye, mii gaye wiin gii-pizhishigozid. Ingoding-sh iidog azhigwa gii-wiijiiwaad iniw nookomisinaaban, mii iniw akiwenziiyan. Miish iw ingoding iizon gaa-izhi-wiidigendiwaad, gaa-izhi-wiijiwaawendiwaad.

[3] Geget iidog o'ow gegoo ogii-ayaan a'aw akiwenzii. Ingezikwenimaa wiin igo. Gii-wenda-onizhishiwan iniw gaa-odayijin bebezhigooganzhiin. Miinawaa gichi-gwanaajiwaninig gaye iniw odapikanan iniw. Wenda-gwanaajiwag ingiw bebezhigooganzhiig. Miinawaash igo gegoo gaye ingii-shawenimigonaan sa go a'aw akiwenzii i'iw. Mii i'iw nookomisiban azhigwa waa-kichi-aya'aawiwaad. Mii eta go gii-wiidookawaad gaye gii-pami'iyangidwaa gaye wiin. Mii go imaa gaye wiin gaa-tanizid a'aw akiwenzii. Ingoding-sh igo, mii azhigwa gaa-wiidigemaad nimaamaanaaban, nookomisiban gaa-wiidigemaad onow akiwenziiyan. Mii gomaa gaye ininiwan besho gaa-taayaang. Anooj igo gomaa apii ingoding ingii-taamin miinawaa da-dagoshinowaad mawidisidiwaad igaye.

[4] Ingoding igo ogii-pizagaabiiginaan bebezhigooganzhiin. Agaashiinyi a'aw bebezhigooganzhiins. Wiikaa wawaabijiizi. Gagidagishin igo waawiyeyaag imaa gagidagishing. Miish i'iw apii ininamawid niin i'iw biiminakwaan bezagaabiiginaad iniw bebezhigooganzhiin. Miish i'iw gaa-izhid, "Mii a'aw giday," indig. Wayaa gichi-minwendamaan niin odayiyaan. Aanishinange indedeyiban nawaj gii-nanaa'itood i'iw bebezhigooganzhiiwigaan. Igaye imaa ogii-ayaawaan odayan indedeyiban. Mii imaa gaye niin gii-asag a'aw. A'aw-sh, mii gii-igooyaan, "Giinish o'ow giga-ashamaa gaye gidoominaa gaye," indigoo. "Giin giga-ganawenimaa giday," indigoo. Miish i'iw, "Aaniish waa-izhinikaanad," indigoo. Miish i'iw ganawaabamag indagonaa, "Giwaabandaanaawaadog iko awiiya zhishigagowed. Mii sa go gaa-izhinawag i'iw inaanzod

called her—"*maamaanaan*." And that is what we call our grandmothers when we talk to them. She had now been widowed for quite some time.

[2] So one time she found someone [new], that old man who would take care of her. That old man was probably from over by the shore. And she was spoiled when he made her his wife. I do have somewhat hazy memories of him. We went there when that old lady was proposed to, that was by that old man I've been speaking about. He was single himself. And one time now my grandmother went with him, that old man. And they married one another, and thus became partners.

[3] That old man really had [many] possessions. I remember him. He had ponies and those horses were just beautiful. And his [horse] tackle was magnificent. Those ponies were just beautiful. And that old man loved us too. He and my grandmother were elders now. He just helped her, too, and they took care of us. That old man stayed there himself. And one time, now my grandmother married him, my grandmother married this old man. And so we lived pretty close together. We lived for some time like this and one time they arrived and visited one another.

[4] One time he was leading a horse with a rope. That pony was small. He had a dapple-colored coat. He was speckled with round dots on his spotted coat there. Then at that time he handed me that rope myself as he led that horse around. Then he told me this, "That's your pony," he tells me. Boy was I ever elated to be a horse owner. My dad made more repairs to that horse stable. My dad kept horses there too. So I put mine in there too. And in regards to him, I was told, "You are going to feed him and furnish his oats too," I'm told. "You are going to take care of your horse," I'm told. And then this, "What do you want to call him," I'm told. Then as I took a fresh look at him, "Do you all see how it [looks] like someone's just puked?" This is what that horse looked like to me in his coloration. "Well, I am going to

a'aw bebezhigooganzhii. Aaniish, mii sa iidog i'iw
Zhishigagowaan inga-izhinikaanaa." Miish i'iw gaa-
izhinikaanag a'aw inday—Zhishigagowaan.

[5]   Aan, aabiding ganabaj eta ingii-pimoomig. Gaawiin ingii-
ayaanziimin gegoo i'iw bimoomigoo-apabiwinang. Mii
go mitaawigan gaa-izhi-bimoomigooyaan azhigwa.
Aaniish, ingii-agaashiny i'iw apii imaa gegaa gaa-naano-
biboonagiziwaanen apii gii-odayiyaan. Mii i'iw inday
Zhishigagowaan gaa-izhinikaanag. Gaawiish igo, inashke
gaawiin nimaamaa odinendanziidog gaa-inikaagobanen a'aw
inday. Gemaa go gaye azhigwa gii-taawag indedeyiban odayan
gaye wiin gaa-tago-adaawaageyaang. Inashke gaawiin ingii-
ayaasiimin endaayaang. Mii gaye ginwenzh opime-ayi'ii
gii-paa-anokiidog indedeyiban gii-naganangidwaa ingiw
bebezhigooganzhiig. Mii imaa gaye, gemaa gaye gaa-
adaawaagegwen indedeyiban iniw odayan miinawaa go gaye
niin a'aw inday. Gaawiin naganag aapiji ingezikwendanziin i'iw.

Gibaakwa'igan Dazhi-anishinaabeg

[1]   Ingagwejimigoo dibaajimoyaan akina wenjibaayaan, ayi'ii sa
iwidi Misi-zaaga'iganiing wiin gomaa indibaajimotaagooyaan
dash o'ow ingii-tazhi-ondaadizinaadog omaa akeyaa
Gibaakwa'iganing akeyaa Nesawegamaag ezhinikaadeg.
Mii iidog imaa gii-wiindamawipan indedeyiban gaa-
tazhi-ondaadiziyaan iidog. Mii azhigwa a'aw indedeyiban wiin
iwidi akeyaa Azhoomog ezhinikaadeg, mii iwidi akeyaa gaa-
tazhi-nitaawigid wiin. Gayesh i'iw imaa azhigwa mayaajii-wiiji-
ayaawaad iniw nimaamaayibanen. Mii iwidi gaa-izhigoziyaan
iidog iwidi, iwidi akeyaa Aazhoomog ezhinikaadeg. Gaawiin
iwidi Aazhoomog ingii-ayaasiimin. Jejajiibaan igo gii-ayaawag
ingiw, ingiw sa go niningwezhinaningodwewaanagiziwaad.

[2]   Inashke a'aw nimishoomisinaaban a'aw. Ayi'iing iwidi jiigibiig
i'iw Nenaandago-ziibi ezhinikaadeg, mii iwidi gii-ayaad wiin
a'aw nimishoomisiban. Mii iwidi gii-ayaawaad iniw gaye wiin
oniijaanisan igaye. Gaye, mii indedeyiban gaa-tedeyijin
miinawaa go inzigosiban miinawaa go bezhig ninzhishenh.
Nimishoome gii-ayaa iidog. Gaawiin ingezikwenimaasiig.

name him Puke." That's what I named that pony of mine—
Puke.

[5]   Oh, I probably only rode on him one time. We didn't have
      anything for that saddle. So I just rode bareback then. Well,
      I was small at that time there, as I must have been almost
      five years old when [I] became a horse owner. That was my
      horse Puke as I called him. But no, you see, my mother
      didn't think much of what that pony of mine was named.
      Maybe then my dad's horses were there too when we sold
      them at that place. You see we weren't at our house. My
      father would have to go off working for long periods of time
      so we left those horses behind. So my dad must have sold
      those horses there including my own pony. I don't recall if I
      left him alone very much.

The Dam Indians

[1]   I have been asked to speak about all the places I'm from,
      to discuss a little bit places such as Mille Lacs and where I
      was born here, towards The Dam, at Shakopee Lake as it is
      called. So my father told me it must have been there that I
      was born. Now my dad, on the other hand, was raised over
      there toward Lake Lena as it's called. And it was there that
      he started going with my mother. I moved over there too
      [later on], over there towards Lake Lena as it's called. But
      we weren't right at Lake Lena there. They were at various
      different locations, each of those different family groups.

[2]   You see that was my grandfather. Over there on the bank
      of the Tamarack River, on the other hand, that's where my
      grandpa was. And that's where his children were too. And
      that was my father's father and my paternal aunt and one
      of my maternal uncles. My paternal uncle was there. I don't
      remember them [all].

[3]   Ayi'iing idash iwidi jiigi-ziibi, gaye niinawind igo ziibi, mii
iwidi gaa-taayaang gibaakweg. Gii-kaanjweba'igeng iko
ogii-kagiibaakwaanaawaan chimookomaanag ziibiwan,
zaaga'iganiin gii-ozhitoowaad dash miinawaa mitigoon
gii-misaaboonaawaad. Mii imaa gii-ayaamagak iidog
gibaakwa'iganing, gibaakwa'igan. Miish i'iw wenji-izhinikaadeg
Gibaakwa'iganing. Mii iwidi gaa-tazhi-nitaawigiyaan gaye niin
azhigwa. Mii iwidi apane gaa-taayaang.

[4]   Iwidi Gibaakwa'iganing ezhinikaadeg, ayi'iing wiin i'iw
giigoonh-odena, iwidi gabeshiwag. Odenawens Jekaakwaag
ezhinikaadeg gii-izhinikaade. Chimookomaanag
wiinawaa *Markville* ogii-izhinikaadaanaawaa—*Markville,
Minnesota.* Mii i'iw ganabaj nishwaaso-diba'igan i'iw apii
gii-tagon i'iw odenawens. Miinawaash imaa akeyaa
aazhawayi'ii adaawewigamigoons gomaa gaye ayaamagad.
Chimookomaanag odizhinikaadaanaawaa *Duxbury.*
Anishinaabeg dash wiin igo gezikwenimagwaa ongow
mewinzha, Eko-biising gii-izhinikaade. Izhinikaade sa go
noongom.

[5]   Inashke, mii iwidi, imaa Gibaakwa'iganing gii-kibaakwa'igaade
i'iw ziibi. Gii-saaga'iganikaadeg idash, mii iwidi *Duxbury* gaa-
ako-biising i'iw gichi-zaaga'igan iidog imaa gibaakwa'igaadeg
i'iw ziibi. Miish i'iw wenji-izhinikaadeg Eko-biising. Mii gaye
niin iwidi akeyaa gaa-tazhi-nitaawigiyaan Jekaakwaag
miinawaa go Aazhoomog, miinawaa iwidi Aazhoomog gwen
iwidi besho odena i'iw agaamiing ezhinikaadeg *Danbury.* Mii
imaa wiinawaa gaa-ondinamowaad omazina'iganiwaan ingiw
Aazhoomog gaa-ayaajig. Mii iwidi gaye niin akeyaa gii-tazhi-
nitaawigiyaan i'iw. Ayi'iing, jiigayi'ii go iwidi Aazhoomog anooj
igo imaa akeyaa noongom geyaabi ayaawag anishinaabeg imaa.
Mii imaa gaa-tazhi-nitaawigiyaan gaye niin o'ow jiigi-gichi-ziibi
go gaye: Gichi-ziibi, *St. Croix River.*

[6]   Ginwenzh o'ow mayaajii-zhaaganaashiimoyaan; mayaajii-
zhaaganaashiimowaad sa go ongow anishinaabeg iwidi
miinawaa gii-ishkwaa-anishinaabewinikaadeg iwidi
Gibaakwa'iganing. Aanishinange chimookomaanag gaa-
izhinikaadamowaad *the dam.* Mii i'iw Gibaakwa'igan.
Mii iwidi gaa-taayaang. Gayesh o'ow noongom anooj
inaajimotawiwaad wii-ani-gikinoo'amawagig ingiw
ojibwemowaad anooj awiiya. Mii gagwejimiwaad, "Aaniish

[3]   And over there on the bank of the river, we lived over there
      at the blockage ourselves. The white people used to dam
      up the rivers where they managed the log shoots, and they
      made lakes where they floated the logs. That's where the
      damming was, the dam. So that's why it was called The
      Dam. Now then I was raised over there myself. We always
      lived over there.

[4]   Over there at The Dam as it's called, there was a fishing
      village, [and] they camped over there. That little village was
      named the so-called Markville. The white people called it
      Markville—Markville, Minnesota. That little village was
      located perhaps eight miles away. And on the other side of
      [the river] there somewhere there was a little store. The
      white people called that place Duxbury. But according to
      these Indians I remember from long ago, it was called
      Eko-biising [end of the water]. It is called so today.

[5]   You see, over there at The Dam, that river is blocked up. And
      it was referred to as a lake, as over there at Duxbury that
      gigantic lake elongated there where that river was dammed
      up. That's why it was called Long Lake. Thus I was raised
      over there towards Markville and Lake Lena and also over
      there by the village near Lake Lena on the other side of the
      river called Danbury. That's where those Lake Lena villagers
      got their papers. So I was also raised over there. Near Lake
      Lena over there today there are still Indians all over there. So
      I was raised there myself and also along the Big River: the
      Big River, the St. Croix.

[6]   It's a long time since I started speaking English; [and] as
      these Indians started speaking English The Dam ceased to
      be called that in Indian. The whites certainly called it The
      Dam. That's *Gibaakwa'igan*. That's where we lived. And now
      when I want to teach some of them to speak Ojibwe they tell
      me things. They ask me, "How come you live way over there
      in the toolies over there where you live 'at the dam,'" they
      say to me. Then I want to tell them about this. We jokingly

iwidi gaa-onjiikogaayan iwidi daayamban 'at the dam,' "
izhiwaad. Miish i'iw wii-wiindamawagwaa. Ingii-izhi-
gadedaamin apane gii-izhinikaanigooyaang i'iw "the damn
Indians." Mii gaye niinawind i'iw gaa-onjiikogaayaang.

Baa Baa Makade-maanishtaanish

[1]   Baa Baa makade-maanishtaanish
Awiiya na maanishtaanishibiiwiin gidayaawaa?
Eya'. Eya'. Niso-mashkimod.
Ingod o'ow mashkimod a'aw indoogimaam.
Ingo-mashkimod wiin indoogimaakwem.
Miinawaa ingo-mashkimod a'aw gwiiwizens
Iwidi miikanensing gii-ani-danademod.

Gaazhagens Miinawaa Naazhaabii'igan

[1]   Inashke gosha, inashke gosha dazhi-naazhaabii'ige a'aw
      gaazhagens.
Miinawaa gaa-izhi-gichi-gwaashkwanid a'aw bizhiki imaa
      dibiki-giizisong.
Imaa endanaapid a'aw animoons waabandang
      menwendaagwadinig.
Miinawaa a'aw onaagan miinawaa emikwaanens
      ginjiba'iwewag.

Jiigibiig Nenaandago-ziibiing

[1]   Mi i'iw bezhig gaa-izhiwebiziyaang iko gii-abinoojiinyiwiyaang.
Ayi'iing, mii iwedi Gibaakwa'iganing izhinikaadeg iwidi
gii-taayaang jiigibiig, jiigi-ziibi i'iw Nenaandago-ziibi
ezhinikaadeg. Mii eta go gaye niin gaa-izhi-gikendamaan
ezhinikaadeg mewinzha. Noongom wiin chimookomaan
Tamarack River odizhinikaadaanaawaa. Mii iwidi gaa-taayaang.
Mii megwaa go gii-pimaadizishid a'aw nimaamaayiban gii-
ayaayaang iwidi. Gaye gomaa apii go gii-ayaamagad i'iw ziibi
imaa gaa-onda'ibiiyaang gaa-ondinamaang sa go nibi.

thought about how we were always called "the damn Indians." And that's where we lived in the tules by ourselves.

Baa Baa Black Sheep

[1]   Baa Baa black sheep,
Have you any wool?
Yes, sir. Yes, sir. Three bags full.
One bag is for the king.
One bag is for the queen.
And one bag is for the little boy
Who lives down the lane.

The Cat and the Fiddle

[1]   Hey diddle diddle, the cat played the fiddle,
And the cow jumped over the moon.
The little dog laughed to see such a sport.
And the dish ran away with the spoon.

On the Bank of the Tamarack River

[1]   This one's about how we used to do things when we were kids. We lived over there on the shore at The Dam as it's called, near the river, the Tamarack River as it's called. And I might be the only one who remembers what it was called long ago. Today the white man calls it the Tamarack River. That's where we lived. We were over there while my mother was still alive. There was a river there then where we fetched water there, where we got water.

[2] Ayaabita go gaye imaa, mii imaa gii-poodawed; indedeyiban gii-poodawanaad giziibiiga'igenid nimaamaayibanen ji-gizhaagamezang nibi. Mii agood a'aw jiibaakwaanaad gegoo imaa. Ogii-ozhitoonaawaa. Miish i'iw, iniw okaadakikoon imaa gaa-agoonaawaajin imaa gaa-tazhi-gizhaabikizang nimaamaayiban i'iw dazhi-gizhaagamezang i'iw nibi imaa aabajitood wii-kiziibiiga'iged. Gaa-izhi-abinoojiinyiwiyaang gii-anoozhiyangid nimaamaayiban i'iw ji-mooshkinebinangid a'aw akik, okaadakik wii-kizhaagamezang nibi. Mii booch epiichi-boodawanaad iniw akikoon.

[3] Mii gaa-onji-batwaadamaang i'iw nibi. Anooj igo wii-tazhi-daayaang igo imaa, inashke ayi'ii gaawiin igo gii-timiisinoon i'iw ziibi imaa noongom ayaamagak gaa-onda'ibiiyaang. Mii gaa-onji-batwaadamaang i'iw nibi. Mii ingiw igaye, bezhig nishiimeyiban a'aw gii-agaashiinyi gaye wiin. Agaawaa go gii-pimose gaye wiin onaagaans gii-takonang gii-naadid nibi. Nawaj omaa aanish indinawemaaganag akikoonsan gegoo gagwe-aawadiiyaang awenen nawaj. Mii gii-aawadood nibi. Gaye miish gii-shiigonamowaad i'iw gii-shiigonang nimaamaa i'iw bengo-bakwezhigan, gigine-bakwezhigan gii-pi-abid mashkimodaang, mii i'iw. Inashke, gaawiin igo aapiji gii-kichi-onjigaasinoon iniw. Gegaa go gii-paabaabasaabiigadoon iniw mashkimodan, apagiwayaaneshkimodan.

[4] Mii gaye niin i'iw gaa-aabajitooyaan mikwendamaan ani-maajii-batwaadamaan i'iw mashkimodaash. Mooshkinebadooyaan, gaawiin igo minik i'iw gii-ako-gashkinamaan gii-piidooyaan gaye niin i'iw ziigwebinamaan imaa akikong i'iw. Gaye, mii gaye niin i'iw mikwendamaan gaa-aabajitooyaan gii-onzibiiyaang gaa-aawadooyaang i'iw nibi.

[5] Booch igo ingoding igo ingii-mooshkinebanaanaan a'aw akik. Gaye ingii-aawadoon. Ingii-tazhitaamin igo dazhitaayaang dazhiikamaang i'iw nibi. Ganabaj onzaam imaa akeyaa iko i'iw awiiya ge-biziigwebakiteshing i'iw nibi, aya'aa ogii-mooshkinebanaan aawanaad dash iko nimaamaayiban i'iw booch igo gii-mooshkinebanangid a'aw akik. Inashke wiin, mii go o'ow apii, ingii-odaminomin igo, dibishkoo i'iw apii noongom wiin anoonigooyaan iko gichi-anokiiwin, gichi-anokiiwinagak i'iw aawadoong, nibinaading sa go gegoo wii-mooshkinebanind a'aw akik.

[2]   About halfway [to the river] he built a fire there; my father
      built a fire for my mother where she washed clothes so that
      she could heat water. She hung it there when she cooked
      things. They built it. That was that tripod kettle they
      suspended there where my mother heated things, heated up
      that water she would use when she wanted to wash clothes.
      When we were kids my mother made us fill up that kettle,
      that [three-]legged kettle when she wanted to heat water.
      Then she really built up the fire around that kettle.

[3]   So that's why we raced after that water. Wherever we lived
      there, you see now it wasn't deep at that river there where we
      fetched the water. So that's why we made a game of running
      for that water. The others [did] too, and one of my younger
      siblings was quite small. And he could hardly walk as he
      grasped that bucket when he went after water. We tried to
      haul water for more of my relative's kettles, whoever [needed
      help]. So he hauled water. Then they emptied it in, my
      mother emptied it from the flour and meal bags. You see,
      they didn't leak very much. Those bags almost tightened up
      around the liquid, those sacks.

[4]   So that's what I remember using myself too when I started
      to fill that old bag. I filled it to no particular level, just what I
      was capable of managing to bring and pour into that kettle
      there myself. So that's what I remember using when I got
      and hauled that water.

[5]   One time we really filled that kettle. I was hauling too.
      We spent quite a bit of time as we were there working on
      [hauling] that water. Maybe all too often there one of us
      would wipe out, spilling that water, and then my mother
      used to fill it, hauling it herself, so we certainly filled up that
      kettle. You see, we played around at times, like when I used
      to get ordered about that hard work because hauling is hard
      labor, fetching water in order to fill that kettle.

[6] Mii imaa aabiding mamikwendamaan i'iw iwidi
Gibaakwa'iganing gii-taayaang jiigibiig i'iw Nenaandago-
ziibi ezhinikaadeg. Mii i'iw minik imaa ezhi-ani-
mikwendamaan ji-inaajimong i'iw. Noongom wiin ganabaj
gaawiin awiiya gey abi ogikendanziin ezhinikaadenig i'iw ziibi,
anishinaabewinik adenig. Niin iko indaa-ani-gagwedwe iko
iwidi izhaayaan. Gaawiin awiiya geyaabi ogikendanziin. Mii eta
go ezhi-gikendamowaad *Tamarack River*. Mii wanising iniw
anishinaabe-izhinikaazowinan. Wanisinoon anooj
gaa-izhinikaade in iniw gaye odenawan iwidi. Noongom
wanisinoon gii- nishinaabewinikaadeg iko mewinzha.

Ikwabin

[1] Anooj igo gegoo ayi'ii nitaawadoon iniw ojibwemong, inashke
a'aw iwidi wayeshkad gii-tibaajimoyaan—giboodiyegwaazon
ezhinikaazod. Mii i'iw, mii i'iw anooj eni-ikidong. Inashke
awiiya namadabid ingoji nandawenimind ingoji bakaan ji-o-
namadabid, gegoo izhi-wiindamawind ingoji bakaan ji-o-
namadabid, ji-namadabisig imaa geyaabi, gaye noongom awiiya
ikidod i'iw, "indaga ikwabin." Mii i'iw enind a'aw awiiya ingoji
bakaan ji-o-namadabid, ikwabing.
[2] Gayesh wiin a'aw, mii ko mewinzha anishinaabeg gii-
odikwamiwaad. Mii i'iw *head lice, body lice.* Mii iniw ikwan gaa-
izhinikaanaawaajin. Gayesh awiiya ikidong i'iw "ikwabin,"
ingod dibishkoo inind awiiya ji-inabid amanj enabigwen
a'aw ikwa. *It's easier to explain that in English because it sounds,
when you say "ikwabin," it means "sit like a louse."* Mii i'iw
anooj initaagwak iniw anishinaabe-ojibwemowinang.

Gidinwewininaan

[1] Ganabaj igo mii geget wanising o'ow ojibwemowin. Gegoo imaa
iwidi bezhig gaa-ozhitooyaan naabisijigan. Noomaya gomaa
ingii-kiizhiikaan gaa-tibaajimoyaan o'ow ezhi-wanitood
a'aw anishinaabe gaa-ina'oonind ji-inwed da-ojibwemoyang.
Geget wanitoowaad; inashke igo gaa-inaadodamaan iwidi
wanitoowaad ezhinikaadenig anooj odenawan, ziibiwan,

[6] So that's my recollection of when we lived at The Dam on the banks of the *Nenaandago-ziibi* (Tamarack River) as it was called. That's the extent of what I can recall to be told of it. Today nobody knows what that river is called any more, how it's called in Indian language. I should ask the next time I go over there. No one knows that any more. They only know Tamarack River. Those Indian names are getting lost. The names of many villages as they were called over there are getting lost. Today it is getting lost how things were called in Indian long ago.

Sit Elsewhere

[1] There are some good [puns] in the Ojibwe language, for example that first one I talked about over there—the [meaning] of the name "pants." There are all kinds of sayings. You see if someone is sitting somewhere and someone wants him to sit somewhere else, he is thus told to go sit in a different place, not to sit there any more, and someone says this, "*indaga ikwabin.*" That's what that person is told in order to go sit in a different place, sit elsewhere.

[2] And a long time ago Indians used to get lice. That's those head lice, body lice. They were called *ikwa*. And so when someone says "*ikwabin,*" it's just like someone is being told to sit however it is that [a] louse sits. It's easier to explain that in English because it sounds, when you say "*ikwabin,*" it means, "sit like a louse." That's how that sounds in the Ojibwe Indian language.

Our Language

[1] Perhaps this Ojibwe language really is being lost. That's what that one recording I made over there is about. Recently I finished telling about how the Indian is thus losing this thing he was gifted with, to have a language for us to speak—Ojibwe. They're really losing it; you see this is what I was talking about over there, how they're losing the

miikanan, anooj igo gegoo ingiw wanitoowaad. Gaawiin awiiya geyaabi ogikendanziin. Gaawiin ogikendanziinaawaa iniw zaaga'iganiin ezhinikaadeg, ojibwewinikaadeg. Mii noongom eta go zhaaganaashiiwinikaadamowaad ezhi-gikendamowaad noongom abinoojiinyag. Ganabaj awiiya gaganoonaad onow abinoojiinyan, maagizhaa odaa-wiikwajitoonaawaa.

[2] Inashke go noongom onow niizhing akeyaa enwejig, wejibwemojig miinawaa go zhaaganaashiimowaad ingoji nagishkodaadiwaad. Niin wiin igo, ingoji nagishkawag, giishpin gikenimag ji-ojibwemod, mii go ojibwemotawag. Inashke, mii go imaa minik gayaagiigidoyaan ge-izhi-ojibwemotaadiyaang. Maagizhaa go miinawaa a'aw naasaab a'aw ingoji waabamag maajii-zhaaganaashiimotaadiyaang, mii go minik ge-mawadisidiyaang ge-zhaagaanaashiimoyaangiban. A'aw nitam gaagidod maajii-ojibwemod, mii go gaye ge-izhi-ojibwemongiban ji-wii-kashkitood. Gaye wiin aapiji ojibwemosig a'aw ge-ganoonind, mii i'iw. Gaawiin aabadasinoon. Wenipanad. Owenipanendaanaawaa noongom abinoojiinyag o'ow zhaaganaashiimowaad.

[3] Inashke go iwidi gaa-ako-gichi-miigaadiing gaye niin gaa-izhaayaan o-dagoshinaan; azhegiiweyaan eshkwaa-miigaadiing i'iw gii-noondawagwaa ingiw abinoojiinyag gaawiin aapiji ojibwemosiiwag. Miish iniw igo niijaya'aag, ingiw indedeyiban oniijaanisan. Ingii-wani'aanaan niinawind nimaamaa. Gayesh wiinawaa, gii-wiidiged a'aw indedeyiban, mii abinoojiinyan wiinawaa gii-ayaawaad. Mii ingiw gaa-izhi-wiikwaji'angidwaa ji-ojibwemowaad. Gayesh igo noongom mii go akina izhi-ojibwemowaad ongow, ongow nishiimeyag, mii ingiw. Niinawind ingii-ojibwemotawaanaanig. Gaye wiin a'aw bezhig gaa-omisenyiyaan waadiged gaye wiin, iniw oniijaanisan bebakaan gii-ayaawag. Gaawiin awiiya ogii-ojibwemotaagosiiwaan. Inashke noongom agaawaa ojibwemowag ingiw, mii ingiw nishimisag miinawaa niningwanisag. Gaawiin ojibwemosiiwag. Ogikendaanaawaa. Nisidotamoog igo. Aanawi gaawiin dash ogii-aabajitoonsiinaawaa. Namanj gemaa gaye agadendamowaagwen ingoji gegoo ji-wanigiizhwewaad. Gegoo ogotaanaawaa awiiya ji-baapi'igowaad.

names of many villages, rivers, roads, and they're losing all sorts of things. Nobody knows this any more. They don't know what those lakes are called, what they're called in Ojibwe. Kids today only call things by their English names since that's all they know. Perhaps if someone talked to these children, maybe they would endeavor to do that [speak in Ojibwe].

[2] You see it's even like that today with bilingual people, when those who speak Ojibwe and English meet one another someplace. As for me, when I meet someone somewhere, if I know he speaks Ojibwe, I speak to him in Ojibwe. You see, when I speak that [language] we end up speaking to one another in Ojibwe. And quite similarly when I see someone somewhere and we start speaking English to one another, the entire time we visit one another we'll speak English. When the first person to speak starts speaking Ojibwe, then he'll succeed in having the [entire] conversation in Ojibwe. However, if he doesn't respond much in Ojibwe when he's spoken to, that's it. It doesn't get used. It's simple. Today the children think it is easier for them to speak English.

[3] You see I went over there, arriving over there for World War II; when I came back after the war was over, when I heard those children, they weren't speaking Ojibwe very much. That [included] my companions, my father's children. We had lost my mother. And those ones, my father had those kids through his [second] marriage. We tried to enable them to speak Ojibwe. And today they all speak Ojibwe, my younger siblings. We spoke Ojibwe to them ourselves. And one who was an older sister to me had gotten married too, so there were different kids. Nobody spoke Ojibwe to them. You see today they hardly speak any Ojibwe, that's my nieces and nephews. They don't speak Ojibwe. They know it. They understand. But in spite of this they don't use it. Perhaps they might feel shy to make some mistake somewhere. They are afraid someone will laugh at them.

[4] Aanawi wii-wiikwaji'agwaa gii-kikinoo'amawagwaa
bemaadizijig ji-ojibwemowaad, mii i'iw apane gaa-inagwaa
i'iw. "Giishpin awiiya wanigiizhwed, gego baapi'aakegon,"
ingii-inaag. Ingii-inaag miinawaa, "Gii-kikinoo'amaagoziyeg
awiiya bi-wiijiiwig apane gaye ge-waabameg. Mii imaa akeyaa
ge-izhi-gaganoonidiyeg," ingii-inaag idash.

[5] Gaye wiin noongom abezhig bezhigod, gaawiin
owiikwajitoosiin wii-aabajitood i'iw, ji-ojibwemod.
Ojibwemotawind igo awiiya, mii gomaa apii ge-izhi-
nisidotang. Miinawaa go, mii gomaa apii ge-izhi-
wiikwajitood ji-ojibwemod.

[6] Inashke iniw gaa-omaamaayikaayaan oozhishenyan ogii-
ayaawaan. Gaye, gaawiin ingiw gii-pi-nitaawigiwaad ingiw
ojibwemosiiwag. Miish a'aw nimaamaayikaan imaa,
niiyawe'enh, a'aw nindedeyiban gaa-wiidigemaajin, ogii-
pami'aan aanind iniw. Apane gii-pamoozhe, mii go apane.
Gaawiin gii-nitaa-zhaaganaashiimosiin. Mii i'iw apane gii-
ojibwemotawaad iniw abinoojiinyan. Inashke, mii i'iw
gomaa apii ingoji ingiw abinoojiinyag gaa-izhi-
zhaaganaashiimowaad. Noongom dash igo ojibwemowag
gaganoonindwaa. Ojibwemotawindwaa ongow
ji-ojibwemowaad. Zhaaganaashiimotawindwaa,
zhaagaanaashiimowag. Mii go niizhing akeyaa izhi-
inwewaad gaagiigidowaad. Daa-gaagiigidowag ongow
abinoojiinyag. Niizhiwag ganabaj netaa-gaagiigidojig.

[7] Wiikwaji'ind igo gaganoonind a'aw awiiya, mii i'iw akeyaa ge-
izhi-gashkitood ji-ojibwemod, nitam ji-nisidotang. Miish
miinawaa ge-izhi-wiikwajitood giishpin awiiya ayaasinig ge-
baapi'igod ingiw wanigiizhwed. Gaawiin onjida odoodanziin
i'iw—wanigiizhwed gegoo gikinoo'amawind. Noongom niin
awiiya noondawag gegoo wani-ikidod, mii gomaa apii ezhi-
wiindamawag imaa gii-ikidod.

[8] Inashke noongom ingiw nishiimeyag, mii go gaye wiinawaa
ezhi-nitaa-ojibwemowaad ingiw. Gaye wiinawaa gegoo ani-
wawanendamowaad, geyaabi ingagwejimigoog. Miinawaa
ingagwejimigoog mii onow akeyaa ekidong, ikidoyaan. Mii
ezhi-wiindamawagwaa akeyaa wii-ikidowaad. Mii ganabaj
akeyaa gii-izhi-gikendang a'aw bemaadizid ji-ojibwemod.

[9] Indayaa owidi ayaapii ishkoniganing gabe-niibin noongom
endaayaan. Mii go omaa, ingii-ani-onji-maajaa. Gichi-

[4]   Anyhow I want to try to enable the people I taught to speak
       Ojibwe, which is why I always tell them that. "If someone
       makes a mistake speaking, don't laugh at him," I told them.
       I also told them, "When you're being taught, always
       accompany someone who can oversee you. In that way you
       will always be conversing," I told them.

[5]   Also today when one person is by himself, he won't endeavor
       to want to use it, to speak Ojibwe. When someone is spoken
       to in Ojibwe, that's when he will come to an understanding
       of it. Then at that time he will also make the effort to speak
       Ojibwe.

[6]   You see my stepmother had grandchildren. And as they were
       raised they didn't speak Ojibwe. Then my stepmother there
       who had married my father, my namesake, they took care of
       them. She was always babysitting, always. She didn't speak
       English too well. So she was always speaking Ojibwe to
       those kids. You see, some time later those kids would thus
       speak English somewhere. And today they speak Ojibwe
       when they are spoken to. Talk to people in Ojibwe so that
       they will speak Ojibwe. When people are spoken to in
       English, they speak English. That's how it is when bilingual
       people speak. These kids should speak. There are probably
       [only] a couple good speakers.

[7]   When someone is enabled to be spoken to, that's the way he
       will be able to speak Ojibwe, to understand first. And then
       he makes an effort when there is nobody there to laugh at
       him if he makes a mistake. He won't do that intentionally—
       make a mistake while speaking something he's been taught.
       Today when I hear someone misspeak, sometime later I just
       tell him what he said there.

[8]   You see now my younger siblings, they also speak good
       Ojibwe. But when they forget something, they still ask me.
       They ask me about how things are said, how I say them. So
       I tell them about what they want to say. That's probably the
       way that a person learns how to speak Ojibwe.

[9]   I have been over here on the reservation all springtime,
       where I now live. So this is why I left here [long ago]. There

odenaang ayaawag ingiw omaa anishinaabeg. Mii wiin omaa,
owiikwajitoonaawaa. Owiikwajitoonaawaa nawaj niibowa
omaa wii-ojibwemowaad. Iwidi wiin ishkoniganing eyaajig
gaawiin aapiji owiikwajitoosiinaawaa. Mii eta go
gii-shaaganaashiimowaad, wiinawaa iwidi bezhig
wiikwajitoowaad. Namanj iidog gemaa gaye
agadendamowaagwen anishinaabewiwaad. Mii akeyaa
ge-izhi-wanitood a'aw anishinaabe odinwewin, agadendang
i'iw anishinaabewid.

Mawadishiwewin

[1] Mewinzha ko gaa-izhichigewaad gii-mawadisidiwaad
gichi-anishinaabeg gii-paa-nanibendaadiwaad. Mii go gaye
awiiya wii-maajaad. Mii go mawadishiwed ingoji gemaa gaye
waaboowayaan ogii-maajiidoon. Aanawi go ogikendaan ingoji
ji-nibe'ind. Mii dash igo gaa-izhi-biidood i'iw konaas igaye
ji-agwazhed. Gaawiish memwech inime'odisaajin memwech
akina gegoo odaa-ondinamaagosiin o'ow wiin gaa-izhi-
bimoondang gaye wii-agwazhed miinawaa go iniw
apikweshimod igaye. Mii eta go gii-waabanda'ind aandi
ji-nibaad miinawaa a'aw gegoo gii-miinind ji-apishimod.
Mii imaa wiinawaa gii-mawidisidiwaad. Akina gegoo ogii-
tazhindaanaawaa.

[2] Inashke giinawind noongom mawadisidiyaang, gegoo
maagizhaa ingo-diba'igan, niizho-diba'igan mawadisang
awiiya. Mii go i'iw. Gemaa go gaye gaa ingii-
kaganoonaasiiwaanaan. Mii i'iw mazinaatesijiganimakak
genawaabandamaang. Mewinzha ko wiinawaa gii-
tadibaajimotaadiwag akina gegoo ezhiwebadinig. Gayesh wiin
noongom gaawiin geyaabi gidizhichigesiimin. Inashke go owidi
noongom gabe-niibin o'ow ayaayaan, mii imaa ayaad a'aw
besho igo a'aw niitaa. Miish naa gayesh, iwidi go ingii-o-naanaa
indawemaagan. Miish imaa nazhikewid jiigi-ayaawid niitaa.
Giishpin ezhaayaan imaa endaad awi-mawidisag, mii eta go
i'iw mazinaatesijiganimakak genawaabandamaang. Mii
go, gaawiin gegoo indinaajimotaadisiimin. Gaye wiin igo
bi-izhaad giishpin gegoo wii-inaajimotaadiyaang,
mii i'iw giigidowin ayaabajitooyaang. Mii gaa-kanoozhid

are a lot of Indians [from] here in the Twin Cities. But un-
like here, they are making a concerted effort. More of the
[people from] here are making that endeavor [there] as
they want to speak Ojibwe. In contrast, the people on the
reservation don't seem to be making much of an effort.
They only speak English, whereas the ones over there are
trying. Maybe they're ashamed of being Indian. So that's
how the Indian is losing his language, by becoming
ashamed of being Indian.

Visiting

[1] This is about what our ancestors used to do a long time ago
when they visited one another and stayed at one another's
homes. Say someone wanted to leave. So he goes visiting
somewhere and he brings a blanket along. Anyway he
knows he'll be offered a place to sleep somewhere. And
so he thus brought that blanket to cover up with. It wasn't
necessary for those hosting him to furnish him with everything, as he would carry with him what he wanted to cover
up with and use for a pillow, too. He was just shown where
he would sleep and given something to lie down on. So they
visited one another there. They talked about everything.

[2] When we visit one another today, it's maybe one hour or
two that we visit someone. That's it. And maybe we don't
even talk to him. We just watch that television set. Long ago
they used to talk to one another about everything that was
going on. But today, however, we no longer do that. You see
I've been staying over here all spring now, near where my
brother-in-law is there. Then I'd go over there and get my
relation [of sorts]. So my brother-in-law is there by himself
next door. If I go to his house to visit him, we only watch
that television set. So we don't really talk to one another.
And instead of coming over, if we want to talk to one
another, we use that telephone. It was he who informed me
of this, revealing how we converse on the telephone when
we want to talk to each other about something. So that's the
only time we visit one another, when we use that telephone

ganawaabanda'iiyaamagak gaganoonidiyaang giigidowining gegoo waa-inaajimotaadiyaang. Mii eta go apii mewidisidiyaang, i'iw giigidowin aabajitooyaang dibaajimotaadiyaang gegoo. Mii imaa akeyaa. Imbaapimin igo. Agwajiing igo niibing ayaayaang eniwek waa-kanoozhid, inaajimotaading.

Gaa-ina'oonind Anishinaabe

[1] Omaa odenaang ayaayaang, gichi-odenaang ayaayaang, ingoding igo omaa gii-pi-giigido bezhig a'aw inini. Ginwenzh igo omaa ayaadog gichi-odenaang. Mii go, mii wiin igo gii-wanitood i'iw odizhitwaawin. Miinawaa gaawiin ojibwemosiin. Gaawiin igaye onisidotanziin. Miish i'iw gaa-izhi-biindigadood iniw chimookomaanan omaa ji-anami'aad gaa-izhi-gikendang, gaa-izhi-gikendang ezhitwaanid iniw chimookomaanan.

[2] Mii go omaa gaye wiin akeyaa gii-wiijii'iwed. Miinawaash igo onow ogitiziiman bezhig owidi gii-ayaawan ishkoniganing geyaabi. Inashke, mii wiin awedi geyaabi gaa-anishinaabewitwaad. Gaye gii-midewi. Gaye wiinawaa onow dewe'iganan ogii-tazhiikawaawaan. Mii iwidi gii-ayaagwen a'aw ganabaj a'aw mindimooyenh, iniw omaamaayan. Gayesh wiin a'aw inini imaa gii-pi-ganoozhid gaye wiin ogii-kikendaan anishinaabewitwaawin.

[3] Miish imaa gii-pi-gagwejimid, "Gidaa-gashkitoomin ina? Gidaa-wiidookawimin ina ji-aabajitooyaang nayenzh igo keyaa onow izhitwaawinan ji-wiiji'indiimagak igo—a'aw anishinaabe odizhitwaawin miinawaa go a'aw chimookomaan odizhitwaawin—i'iw anami'aang miinawaa midewing? Gidaa-gashkitoomin ina ji-wiiji'indiimagak igo nayenzh iniw akeyaa da-izhi-aabadak?" Ingii-kanoonig imaa ji-bi-gaganoonag gaye niin i'iw aaniin akeyaa ge-izhichigewaad ji-gashkitoowaad ji-wiiji'indiimagadinig iniw izhitwaawinan—anami'ewin miinawaa midewiwin. "Aaniish," ingagwejimigoog.

[4] Mii gaa-izhi-wiindamawagwaa. "Mii go izhi-booni'itoog," ingii-inaag i'iw apii. "Gaawiin gigashkitoosiinaawaa." Aanawi go, "Mii i'iw gegaa naasaab ezhi-gikenimang a'aw manidoo geganoonang. Bezhigoo a'aw omaa gaa-pagidininang," mii

to discuss things. That's how it is there. We laugh about it. We go outside a little more in the summer when he wants to talk to me, making conversation.

How Indian People Were Gifted

[1] When we were in the city here, when we were in Minneapolis, one time a certain man came to speak here. He must have been here in the Twin Cities a long time. So, in any event he had lost his religion. And he didn't speak Ojibwe. He didn't understand either. Then he had brought [Indian ways] into the white man's church here [or] what he knew of it, as he thus came to know how the white man worshipped.

[2] And so in this way he always accompanied those [people]. And one of his parents was over here on the reservation yet. You see she still followed the Indian religion. And she had been initiated into the medicine dance. And they had been involved with these [ceremonial] Drums. That old lady must have been over there, that's his mother. And that man came to talk to me there even though she also knew about the Indian religion.

[3] Then he asked me there, "Could we do it? Could you help us to use both religions to work them together—the Indian's religion and the white man's religion—church and medicine dance? Would we be able to blend them both together so that they could be used that way?" He beseeched me there to talk to him myself about what they might do to be able to weave together those religions—church and medicine dance. "Well," they asked me.

[4] So I told them this. "Leave it alone," I told them at that time. "You will not be able to do it." In spite of that, "It's almost the same thing how we know and talk to the spirit. There is only one [faith] here that we were offered," that Indian guy said. The white man he spoke to somewhere said

ikidod a'aw anishinaabe. Chimookomaan igo gaye wiin, mii iniw genoonaajin ingoji gegoo ekidod: "Gaawiin dash daaginigawisinzinoon iniw izhitwaawinan." Mii gaa-inagwaa, "Gaawiin gidaa-gashkitoosiinaawaa. Mii go izhi-booni'itoog i'iw wii-wiikwajitooyeg ji-wiiji'indiimagak miinawaa go ji-ginigawi'ind ezhitwaad a'aw bemaadizid. Gaawiin daa-gwayakosesinoon."

[5] Bebakaan gii-inaawag ongow bemaadizijig. Odizhitwaawiniwaa o'ow gii-miinaawag ji-aabajitoowaad ingiw. Anishinaabe gii-miinind igaye onow dewe'iganan miinawaa i'iw midewiwin miinawaa asemaan ji-aabaji'aad. Mii wiin gaa-ina'oonind a'aw anishinaabe.

[6] A'aw dash chimookomaan akina gegoo wiin gekendang mazina'iganing ogii-ozhitoon. Mazina'iganing ogii-ozhibii'aan. Miish igo akina awiiya noongom gaawiin onisidotanziin. Gaawiin igo gegoo odaa-agindanziin i'iw. Gaawiish gegoo wiin imaa odaa-ondinanziin i'iw mazina'iganing ji-agindang. Noongom aano-gikendaasod; gaawiin odaa-gashkitoosiin ji-gikendang i'iw enamanji'od a'aw anishinaabe imaa isa wiin gaa-ina'oonind. Gaye gaawiin wiin ingoji oganawisinzininig ogii-ozhibii'anziin.

[7] Gegapii ina'oonind geget ayi'iing gii-ozhitood gii-kikinawaajitood akeyaa ge-ani-izhitwaad. Wiigwaasing wiin ogii-ozhibii'aan i'iw. Gaawiin wiin ikidowinan ogii-ozhibii'anziinan. Iniw amanjidoowinan ayaabaji'aajin gegoo izhichiged; mii iniw gaa-ozhibiiwaajin. Gemaa wiigwaasing gaawiin gegoo ikidowin imaa ogii-ozhibii'anziin. Mii eta go gii-ozhibii'ang aaniin akeyaa ge-ini-inikaad a'aw anishinaabe. Gaye, mii imaa wiin a'aw anishinaabe gikendang i'iw aaniin enaabadizid a'aw awesiinh gaye. Mii ezhi-manidoowid. Aanish akina gegoo wiin ogii-manidookaadaan a'aw manidoo azhigwaa wezhi'aagobanen anishinaaben. A'aw wiin wayaabishkiiwed binaanoondang mazina'igan i'iw ayaabajitood wenji-gikendang noongom i'iw ba-izhitwaad. Gayesh igaye ayaapii odani-aanjibii'aan i'iw mazina'igan.

[8] Mii gaa-inagwaaban imaa gii-pi-gagwejimiwaad ji-ginigawisidooyaang i'iw ayi'ii izhitwaawin gaa-ina'oonind a'aw anishinaabe miinawaa a'aw chimookomaan. Inashke bebakaan wiinawaa gaye gii-ina'oonaawag agaami-gichi-gamiing eyaajig. Gaye ingiw zhodaawininiwag gaye wiinawaa bakaan

the same thing, though: "But you can not mix those religions." I told them, "You won't be able to do it. Just abandon your endeavor to work them together and mix up the people's religious beliefs. That can't be right."

[5] Each [group of] people was told something different. They were [each] given religions for their use. The Indian people were given these Drums and the medicine dance and tobacco to use. That is how the Indian people were gifted.

[6] And on the other hand, that white man created his knowledge of everything from a book. He wrote it down in a book. But today all people don't understand it. The [Indian] shouldn't read things in that. And he shouldn't derive things from that book for his study. Now that would be education to no avail; one would not be able to learn about the status of the Indian there in how he was gifted himself. And he couldn't write down somewhere things that were not to be written.

[7] Eventually as he was so gifted the [Indian] made a certain way of marking things about his religion. However, he wrote that on birch bark. He didn't write down words. Symbols were used about what he did; those were the inscriptions. He did not write words on the birch bark there. So he only wrote about how the Indian's life would turn out. Also [put] there was the Indian's knowledge of how the animal was to be used. So it was spiritual. Well, everything relating to how the spirit made Indian people was considered spiritual. The white man, however, uses the passages in that book to get his knowledge of how he believes today. And also from time to time he writes changes to that book.

[8] So that's what I told them there when they asked me about integrating the religion gifted to the Indian and that of the white man. You see each people was gifted differently including those who are on the other side of the ocean. And those Jewish people have different religious beliefs

izhitwaawag. Miinawaa ongow aniibiishikewininiwag gaye
wiinawaa bakaan izhitwaawag. Aaniish imaa waa-izhi-
wiikwajitood o'ow chimookomaan wii-makamaad iniw
anishinaaben i'iw odizhitwaawininig gaa-ina'oonimind. Mii
gaa-wii-inaajimotawagwaa iwidi. Miish igo ishkwaaj i'iw apii
gii-pi-gagwejimiwaad. Gaawiin miinawaa niikaanag ingii-
nandomigosiig ji-o-ganoonagwaa azhigwa akina gegoo gaa-
wiindamawagwaa aaniin ezhi-gikendamaan.

themselves. And these Asian people have different religious beliefs too. Well, the white man wanted to try to take the Indian's [god-]given religion away from him. That's what I wanted to tell them over there. That was after that time they came to ask me about that. My brethren didn't call upon me again to go over and talk to them as I had now told them everything about why I know that.

MELVIN EAGLE

MELVIN EAGLE (b. 1931), whose Anishinaabe name is *Miskwaanakwad* (Red Sky), is a gifted oratorical artist. He grew up hearing legends told by his grandfathers Chief Migizi and Jim Littlewolf, both of whom were prominent religious and political figures in their community. When he was a boy, his uncles and a number of older men from the community at Neyaashiing forced him to sit and listen to their stories about history, culture, and daily life.

When he was first sent to day school at Onamia, Minnesota, Melvin spoke nothing but his first language, Ojibwe. The school was conducted entirely in English, and, through the power of immersion and embarrassment, Melvin quickly acquired knowledge of the English language. However, he never forgot Ojibwe, and, throughout his schooling in reading, writing, and arithmetic, Melvin continued to be instructed about Big Drum, hunting, fishing, and ricing by numerous elders in his community.

As a young man, Melvin was commissioned to hold one of the permanent seats on the Mille Lacs Big Drums. There he began his formal education in the songs and speeches used at the ceremonial dances. He would eventually become a member on the Ladies Drum at Mille Lacs and two more Big Drums. The miraculous story of his healing at the Drum and his reaffirmed faith in Ojibwe culture is detailed in the following narratives.

As Melvin approached middle age, his knowledge of the Drum and fluency in the language proved to be assets well appreciated by his peers, and on one of the Big Drums Melvin was raised up to the position of Drum Chief. From then on, Melvin was to be not only a student of Indian ways, but also an increasingly recognized and respected teacher of Ojibwe culture.

Melvin worked several jobs, sometimes as far away as Minneapolis. However, he never relinquished Mille Lacs as his home base and spiritual center. In his retirement, Melvin is busier than ever. He was recently seated as the first *Oshkaabewis* on the Big Drum at White Earth, and he uses that position to teach the proper means of conducting the ceremonies. He also travels frequently to participate in Drum ceremonies at Round Lake, Lake Lena, East Lake, and elsewhere.

In December 1997, I was in Mille Lacs for the dance at which Melvin's Big Drum was being used. I stayed at Melvin's house to visit and to record some Ojibwe stories. As I flipped on the tape and Melvin began to speak, I was astounded by the depth of his knowledge and experience, as well as his gift for gab. Melvin filled up one side of my 120-minute tape and, when I flipped over the tape, he continued to speak, nearly filling the second side as well. He only used one English word—Batiste—the name of a Mille Lacs elder. Everything else was unwavering, fluent Ojibwe, full of inspiring thoughts about the importance of language and culture as well as humorous reminiscences about Melvin's learning process and the actions of various elders around him. I had goose bumps at parts of his story and laughed out loud at others.

By the time he was finished speaking, Melvin had shared a great deal of information about numerous learned elders—*gekendaasojig*—and the process of acquiring their knowledge himself—*gikendaasowin*. Ultimately, we broke his long narration into several stories for ease of access and reference. However, all of Melvin's stories in this book were originally connected as one piece of verbal art. Humble, open, and very entertaining, the stories vividly describe Ojibwe cultural beliefs from hunting to Big Drum ceremonies—the Anishinaabe gift of *gikendaasowin*.

Gimishoomisinaan

[1] Ahaaw-sh iwidi mewinzha go daa-gii-pi-agaashiinyiyaan iko gii-pabizindawagwaa akiwenziiyag gii-pizindawagwaa ko waawiindamawiwaad gegoo iwidi ko mewinzha o'ow indazhindaan. Owidi mewinzha ko gii-kichi-naaniimi'idiiwaad Gaa-waababiganikaag gii-izhaa gii-pi-onjibaad gaa-onji-ondaadiziyaan gaye niin. Wa'aw akiwenzii iwidi Gaa-waababiganikaag gii-onjibaa. Owidi gii-pi-niimi'idiid omaa, omaa o'ow ikwe-dewe'igan omaa gii-tibendaagozi omaa nookomis. Miish imaa nimishoomis gaye gii-pi-wiidigemaad gii-pi-niimi'idiiwaad ko. Mii imaa gaa-izhi-ondaadizid nimaamaa.

[2] Miinawaa-sh gegoo nisiwag ingiw gwiiwizensag imaa, iwidi Gaa-waababiganikaag. Ma'iingaansag gii-izhinikaazowag. Miinawaa aya'aa iwidi bezhig a'aw wiijikiwending. Gaawiin ingikenimaasiin ezhinikaazod a'aw akiwenzii gii-wiidigending Gaa-miskwaawaakokaag. Mii gaye wiidiged imaa-sh gaye wiin akiwenzii imaa-sh besho iwidi Gaa-waababiganikaag. Mii iwidi gaa-onjibaawaad ingiw Ma'iingaansag gaa-izhinikaazojig.

[3] O'ow dash akiwenzii imaa ingii-waawiindamaag ko gii-pi-naaniimi'idiiwaad iko biboong gii-paa'igoowaad iko miinawaa go sa ingoji aabita gii-tazhi-daawag ko gii-pi-azhegiiwewaad imaa gii-pi-niimi'idiiwaad. Mii eta ko gii-pi-anokiiwaapan gii-niimi'idiiwaad miinawaa go mawadishiwewaad gaye wii-ishkwaa-niimi'idiiwaad gigizhebaawagak. Miinawaa aangodinong ko niiyogon ko gii-niimi'idiiwag omaa. Mii omaa Neyaashiing akeyaa gii-kichi-naaniimi'idiiwaad iko ongow dewe'iganag.

[4] Mii iwidi akeyaa dewe'iganag gaa-pi-onjibaawaad bwaanakiing. Niibowa eyaajig omaa o'ow dash dagoshinowaad omaa ingiw dewe'iganag. Mewinzha ko ongow anishinaabeg gii-miigaanaawaad iniw bwaanan. Gaawiin igo sa gikendanziiwag. Gii-maanendiwag apane ingiw bwaanag miinawaa go anishinaabeg, gii-miigaanaawaad iniw bwaanan. Gaawiin ongow anishinaabeg odaa-gii-miigaanaasiiwaawaan iniw bwaanan. Ayi'iin dash iniw baashkiziganan ogii-ayaanaawaan wiinawaa go anishinaabeg iwidi gii-pi-onjibaawaad akeyaa wendaabang. Omaa gii-pi-dagoshinowaad gii-

Our Grandfather

[1] All right then, a long time ago when I was a child I used to listen to the elderly men, listening to them in what they told me about different things over there a long time ago, this [is] what I'm talking about. A long time ago they used [to] have huge Big Drum ceremonies over there at White Earth; the people went there where they came from just as I originate from there myself. This one old man was from over there at White Earth. My grandmother was a member of the Ladies Drum here [at Mille Lacs] when they were having a Big Drum Ceremony over here. And then my grandfather married her while they were having [a] Drum Ceremony. That's where my mother was born.

[2] And there were three boys there too, over there at White Earth. They were called the Littlewolfs. And with that one guy over there, they were all brothers. I don't know that one old man's name who got married at Cass Lake. And that one old man got married there, but that's close over there to White Earth. That's where they were from, those Littlewolfs as they were called.

[3] That old man there told me this here about how they used to have Drum Ceremony in the winter and they would go along until somewhere about halfway there where they would stay and then return there when it came to be time for the Dance to be held. They only used to work when they had Drum ceremonies and then they visited after they had the dance in the morning. And sometimes they used to hold a dance for four days here. Right here by Neyaashiing they used to have really big Drum ceremonies with these Drums.

[4] The Drums originated over there in the Sioux lands. There were a lot of them here when those Drums came here. A long time ago these Indians used to fight those Dakotas. They don't know why. The [Ojibwe] Indians and the Dakotas hated each other, and they fought those Dakotas. These Indians shouldn't have fought the Dakotas. But the Indians had acquired guns for themselves from the east where they came from. When they arrived here they liked this land. That's why they fought those Dakotas. And those Dakotas went out there towards the west where the

minwendamowaad o'ow aki. Mii gaa-onji-miigaanaawaad iniw
bwaanan. Gayesh imaa gii-izhaawaad ingiw bwaanag akeyaa
bangishimog gii-kiizhikawaawaad. Gayesh ingiw bwaanag
gaa-shawenimaawaad iniw dibishkoo gii-maanendiwag sa
go. Miish ingiw bwaanag gaa-izhi-inendamowaad i'iw wii-
miinaawaad iniw dewe'iganan, dibishkoo go akeyaa o'ow
apane gii-miigaadiwaad dibishkoo go gii-shawendiwaad;
gii-shawenimaawaad iniw anishinaaben i'iw gii-
niimiwenigoowaad. Mii gaa-pi-onji-maajii-izhaawaad ingiw
dewe'iganag imaa gii-pi-dagoshinowaad ingiw dewe'iganag.

[5] Dibishkoo go i'iw gii-ani-miinaawaad; iwidi ingiw
bwaanzhii-dewe'iganag imaa wenji-ayaawaad, weweni ji-
ganawendaagozinid iniw anishinaaben. Mii imaa wenji-
ayaawaad ingiw dewe'iganag. Biinish igo iwidi akeyaa gii-
izhaawag akeyaa iwidi akeyaa bangishimog gii-pi-maajaawaad
bangishimog gii-izhaawaad akeyaa. Mii eta go bezhig i'iw apane
ezhaad a'aw dewe'igan iwidi akeyaa wendaabang. Gaawiin daa-
gii-azhegiiwesiin imaa, iwidi.

[6] Imaa gaye wiinawaa ingiw Waawiyegamaag, mii imaa gaye
wiinawaa ongow anishinaabeg gii-shawenimaawaad
anishinaaben iwidi Waawiyegamaag. Biinish igo iwidi
akeyaa iwidi waasa gii-izhi-izhaawaad dewe'iganag gii-
kikinoo'amawaawaad gaye wiinawaa gii-shawenimaawaad,
gichi-ganawenimigoowaad iniw dewe'iganan. Mii gaa-
onji-ayaad dewe'igan ji-wiidookawaawaad zhawendaagozinid
anishinaaben.

[7] Mii sa go gaa-onji-gikendaasoyaan gaye niin gaa-wiindamawid
a'aw akiwenzii, a'aw moozhag gaa-waawiindamawid gii-
agaashiinyiyaan. Gaawiin go ingii-izhi-mikwendanziin go
wiin. Iwidi go wiin-sh chi-aya'aawiyaan, niin maagizhaa
gikendamaan iko wiindamawid akiwenzii. Dibishkoo go
bijiinaago, awasanaago indinendam ko gii-waawiindamawid
a'aw akiwenzii, akeyaa gaye manidoo akiwenzii gaa-
wiindamawid akina go gegoo omaa miikana gaa-agoojigewaad,
gaa-adaawaagewaad wiigwaasi-mazinigwaasowaad. Miish
gegoo gii-pi-maajaawaad bi-izhaawaad adaawewigamigong.
Mii go akiwenzii ganoozhid, "Hey! Omaa bi-izhaan. Omaa
bi-izhaan, ishkwaaj biindigen. Wewiib bi-izhaan omaa."
Namadabiyaan, "Haa namadabin. Aniibiish minikwen." Mii eta
go aniibiish minikwed. Mii go omaa ashamigooyaan, niibowa
ashamigooyaan gaye.

[Ojibwe] chased them. And then the Dakotas loved them just like they used to hate one another. Then it occurred to the Dakota to give them the Drums, and they loved one another the same way they used to hate one another; they really blessed those Indians in making such a gift as that. That's how those Drums came there, how those Drums arrived.

[5] It was just like that when they bestowed the gift on them; that's why those Sioux Drums are there, when the Indian people are looked after so well. That's why these Drums exist there. So they went over that way, out there toward the west, they left going out west. The Drum always only goes over there toward the east. It can't return over there.

[6] And the ones over there at Round Lake, these Indians here blessed them at Round Lake. The [Dakotas] themselves taught about them, too, up until the Drums went a long ways away over there and they loved them and wanted the Drums to be given the very best care. That's why the Drum came into being so that they could help the Indians in their blessing.

[7] This is how I became so learned myself about what that old man told me, as he was always telling me things when I was small. I couldn't remember then. But as I am now an elder myself, maybe I remember what that old man used to tell me. It's just like yesterday or the day before when I think about what that old man used to tell me about, as he told me about all spiritual matters and everything about this road—when they were hanging out their baskets for sale and working on birch bark embroidery. They would leave and go to the trader's shop. So this old man converses with me, "Hey! Come here. Come here, come in. Get over here quick." Then I would sit down, "All right sit down. Drink some tea." He only drank tea. I got fed there, and I got fed a lot.

[8]   Mii gaa-izhi-waawindamawiwaad i'iw aaniin ji-
gikendaasoyaan, o'ow gaagiigidoyaan imaa niimi'idiing.
Ingii-waawiidookawaag inendaagoziyaan, iniw manidoon
o'ow gii-waawiindamawiwaad. Mii moozhag. Mii omaa
gii-izhi-aajimod a'aw akiwenzii bezhig. Haa ani-maajaayaan,
mii go miinawaa gomaa apii miinawaa ani-izhaawaad
dagoshinowaad ani-agoojigewaad. "Hey, omaa bi-izhaan.
Omaa bi-izhaan, nishiimens." Indizhinikaanigoog ishkwaaj.
"Hey, omaa bi-izhaan." Mii go omaa biindigeyaan miinawaa
imaa. Gaawiin igo wiigiwaamens—wiigiwaamiin
ogii-ayaanaawaan. Mii go omaa, "Haa, namadabin. Aniibiish
minikwen." "Gaawiin ganabaj igo niin." Ingii-naanoogishkaa
gaa-wiindamaagooyaan akina. Gaawiin gaye naasaab
indibaajimotaagoosiin. Mii booch igo gii-kikendamaan
igo, miish ginwenzh. Gaawiin ingii-mikwendanziin.
Imaa-sh ezhi-gichi-aya'aawiyaan ezhi-ani-gikendamaan
gaa-waawiindamawiwaad ingiw akiwenziiyag. Miish i'iw
wenji-gikendaasoyaan gaye niin o'ow. Gaawiin go akina
go ingikendanziin. Maagizhaa gaye ingoding booch
inga-gikendaan i'iw gaa-wiindamawiwaad ingiw akiwenziiyag.

[9]   Mii sa go ani-maajaayaan, "Wayaa niin indebisinii." "Hey
gomaa indaakoshkade," indinendam ko mooseyaan, "niibowa
dash." Gaawiin indaa-ikidosiin. Apiichi-apiitenimadwaa ingiw
waawiindamokwaa, biinish go gii-miinadwaa gidasemaan
ishkwaa-waawiindamokwaa. Ishkwaa-wiindamaagooyaan
gegoo, o'ow isa ani-maajaayaan miinawaa indaakoshkade,
wii-ani-maajaayaan. Booch igo miinawaa chi-ganoozhid a'aw
akiwenzii, gaye aaniish gaa-onji-izhichigewaad ingiw
akiwenziiyag.

[10] Maazhaa ingii-kikenimigoog miinawaa naagaj ji-ani-biinag
dewe'igan ji-ani-gikendamaan. Mii imaa gaa-onji-
waawiindamawiwaad ingiw, o'ow isa akiwenzii gii-
waawiindamawid a'aw. Gaawiin igo wiinawaa apane
ingii-kaganoonigoosiin. Aya'aa Dedaakam, aya'aa abezhig
akiwenzii Medwe-ganoonind gii-izhinikaazod, mii gaye weweni
gaa-wiindamawid ge-izhiwebak dewe'igan sa go. Weweni iko
gii-maajiibizoyaang gii-niimi'idiiyaang owidi Waawiyegamaag.
Mii go ani-maajaayaang, ani-maajii-gaagiigidod a'aw
akiwenzii. Mii iwidi booch igo dagoshinaang, mii iwidi geyaabi
waawiindamawid o'ow isa dagoshinaang, wii-kabaayaang.

[8] He would tell me about things that would make me smarter, like the talk I give there at the Drum Ceremony. I helped them when I was thought of, and they would tell me this about those Spirits. This was all the time. That one old man would tell me things here in a certain way. And when I prepared to leave, a little while later he would get ready to take off and show up where they were hanging the laundry. "Hey, come here. Come here my little brother." That's what they called after a while. "Hey, come here." So I would go inside there again. Not some little hut—they had huge *wiigiwaams*. So in here, "All right, sit down. Drink some tea." "Maybe not for me." I had [already] stopped by from time to time when he told me about all these things. But he wouldn't tell me about the same things. So I certainly learned, and for a long time. I didn't remember then. But as I came into my old age, I arrived at an understanding of what those old men had been telling me about. And that's why I'm so knowledgeable about this myself. I don't know everything. But maybe sometime I'll certainly come to understand that which those old men told me.

[9] So I would get ready to leave, "*Wayaa* am I ever full." "Hey I even got a little stomachache," I used to think as I was crawling, "very much so." But I couldn't say that. When you hold them in such high regard for what they've told you, you give them your tobacco after they tell you about things. After I was told about these things, when I prepared to leave and had a stomachache [from overeating], then I would go. And that old man really gave me a talking to, and that's why all those elderly men did that.

[10] Perhaps they knew my [destiny] was to carry a Drum and come to know about it. That's why they told me about stuff there, why that old man told me about this. I wasn't told about this constantly. But that *Dedaakam* and that one old man named *Medwe-ganoonind*, he's the one who told me what would happen with the Drum. We used to start driving to Big Drum ceremonies over there at Round Lake. And as we prepared to leave, that old man started talking. Over there when we arrived, he was still jabbering at me when we got there, even when we disembarked. He was there first thing that morning—unbelievable. That's how

Zhebaa akawe gii-ayaa—gaawesh. Mii gaa-izhid akiwenzii. Mii go miinawaa maajaayaang, gaawiin go naasaab miinawaa inaajimotaagozisiin, apane go bakaan gii-inaajimotawid. Mii go omaa dagoshinaang, mii go omaa geyaabi gii-wiindamawid a'aw akiwenzii akeyaa gaa-izhi-gikendaasod a'aw akiwenzii. Mii i'iw wenji-gikendamaan ingiw dewe'iganag gaye niin gaa-onji-ininendaagoziyaan ji-bimiwinag a'aw dewe'igan, maagizhaa gikendaagoziwaanen o'ow ji-gikendamaan gegoo akiwenziiyag gaa-waawiindamawiwaad. Booch igo ingii-kaganoonigoog ingiw akiwenziiyag, akeyaa gaye bezhig akiwenzii.

Zhimaaganish Ezhinikaazod

[11] Bezhig oshki-gwiiwizens gaa-wiijiiwag apane—niwiijii'idiimin sa go, ingikinoo'amaagoomin gaye. Aabiding imaa naaniibawiyaang jiigikana, haa imbaapi'idimin, gaagiigidoyaang imaa imbaapi'idimin. Aanish bimosed a'aw Zhimaaganish gii-izhinikaazod a'aw akiwenzii, haa sa naa miinawaa imbaapi'idimin maanoo ji-ikidoyaang. Wa, bimosed a'aw akiwenzii, wa gwashkibagizo imaa gaa-waabamiyangid. Zaka'onan, miish iniw dekonang gaye. Ezhi-waabamiyangid i'iw, ingii-inenimigoonaan gii-paapi'angid. "Aaniin dash wenji-baapiyeg," indigoonaan a'aw akiwenzii. Waa-ayiizhino'wiyangid i'iw, ingii-segizimin sa go. Gaawiin ingii-inaasiin a'aw akiwenzii i'iw apane gaa-inaabamiyangid i'iw, gaa-pi-izhi-maajii-apa'iweyaan daa-awi-giiweyaan. Gaawiish. Wiindamawagaa indedeban nimaamaam eyaawaad, "Wiin a'aw akiwenzii, niinawind a'aw Biindige-gaabaw ingaagiigidomin jiigikana. Imbaapi'idimin miinawaa bimosed a'aw Zhimaaganish, a'aw ingii-inenimigoonaan ji-baapi'angid, gii-ikido. Gaawiin gidaa-baapi'aasiig gichi-aya'aag; mii gaa-inendamaan i'iw. Miish, ingii-nishki'igoonaan a'aw akiwenzii. Miish miinawaa waabamiyangid mitigong." "Gaawiin dash," wiindamawid nimaamaam. "Ambe wewiib, wewiib asemaan iwidi awi-miizh a'aw akiwenzii wiindamawad gii-paapi'aasiwad. Wewiib igo. Maajaan igo. Wii-piiskaayan igo dash, maajaan igo endaad igo. Biindigen," gii-ikido.

the old man talked to me. And when we left again, he didn't tell about the same things again, he always told me about something different. When we arrived here, that old man was still telling me about his knowledge of things as an elder man. That's how I know about these Drums and why I was thought of to carry that Drum, as maybe I must have been known to have learned about these things from the old men who talked to me. Certainly those elderly men were always conversing with me, particularly that one old man.

The One Called Zhimaaganish

[11]   There was one young boy whom I accompanied all the time—we were always together, and we went to school together too. One time we were standing around near the road, laughing with one another, as we were talking and laughing together there. Well that elder man named *Zhimaaganish* came walking by, and we were laughing together, letting ourselves say whatever [came to mind]. *Wa*, as that old man was walking, he turned around just startled there when he saw us. And he was holding onto those canes too. As he saw us, he thought we were laughing at him. "So why are you guys laughing," that old man says to us. As he pointed at us with [his cane], we were scared. I didn't tell that old man anything as he just stared at us the whole time, so we started to run away to go home. But no. I told my father and mother where they were, "That old man, *Biindige-gaabaw* and I were talking by the road. We were laughing together and that *Zhimaaganish* walked by. He thought we were laughing at him, he said. You shouldn't laugh at elders; that's what I was thinking. Then that old man got mad at us. Then he saw us again by the tree." "Oh no," my mom tells me. "Come quick, hurry up, go over and give that old man tobacco telling him you were not laughing at him. Hurry up. Go on. As fast as you can, go over to his house. Go inside," she says.

[12] Naa miinawaa-sh biindigeyaan wii-paabaagoo'igekeyaan biindigeyaan igo jiishkimag namadabid a'aw akiwenzii. Wa, apane ge-inaabamid a'aw, o'ow debaabandang ozaka'on. Aan wiindamawag, "Hey Zhimaaganish. Gaawiin gibaapi'igoosiin iwidi. Miinawaa ingii-paapi'idimin." Imaa go miinind asemaan a'aw, "Gaawiin ji-maanenimigooyaan igo gibaapi'isinoon i'iw." Wa, mii a'aw akiwenzii gii-paapid gaye. "Ho, ho, ho, ho, noozis. Weweni, weweni gaye weweni wii-pi-izhichigeyan," ikido. "Gaawiin gigikenimisinoon. Weweni giinawaa gigii-paapim, indinendam," gii-ikido a'aw akiwenzii. Mii bijiinag gii-minwendamaan gii-ani-giiweyaan. Wa, naa imbaabaapi'aa miinawaa nagamoyaan ani-maajaayaan. Mii go bijiinag gii-miinag asemaan. Gaye go, miish imaa gii-wiindamawid a'aw indedeban miinawaa nimaamaaban, "Gego wiikaa aapiji gaye ingoji niibawiyan baapi'aaken ingiw akiwenziiyag miinawaa mindimooyenyag," gii-ikido. "Gichi-apiitenimad gichi-aya'aa," gii-ikido. "Gaye ingoding igo giga-ganawenimigoog gichi-aya'aag. Gegoo giga-ganawenimigoog," ingii-ig. Miish i'iw gaa-izhi-debwewaad.

Gekendaasojig

[13] Miish i'iw wenji-gikendaasoyaan gaye niin. Indinaa sa gikendaasoyaan. Gaawiin go akina gegoo indaa-gikendanziin. Indinendam igo debinaak, debinaak o'ow inendamaan wiidookawiwaad ingiw manidoog wii-kaagiigidoyaan. Gegoo gaa-wiindamoonaan i'iw gegoo biindigeyaan imaa niimi'idii'wigamigong niimi'idiing. Gaawiin gegoo indaa-gikendanziin igo. Niwiidookaaz sa nagamong. Ingoding sa go ininendaagoziyaan iwidi wii-gaagiigidoyaan, mii iwidi bezhig gikendamaan waa-ikidoyaan. Gaawiin memwech indaa-mikwendanziin waa-ikidoyaan, mii go ba-izhi-dagoshinaan imaa gaye waa-inaajimoyaan.

[14] "Gegoo naagaj igo gaye giin ge-izhiwebiziyan, maagizhaa-sh, mii go gaye ezhiwebiziwanen azhigwa, mii go. Giga-zhawendaagoz i'iw bimiwinad dewe'igan enaginzoyan gidewe'igan dibendaagoziyang i'iw oshkaabewisiwiyan. Mii gosha gii-kikendaagwak ji-minoseyan. Gigikendaanan gaye giin iniw nagamonan. Akina go weweni gigikendaan gaye.

[12] And so I went inside, wanting to be as timid as possible. As I
entered I nudged that old man where he was sitting. Boy, he
just stared at me, and kept an eye on his cane. So I told him,
"Hey *Zhimaaganish.* You weren't being laughed at over there.
We were just laughing at one another again." He was given
tobacco then, "So I won't be thought of in a bad way
because I wasn't laughing at you." Boy, then that old man
laughed too. "*Ho, ho, ho, ho,* grandson. It's good, in a good
way that you come to do this," he said. "I don't know you.
But I think you guys were laughing in a good way," that old
man said. So for the first time again I was happy when I
prepared to go home. Golly, I laughed [with] him and I was
singing again as I left. That was the first time I gave him
tobacco. Then my father told me, and my mother too,
"Never ever laugh at those old men and old women when
you're standing around someplace," he says. "Hold the elder
in high regard," he said. "One time the elders are going to
watch over you. They'll take care of you in various
endeavors," he told me. And they spoke the truth.

The Learned Ones

[13] And that's why I'm so learned myself. I tell [people] about
the things I know about. I can't know everything. I think in
a number of ways, a variety of ways in my thinking, the
Spirits help me when I want to talk. I told you something
about when I went in the dance hall there during the Big
Drum Ceremony. I didn't know anything. Yet I'm helped by
the singing. One time I was thought of over there to give the
speech, right at once I knew what I was going to say. It's not
necessary for me to remember what I'm going to say, when I
come to that point there I simply speak.

[14] "You'll fare this way yourself later on, and maybe this must
be how things are with you right now. You will be blessed in
that you'll carry a Drum and you'll be counted among the
membership of your Drum just as you're its messenger. It
was already known that you would have good fortune. You
know those songs yourself. And you know everything very

Gidinendaagoz ji-gikendaman iniw nagamonan miinawaa
ge-ikidoyan sa go. Mii i'iw wiidookawag inendaagoziyan.
Gimanidoog giwiidookaagoog gegoo go wii-izhichigeyan."
Mii gaa-pi-izhid akiwenzii, gichi-aya'aa.

[15] Ingii-kaganoonigoog weweni ingiw akiwenziiyag. Gaawiin
wiikaa indaa-wanenimaasiig i'iw gaa-pi-izhi-ayaawaad
ingiw akiwenziiyag. Miinawaa aangodinong igo gegoo
gii-koshkoziyaan gigizhebaawagak, mii dash zhayiigwa i'iw
gegoo i'iw mikwendamaan gaa-wiindamawiwaad. Gaawiin gaye
apane naasaab indaa-izhi-mikwendanziin. Miinawaa go gegoo
gaye a'aw dewe'igan imaa genawendamaageyaan wiipemag
imaa indabiwining. Mii go i'iw gegoo aaningodinong
gigizhebaawagak goshkoziyaan, maagizhaa gaye dibikak
onishkaayaan, mii dash mikwendamaan iniw nagamonan
gaa-pi-noondamaan. Maagizhaa gaye imaa wiidookawag
inendaagoziyaan ezhi-gikendamaan niibowa iniw nagamonan.
Niibowa ingikendaanan iniw nagamonan. Gaawiish
indaa-gashkitoosiin iniw ji-maajii'amaan akina go iniw
nagamonan indaga ininendaagoziyaan imaa dibendaagwak
iniw nagamonan. Ingikendaanan akina go. Gaawiin dash
wiin indaa-mikendanziinan apane. Aaningodinong
imbwaanawitoonan iniw ji-maajii'amaan, namanj sa
maagizhaa gaye bagijigewaanen, namanj iidog.

[16] Mii sa go i'iw, mii sa go i'iw gaa-izhid a'aw akiwenzii, "Mii go
naagaj igo ji-ani-gashkitooyan." Gegoo a'aw bezhig akiwenzii
imaa gaa-tewe'iganid iniw, Waabishki-bines ge-bimiwinaad
iniw dewe'iganan. Negwanebii gii-izhinikaazowag. Negwanebii,
mii a'aw akiwenzii gii-tibenimaad iniw jibwaa-dibenimaad a'aw
Waabishki-bines. Mii gii-wiindamawid a'aw akiwenzii iwidi
Waawiyegamaag. Ingii-izhaamin. Mii i'iw oshki-bimiwinag a'aw
dewe'igan, ingii-wiijiiwaag iwidi gegoo. Gaawiin igo ingii-
kikendaagozisiin awashiime Medwe-ganoonind, ikwe,
miinawaa-sh a'aw Negwanebii gaa-inind, miinawaa a'aw
Wewanabi. Mii niiwiwaad ingiw dayewe'iganjigejig gii-
izhaawaad iwidi. Gayesh goshkoziwaad inindwaa ingiw
niiwin, ingiw dewe'iganag, owidi gii-izhaawaad. Gayesh a'aw
Bezhigoogaabaw gii-izhinikaazod a'aw akiwenzii. Iwidi *Moose*
gaa-inind, Bezhigoogaabaw gii-izhinikaazo. Oon Niibaa-
giizhig, mii a'aw gaa-waawiindamawid. Awegwesh a'aw
gaa-wiindamaagoogwen a'aw akiwenzii. Ganabaj a'aw bezhig

well. You are thought to know those songs and what to say as well. That's how I help when I am thought of. You are helped by your Spirits in the things you will do." That's what an old man told me, an elder.

[15] I was spoken to by those elders in a good way. I'll never forget how those old men were. Sometimes when I wake up in the morning, then already I remember certain things that they told me. But I can't always remember those same things. And it's the same thing again with that Drum I watch over and sleep with there in my room. And sometimes when I wake up in the morning, or maybe if I get up at night, then I remember those songs I came to hear. And maybe I help him there when I am thought of to do so as I remember a lot of those songs. I do know a lot of those songs. But I am unable to start off all of those songs, all those position songs, when I am thought of to do so. But I know them all. I just can't remember them all the time. Sometimes I'm unable to lead them out, I don't know maybe if I might make an offering, I don't know.

[16] That's it, that's what that old man told me, "Later on you'll be able to do that." That elder man was a Drum Keeper there, *Waabishki-bines*, and he would carry those Drums. They were called *Negwanebii*. *Negwanebii*, he was owner of that one before *Waabishki-bines* became the caretaker. That's what that old man from over there at Round Lake told me. We went. When he first carried that Drum I went around with them over there. I wasn't known then nearly as much as *Medwe-ganoonind*, that woman, and that one called *Negwanebii*, and also that *Wewanabi*. There were four of those Drum Keepers that went over there. And as those four were called, they got up for those Drums, over there where they went. And there was one old man named *Bezhigoogaabaw*. Over there he was called Moose, but his name was *Bezhigoogaabaw*. *Niibaa-giizhig*, he's the one who told me about this. Someone told that old man. Perhaps one of the other Drum Keepers talked to him and told him that I was

akiwenzii gaa-tewe'iganinijin ogii-pi-wiindamaagoon,
gii-wiindamawaad iniw gii-pazhitoonigooyaan imaa.
Onishkaad a'aw akiwenzii. "Ambe omaa. Niwanichige omaa,"
ikido. "Ambe sa go naadig a'aw bezhig imaa dewe'iganid
bemiwinjiged aya'aa gaa-pezhigoo'oonang," gii-ikido akiwenzii.
Mii sa go omaa maajaawaad akina ingiw, akina ongow gaa-
piindigewaad endashiiwaad akina go anishinaabeg, akina ingiw
biitoowaajigan bi-dagoshinowaad waa-ani-aabideg, waa-
ani-gwapideg i'iw gaa-apwakozidamaagooyaan niin eta go, ji-
niibawid. Niibawi minik gaye, minik wiinawaa niiwin gaa-
tewe'iganijig. Mii genoozhid-sh gaa-pibideg iwidi gii-
wanenimigooyaan imaa. Inashke gii-ikidowag. "Gaawiin
dash indizhaasiin iwidi. Gaawiin ingikenimaasiig ingiw
dayewe'iganijig iwidi," gii-ikido a'aw akiwenzii.

[17] Miish a'aw Negwanebii, niwiidabimaa imaa, nimamaag iniw
asemaan wiindamawag, "Haa, gaagiigidotamawishin." Wa,
gichi-ganawaabamid a'aw akiwenzii. "Tayaa! Gidoodoon-sh
ji-gaagiigidoyan," indig. "Gaagiigidon gaye waa-izhi-
miigwechiwitaagoziyan igo." Mii sa i'iw gaa-izhi-bazigwiiwaad
dash i'iw baapish gii-maajii-giigidoyaan. Gaawiin dash wiikaa
ingii-kaganoonaasiig ingiwejig, akiwenzii gaa-toodawid.
"Atoon gaye gidayaan ji-gaagiigidoyan," indig. Gegaa anooj
ingii-toodawaa a'aw akiwenzii, booch igo, booch igo gaye.
"Mii sa i'iw baa-wiindamawad maajaayang." Niin eta ishkwaa
akawe. "Iwidi izhichigeyan weweni i'iw ji-miigwechiwi'ad
giijanishinaabe gegoo memwech. Gego gaganoonaaken," ikido.
"Akeyaa gaye gigaganoonig, gaganoonik ji-aaniikanootawad.
Wii-miinag asemaan, gego wiin inaaken. Wewiib igo ge-izhi-
bazigwiiyan igo ji-wiindamawad. Mii i'iw ge-izhi-gikendaagwak
i'iw waa-ikidoyan," ingii-pi-wiindamaag a'aw akiwenzii.

[18] Mii go gaye baa-wiindamawid. Mii sa wenji-baa-gashkitooyaan
ji-gaagiigidoyaan dibishkoo go giin igo. Gii-kaagiigidoyaan
imaa, "Gaa gidaa-gaagiigidotamaagoosiin," indig. Gaawiin
gii-ayaasiin go apii gii-maajii-inenimag. Ganabaj igo miinawaa
go niin nitam ingii-taso-biboonagiz i'iw apii ganabaj igo.
Gaawiin nisimidana gii-taso-biboonagizisiin apii gaa-
bimiwinaad dewe'iganan. Gaye niin nisimidana ashi
ningodwaaso-biboonagiziyaan gii-maajii-bimiwinag a'aw
dewe'igan. Maajii-dibinendaagoziyaan sa go ingiw dewe'iganag,
akeyaa gaye a'aw ikwe-dewe'igan, indibendaagoz imaa

being neglected there. That old man got up. "Come here. I made a mistake here," he says. "Come fetch that one Drum Keeper there who carries [that Drum] that's been left by himself," the old man said. So they all left here, and they all came in, however many Indians there were, and all of them putting blankets there as they arrived, it was getting huge as they prepared that bundle just for me, as he stood there. He stood for a certain amount of time, then all four Drum chiefs themselves. And he talked to me where it was resting there about how I was forgotten there. They spoke. "I don't go over there. I don't know those Drum Keepers over there," that old man said.

[17]   Then that *Negwanebii*, I sat with him there, I picked up those tobaccos and told him, "Hey, speak for me." Golly, that old man really looked at me. "*Tayaa!* But you do that speaking," he tells me. "Give a speech about what you want to express thanks for." So they all stood up when I started to speak. I never talked to those other ones on account of what the old man did to me. "And put down whatever you've got to give your speech," he tells me. I almost did all kinds of things to that old man, really, truly. "You talk to him when we start." I was the only one left. "It's necessary for you to do this in a good way over there to express thanks to your fellow Indian. Don't just converse with him," he says. "That's how they will come to you, as he'll ask you to translate for him. I want to give him tobacco, but don't tell him. You'll stand up right away to talk for him. That's how the understanding will come when you speak," that old man said to me.

[18]   And that's what he went around telling me. That's how I became able to give speeches just like you. When I spoke there, "You don't have to be spoken for," he tells me. He wasn't there at times when I started to think of him. Maybe then I was the oldest at that time perhaps. He wasn't even thirty years old when he first started to carry the Drum. As for myself, I was thirty-six years old when I started to carry that Drum. When I started being a member of these Drums, it was that Ladies Drum, and I'm a member of *Negwanebii*'s Drum and there on *Chi-aanakwad*'s Drum I'm a member

miinawaa Negwanebii odewe'iganan miinawaa Chi-aanakwad
odewe'iganan imaa-sh wa'aw niin dibinendaagoziyaan—niswi
bwaanzhii-dewe'iganag miinawaa bezhig a'aw ikwe-dewe'igan
dibinendaagoziyaan i'iw. Mii go gii-siigwang, nisimidana ashi
ingodwaaswo-biboon ganabaj gii-maajii-agimigooyaan imaa
dewe'iganag.

[19] Baamaa naagaj ingii-pi-miinigoog. Ingii-meshkwadabi'ig
iwidi ko bimiwinag. Iwidi akeyaa wendaabang akeyaa ingii-
neskwaakide'wig akeyaa. Ingii-namadab ajina go omaa, mii i'iw.
Miish a'aw Naawigiizis ezhinikaazod, maajaawan odedeyan.
Mii a'aw dayewe'iganid a'aw gaa-izhinikaazod akiwenzii.
Miish i'iw gaa-tewe'iganid. Booch igo inga-mikwenimaa a'aw
naagaj. Miish i'iw gaa-izhi-ikidod, "Wiin odaa-bi-miinaan iniw
Naawigiizis ezhinikaazod odewe'iganan." Miish
gaa-izhi-ikidod, "Gaawiin niin indaa-aashki'aasiin ji-miinag
a'aw dewe'igan; indawaaj igo bezhig omaa debinendaagozid.
Asig," gii-ikido. Mii sa a'aw ogichidaakwe bezhig gaa-ikidod
niin maajii-asigooyaan. Miish imaa gii-aandabii'igooyaan.
Aagawaat gaa-izhinikaazod a'aw gaa-wiidabimag. Mii gaye
gii-wiidabimag o'ow isa gii-inendamaan igo ji-wiidookawid
a'aw nitam, a'aw nitam akiwenzii gii-maajaad imaa gii-
namadabii'igooyaan. Gaye a'aw go nitam gaye, mii nitam
waa-kaagiinisigeg, gekoonisookideg. Mii iwidi wendaabang
akeyaa; mii iwidi gii-namadabii'igooyaan.

Dewe'igan Meshkawiziid

[20] O'ow dash gegoo ezhi-manidoowaadiziwaad gidewe'iganag
imaa ko gii-anokiiyeg daashkiboojiganing imaa awas akeyaa
agaaming gemaa gaye anokiiyaan, miish i'iw. Miish a'aw
nabagisag wasigone-ombinag, ingii-chagitaan bikwan. Mii
gaa-izhi-bwaanawitooyaan. Mii gaa-izhi-mashki'inigooyaan
gaa-izhi-waabamag. Hay'! Mii i'iw giizhiitaamagak dibi go.
"Gaawiin wiikaa gidaa-gashkitoosiin iwidi ji-ayaayan.
Giga-mashki'inin," miish imaa bi-niimi'idiing. Mii imaa.
Mii jibwaa-dibinendaagoziyaan ingiw dewe'iganag imaa bi-
biindigeyaan imaa dash niimi'idiing. Mii a'aw medwewed
biindigeyaan, omaa babaa-naazikawid a'aw Aagawaat megwaa
gii-pi-maajiid a'aw akiwenzii gaa-inaabishkawagiban. Mii dash

myself—that's three Sioux Drums and one Ladies Drum I belong to. Last spring it was perhaps thirty-six years since I've been counted among the membership of the Drums there.

[19] Later on they gave it to me. He put me in a different position so I could be the carrier. He removed me from the east [stick]. I had been sitting here for just a little while, that's it. Then that guy called *Naawigiizis*, his dad passed away. That old man had been named the Drum Keeper. He was the Drum owner. I'm certainly going to remember that guy. Then he said this, "That guy called *Naawigiizis* should be given his Drum." Then he said, "I can't take care of him or give [enough] to that Drum; it's best to use someone who's already a member here. Seat him," he said. So that one warrior woman said that I was starting to be seated myself. Then I was shifted over there. I sat with *Aagawaat* as he was called. As I sat with him I thought he would help me at first, as that old man who had passed away where I was sitting was first. And first of all it was going to be the third stick, the third stick it was. It was over there in the east; it's over there that I had been seated.

The Power of the Drum

[20] And your Drums are sacred things even there in the saw-mill where you used to work or where I worked myself on the other side of the lake. As I was lifting a wooden beam, I pulled a muscle in my back. I was just unable to do it. I thought I was strong enough when I saw it. Too bad! That's all done with now. "You could never manage being over there. I'll give you strength," that's [what I was told] there at the Big Drum Ceremony. Right there. This was before I was a member on those Drums, when I came inside the Drum ceremonial there. The [Drum] was sounding out as I came in, and in the middle of leading out a song that old man *Aagawaat*, whose position I would assume, came after me

i'iw bezhig a'aw Nitamigooneb gaa-izhinikaazod a'aw
akiwenzii. Nitamigooneb gii-izhinikaazo, geyaabi go gii-
inaabishkawag. Miish gaa-izhi-izhid, "Haaw. Dibendaagozin
imaa. Gigagwejimin ji-dibinendaagoziyan. Haaw sa giin
inakomag." Mii gaa-izhid a'aw akiwenzii, "Gego gaagiigidoken
wii-kagwejimigooyan ji-dibinendaagoziyan dewe'igan.
Giniijaanisag miinawaa gidinawemaaganag weweni da-
dibendaagoziwag. Mii sa go gaawiin da-maazhisesigwaa,
weweni ji-ani-bimaadiziwaad."

[21] Gayesh indaakoz. Imbikwan indaakoz. Wayaa! Mii ezhi-
bwaanawitooyaan wii-mino-ayaayaan, azhigwa miinawaa go
gaye wii-izhi-ayaayaan bimoseyaan. Aanish naa, mii gaa-
wiindamawid a'aw Mashkiin. "Gaawiin wiikaa giga-minosesiin
gibikwan," ingii-ig. "Aaniish iniw nagamonan i'iw eko-nising,
haa gidaa-niimi'aawaa," ikido. Medwe-ganoonind igo oshki-
niimi'iweng imaa. "Niimig." "Haa sa ezhi-gashkitooyaan
ji-niimiyaan," indinendam. Ingii-naaniim iko. Ingii-
pwaanzhii'igoo naaniimiyaan. "Haa niimig," ikido. "Nagamon
gegaa imaa giizhibaashiwan imaa," indig. Gegaa go, gegaa go
ingashkitoon bimoseyaan, anooj igo aakoziyaan imbikwan
oseyaan. Zhayiigwa apii go niizhing gaa-izhibaataayaan, aanish
miinawaa imaa go bakaadendamaan imaa dash gaa-izhi-
gashkitooyaan miinawaa naaniimiyaan. Azhigwa omaa nising
ge-izhibaashkaayaan o'ow gaa-niimi'igooyaan, weniban
aanh miinawaa gii-aakoziyaan. Indig wa'aw, "Wa, hay'!"
Wii-paa-apagizoyaan igo ani-mino-ayaayaan sa go omaa
bakaadendamaan i'iw aandiish sa go naa indigooban a'aw
Mashkiin. Indig a'aw, "Gaawiin izhisinoon gibikwan. Mii
giizhiitaamagak," ingii-ig. Mii i'iw Mashkiin inind. Mii gaa-
izhi-gagwejimag a'aw akiwenzii, niyawe'enh gii-wiiyawe'enyid
ko gii-abiigizigewininiiwid. Mii imaa Giiyoganebii gii-
izhinikaazod, mii a'aw gaa-niimid. Haaw sa naa gaa-izhi-
ayaayaan imbikwan. Indinaa imbwaaniwinaaban. "Enh," indig.
"Mii i'iw dewe'igan, dibishkoo ingii-nanaandawi'ig," gii ikido.
Miish i'iw gii-kikendamaan i'iw gegoo ingiw dewe'iganag ji-
wiidookawiyangidwaa. Gegaa imaa, gaawiin ingii-pi-aakozisiin
imbikwan. Indizh, gaawiin igo wiin igo naasaab, ginwenzh
namadabiyaan imaa niimi'idiing. Zanagad igo ginwenzh
nagamong imaa. Ingikendaan igo. Mii sa go ajina go indaakoz.
Gaawiin igo indaakozisiin; indashkawigam eta go. Gaawiin

here. Then that one guy, that old man who was called *Nitamigooneb*. *Nitamigooneb* was his name, and I still have his old position. So he tells me, "All right. Take your position there. I am asking you to be a Drum member. All right, you answer him yourself." That's what that old man told me, "Don't speak as you are being asked to become a member on the Drum. But your children and your relatives will have a place at the Drum too. They won't have any misfortunes, and will come live in a good way."

[21] And I was in poor health too. My back was ailing me. Holy buckets! Although I was disabled I was going to be healthy, that's how I was going to be now when I started walking again. Well now, that's what *Mashkiin* told me. "You will never have good luck with your back," he told me. "But for these songs, you should dance for him that third one," he says. *Medwe-ganoonind* was just starting to dance there. "Dance." Well [I was uncertain] whether I'd be able to dance, I'm thinking. I used to dance. I was a traditional war dancer when I danced. "Well, dance," he says. "That song there is almost done there," he tells me. Barely, I'm barely able to walk, as there were all kinds of things messed up in my back when I got to my feet. Now at this time I had circled [the Drum] twice, and again there things changed for me, as I was able to dance again. I had now circled around three times here as I was dancing, and then my ailments were gone. I am told by him, "Boy, unreal!" I flopped down here in perfect health with everything changed around for me while I was being talked to by that *Mashkiin*. He tells me, "Your back won't act up now. It's all over," he told me. That was *Mashkiin* as he's called. So I asked that old man, my namesake, if he would be a namesake for me as well as that one who was a Drum Warmer. That there was *Giiyoganebii* as he was called, the one who had danced. All right, that was how things were with my back then. I told him I was feeble. "Yes," he tells me. "But it's like that Drum doctored you," he said. It was then that I knew something about how these Drums help us. I was barely even ailing there in my back. So you might tell me it's not the same, as I sit for a long time at the Drum ceremonies there. But singing for a long time there is difficult. I know. I only get sick for a little while. I'm

wiikaa miinawaa imbi-aakozisiin imbikwan—gegoo gaa-izhi-
minoseyaan imaa gii-nakodamaan dibishkoo go ingiw
dewe'iganag wiidookawiwaad igo gegoo go. Gegoo gaye
epiichii-manidoowaadiziwaad ingiw dewe'iganag, a'aw
ikwe-dewe'igan.

[22] Miinawaa a'aw noozhishenh owidi gii-paashizwaa
Gakaabikaang omisadaang. Yo'ow dash ayi'ii o'ow—aaniin
ezhinikaadeg i'iw—opikwanding, mii iwidi gii-ani-aabideg
anwii. "Gaawesa. Gaawiin," gii-ikido mashkikiwinini. "Gaawiin
gaye nanaandawii'iwewinini odaa-gashkitoosiin i'iw."
Miinawaa odaa-gashkitoon igo gegoo. "Gaawiish odaa-
bimosesiin," ingii-ig. "Ojiitaad gii-pagisin. Zegosin imaa,"
gii-ikido, "anwii." Miish i'iw gii-piindaakoojigeyaan, miinawaa
gii-atooyaan onaagan ikwe-dewe'igan. Mii go apii gii-chi-
niimi'idiing imaa, gii-shingishing iwidi aakoziiwigamigong
gichi-aakozi. Miish i'iw gegoo gii-naano-giizhigak gii-
paashkizwind, mii sa go gaa-izhi-wiindamawid a'aw. Mii go
gaa-niizho-giizhigak, mii gii-pi-giiwed. Mii i'iw gii-pi-bimosed.
Mii go ikidong, "Giwii-kagwejimin." "Ingikendaan," indig.
"Awegonen?" "Awiiya imaa zhingishinaan ingii-paa-ayaawaa,"
ikido. "Mii gaa-izhi-gikenimag imaa inaabiyaan. Gaawiin
bakaan awiiya imaa ayaasiin. Mii eta waa-izhi-gikenimagwaa
ongow awenenag imaa eyaagwenag aya'aag zhingishinaan.
Mii sa go maajii-mino-ayaayaan igo," ikido. "Gaawiin
zhaaganaashiimosiiwag. Gaawiin gaye ninitaa-
anishinaabe-gaagiigidosiin omaa." Gaye imaa, mii imaa
gii-piindaakoojigeyaan imaa gii-kanawenimigod iniw
manidoon gii-kagwedweyaan miinawaa gaye. Miish a'aw
gwiiwizens gii-mino-ayaad, mii a'aw geyaabi bezhig.

[23] "Mii doodoobik. Gigii-aanawi-maw bikwanaang; gaawiin
wiikaa gaa-pimigaadesinoon. Miinawaa gaa-pimigaadenig,
daa-niboose." Mii gaa-ikidod a'aw nanaandawii'iwed imaa.
Gaye go, miish igo nawaj igo gegoo, mii nawaj igo wenji-
gikendamaan i'iw ji-wiidookawag inendaagozid a'aw
anishinaabe iniw asemaan biindaakoonaad dewe'iganan.
Niigaani-manidoog bemiwinaad iniw dewe'iganan, moozhag
igo ingii-pi-wiindamaagoo. Mii i'iw dewe'iganag bemiwinikwaa
sa go dibi go ezhaayan gaye o'ow ingoji sa go, ingoji wii-
izhaayan biindaakoojigeyan. Mii genawinendaagoziyan i'iw.
Miinawaa go ongow gegoo gaagiigidoyaan, ongow

not ill; I only get minor ailments. And I've never had
problems with my back again—I've had good fortune there
in being answered just like those Drums helped me through
things. Those Drums have the utmost spiritual power, [like]
that Ladies Drum.

[22]   And one of my grandchildren was shot in the stomach
over here in Minneapolis. And this body part right here—
what's it called—the spine, the bullet lodged itself right
there. "There's no way. No," the doctor said. "And an Indian
doctor won't be able to do anything about it." But he was
indeed able to do things. "He'll never walk," he told me. "His
spinal cord has been severed. The bullet is lodged there,"
he said. Then I made a tobacco offering and put a bowl
down at the Ladies Drum. At that time they had a really big
dance there while he was stretched out there in the hospital,
terribly ill. He was shot on a Friday, or so he told me. And
then on Tuesday, he came home. He was already walking
then. So he says, "I want to ask you something." "I know,"
he tells me. "What is it?" "When I was laid out there
someone came to be with me," he says. "When I peeked
there I knew who he was. There was nobody else there. I was
only going to know these beings that were there while I was
lying down. Then I started to get well," he says. "They didn't
speak English. And I'm not good at talking Indian here." So
there, right there I made a tobacco offering and I requested
that he be watched over by the Spirit. Then that boy was
healthy, and he is still.

[23]   "This is what's been done. Despite your crying about your
back, nothing ever came of it. And this is despite the fact
that what did happen could have caused paralysis." That's
what that Indian doctor said there. And then to a greater
extent, to a much higher degree did I come to understand
how [critical] it is to help the Indian when he thinks of his
tobacco to make an offering of it at the Drums. The head
Spirits carry those Drums, that's what I was always told.
And those Drums in turn carry you wherever you go and
wherever it might be that you want to go as you make a
tobacco offering. That's how you are looked after. Again

gagwedwetamaageyaan ingiw bemiwinikwaa, ingiw
ji-dagoshinowaad weweni ji-dagoshinowaad. Ingoji maajaayan
gaye gizaagi'aag weweni ji-ani-waabamadwaa miinawaa. Mii
gaa-pi-wiindamaagooyaan.

Nandawenjigewin Gechitwaawendaagwak

[24] Hey, gayesh bangishenh wiin o'ow waa-wiindamoonaan omaa.
Geyaabi go nawaj igo, geyaabi go gigizhebaawagak ezhi-
gikendamaan igo gaa-pi-izhiseg. Miinawaa go gegoo, gaye a'aw
bezhig nimaamaayiban iniw oshiimeyan gii-shawendaagozinid
iniw. Zhaangaswi waawaashkeshiwan gii-nisaad a'aw
nimaamaayan oshiimeyan, Animikiins gii-izhinikaazod,
gaa-izhi-nisaad iniw zhaangaswi waawaashkeshiwan; nishiwed
iniw waawaashkeshiwan. Ingoding sa go, mii midaaswi ji-gii-
nisaapan iniw gaa-izhi-waabamaad iniw ayaaben imaa, mii
aazhooshkaayaang imaa biiwaabikoo-miikanaang. Miinawaa sa
go naa wii-paashkizwaad. "Baamaa dash gaa-izhi-niibawid
imaa zhaadigewining," gii-ikido. "Apane gaa-inaabamag,"
ikido. "Namanj sa go naa izhichigewaanen," ikido. "Weniban
imaa gii-shaadigeng gii-niibawid imaa waawaashkeshi,
wa'aw gichi-ayaabe," gii-ikido. Miinawaa gaawiin ogii-
paashkizwaasiin. "Mii dash gaa-izhi-maajiibatood," ikido.
"Gayesh ingii-inendaagoz i'iw." Onzaam niibowa ogii-nisaan
iniw. Gegoo da-izhiwebizi giishpin nisaad iniw midaaswi.
Weweni ji-ganawinendaagozid i'iw ge-izhi-inang gegoo; gegoo
asemaan gii-asaad ko endaso-giiyosed asaad iniw asemaan i'iw
gaye. Mii gaa-izhi-wiidookawag inendaagozid i'iw. Maagizhaa
daa-gii-izhiwebizi a'aw akiwenzii.

[25] Moozhag igo gaye niin iko ingii-kiiyose, gaawiish geyaabi.
Omaa akeyaa bagijishkamaagooyaan, ingiw chimookomaanag
imbagijishkamaagoog. Indakandoon imaa sa bidaakiing
miinawaa ge-izhi'igooyaan. Gaawiin gegoo gaa-noondamaan
o'ow isa, miinawaa megwaa bimosed a'aw gichi-ayaabe
gaa-noogishkaad besho go. Gaawiin igo waasa, besho imaa
niibawi apane. Gaa-inaabamag, wayaa wenda-onizhishi.
Indaa-waateshkaagoo dibishkoo o'ow isa apane ba-inaabamid,
inaabamid iwidi, inaabamid akeyaa apane gaa-inaabamid.

when I give speeches about these things, when I make requests to these [Spirits] that you'll be carried so they will come, come in a good way. And when you leave somewhere you care for them in a good way so that you'll see them again. That's what I was told.

The Sacred Art of Hunting

[24] Hey, I want to tell you a little bit more about this here. There is still more that I remember in the morning about what has come to pass. Again in these things my mother's younger brother was blessed as well. My mother's younger brother killed nine deer, that *Animikiins* as he was called, he killed nine white-tailed deer; he killed all those deer. Then one time as he prepared to kill the tenth one, he saw a buck there, right there as we were crossing the highway. And so he shot him. "But after a while he was just standing there in the shadows," he said. "I just stared at him the whole time," he says. "What the heck am I doing," he says. "Then that deer there disappeared as he was standing there in the shade, this big buck," he said. He didn't shoot him again. "Then he took off running," he says. "And I was considered [blessed] in that." He had killed too many of them. Something would have happened to him if he had killed that tenth one. So he was being watched over in a good way, at least that's what he came to say of it, and he used to put tobacco down every time he went hunting; he would put that tobacco out. I used to help him when he was being considerate like that. Maybe that's how that old man should have been.

[25] I used to hunt all the time myself, but not any more. Over this way I was having drives made for me, those white guys were making drives for me. I'm waiting in the stand there on the top edge of a slough again where I was put. I hadn't heard a thing when a great big buck stops in mid-stride just close. It wasn't far; he stood close there the whole time. When I looked at him, boy he was just beautiful. I was all decked out in blaze orange, but it was just like he stared at me the whole time, as he stared at me over there, and he

Miish igo omaa eteg baashkizigan. Gaawiin gaye nimamoosiin, apane gaa-inaabamag. Wa, chi-weweni bimosed besho; chi-weweni apane gaa-ako-waabishkikiing apane. Naa sa naa gii-izhiwebiziyaan, indinendam isa ogoopimaanaawaan ingiw chimookomaanag waa-pagidinishkawaawaad. Wa, bi-dagoshing a'aw chimookomaan indizhi'aa imaa gaa-pi-izhaad a'aw.

[26]   Besho imaa ingaganoonig ojibwemong. "Besho omaa, besho omaa izaabamaad awedin waawaashkeshiwan," indig. "Enh," indinaa. Miinawaa indoojibwemotawaa. "Geget," indinaa. "Geget besho omaa ninandawaabamaa. Ninandawaabamaa weweni ji-gii-nisagiban," indinaa. "Apane gaa-inaabamag," indinaa. "Wenda onizhishi a'aw waawaashkeshi. Gaawiin gaye aagawaateshkaasiin," indinaa. "Weweni bimose jekaakwa'ang." Gaa-izhi-gagwejimag a'aw, indinaa gaa-izhi-gagwejimag a'aw ji-ganawaabamag miinawaa bangii bimaadiziyaan. Mii gaa-izhi-gagwejimag, "Aaniin ezhiwebiziyaan," indinaa. "Enh," ikido. "Gaawiin. Gaawiin inendaagwasinoon ji-nisad onow," ingii-ig. "Gego miinawaa wiikaa nisaaken onow," ingii-ig. "Gizhawenimaa a'aw awesiinh," gii-ikido. "Gizhawenimigoog giin igo. Manidoog i'iw oga-zhawenimaawaan giniijaanisan," gii-ikido. "Gego miinawaa wiikaa omaa nisaaken eta noo onjida," ingii-ig. "Giga-naganigoz. O'ow manidoog giga-naganigoog onjida nisadwaa," gaa-ikidod. "Aan naa manidoog ingiw, mii ingiw awesiinyag ezhinikaazojig, waawaashkeshiwag. Gegoo ezhiwebak biindaakoojigeyan igo gaye, mii ezhi-gikendaagwak gegoo ji-izhichigesiwan."

Wenji-ganawendamang Gidakiiminaan

[27]   Mii gaye akiwenzii gaa-wiindamawid: "Mii ingoding, mii ezhi-gikendaman igo gegoo, maagizhaa gaye ji-giiwaadiseyan," gii-ikido a'aw akiwenzii. Mii sa gaye, mii sa apane wii-inendamaan i'iw gegoo. Gegoo niwii-izhaanendaan sa go gegoo. Wii-wanichigeyaan ji-wanigiizhweyaan gaye ayaapii, gaawiin igo ingotaayisiin, eta go bangii niizhaan eta, gaawiish gegoo. Gegoo gaa-izhid a'aw akiwenzii. "Gego, gego gaye. Gaawiin gaye gidaa-giiwanimosiin gegoo," ikido. Ingii-wiindamaagoz i'iw gaagiigidod i'iw, "Gego agajiken gaye da-

stared and stared. Then my rifle was here. But I didn't grab it, as I just kept my eye fixed on him. Boy, he [looked] so fine as he walked up close, just regal and right by the slough the whole time. Well, what am I doing, I thought as those white guys were so upset about [the deer] they had permitted to pass by them. Gee, that one white man showed up and I had him go over there.

[26] Then somebody talked to me close by in Ojibwe. "Near here, right near here he was so close to that deer over there," he tells me. "Yeah," I say to him. Again I spoke Ojibwe to him. "Truly," I tell him. "I am tracking him down really close here. I'm searching for him so I can properly kill him," I tell him. "I saw him the whole time," I tell him. "That deer was just nice. I never let him out of my sight," I tell him. "He walked by just dignified and then went off in the woods." Then I asked that guy, I told him as I was asking him that I look after him a little bit in my life. So I asked him, "What am I doing," I tell him. "Yes," he says. "No. It wasn't meant for you to kill this one," he told me. "Don't ever try to kill this one again," he told me. "You love that animal," he said. "And they'll love you too. The Spirits will bless your children," he said. "Never intentionally kill one again," he told me. "You'll get abandoned. The Spirits will abandon you if you kill them intentionally," he said. "Now those Spirits are animals and the so-called deer. Something will happen when you make a tobacco offering too, that's how it will become known what you have not done."

Why We Take Care of Our Earth

[27] That old man told me this too: "One time as you come to know about things, maybe you will have that kind of fortune too," that old man said. That too, I think about all the time. I want to let my thoughts go to a certain place. If I'm going to make a mistake or misspeak at times, I'm not scared, only a little bit, but not really. That old man told me other things too. "Dos and don'ts. You shouldn't lie about things," he said. I was told that when he gave a speech, "Don't be bashful to speak." That's what that old man said.

gaagiigidoyan." Mii gaa-izhid a'aw akiwenzii. Moozhag go ingii-paa-wiindamaagoog ingiw akiwenziiyag i'iw. "Gego babaamendangen gegoo ji-wanigiizhweyan gaye," gii-ikido.

[28] Gegoo ingoding, ingoding igo gaye gaa-ani-bimiwinagwaa dewe'iganag, ingii-igoog ingiw akiwenziiyag. Gayesh igo geget, gayesh bimiwinagwaa ingiw dewe'iganag, wiidookaazoyaan ji-bimiwinag wa'aw dewe'igan. "Onjida go noondaagozi ji-bimiwinaad ji-gikendang iniw dewe'iganan." "Da-zhawinendaagoziyan sa go, giiyaw da-zhawendaagwad. Miinawaa giniijaanisag, goozhishenyag, gidaanikobijiganag, gegoo akina giijikiwenyag, miinawaa go gidinawemaaganag sa go akina—mii akina ingiw ge-zhawendaagozijig gagwejimadwaa ongow manidoog miziwe eyaajig genawendangig o'ow aki. Mii sa gaye, gaawiin giinawind gidibendanziimin o'ow aki. Gaawiin sa go gidaa-dibendanziin. Giganawendaamin eta go. Gayesh wiinawaa chimookomaanag, 'Hey indibendaan o'ow aki.' Hey, gaawiin gidibendanziinaawaa. Maagizhaa gaye, maagizhaa gaye niisininig da-dibendamowaad. Gaawiish odaa-dibendanziin. Gaa odaa-ikidosiin owidi da-dibendang. Anishaa gidabiitaan mino-aki. Gizhe-manidoo gigii-izhi-igoonaan ji-ganawendamang o'ow, ji-ganawendamang o'ow aki ji-ganawenimangwaa ongow, weweni ji-ganawaabamangwaa ongow awesiinyag, miinawaa ingiw binesiwag, miinawaa giigoonyag, miinawaa zaaga'igan, mitigoog, akina sa ingiw." Mii gaa-izhid a'aw ani-igooyang ji-ganawendamang.

[29] Gayesh noongom ingoji go naabe izhind akina ingoji ji-asinajigaadeg o'ow aki. Gegoo omaa zaaga'igan ingoding igo, ingoji go ingii-ashi-naanobiboonagiz gemaa ingii-ashi-niiyo-biboonagiz go, gii-paa-kikinoo'amaageyaan i'iw giigoonyag gii-pi-miinagwaa sa chimookomaanag ingiw wii-tiba'amawiwaad gaye ji-gikinoo'amawagwaa iniw giigoonyan ayaanid. Gegoo iwidi akeyaa Neyaashiing ingii-wiindamaagoo maagizhaa go gaye midaaso-ashi-niiyogozid. Mii go dash debaabandamaang ingiw giigoonyag gaa-tebaabamangidwaa babaamakwazhiwewaad. Noongom dash ezhaayaan iwidi, gaawiin iwidi gidaa-debaabandanziin i'iw gichi-wiinagamiginig bimi-izhi-naajigaadeg. Gegoo ongow chimookomaanag—i'iw medwebizod i'iw isa waasakonenjiganaaboo, mii inetood a'aw—ani-atoowaad i'iw ongow chimookomaanag ezhinikaazojig.

Those old men always used to come around telling me that. "And don't worry about things like making a mistake while speaking," he said.

[28]   One time, one time when I was starting to [help] carry these Drums, I was talked to by those old men. That's for sure, it's when I was just starting to [help] carry those Drums, helping out and then carrying that one Drum myself. "He is being heard on purpose so that he'll carry these Drums and know about them." "You will be blessed, your body will be blessed. And your children, your grandchildren, your great-grandchildren, all your friends and all your relatives—they will all be blessed when you ask the ever-present Spirits that take care of this earth. And also, we don't own this land. You can never own it. We only take care of it. But those white people, 'Hey I own this land.' Hey, you guys can't own it. Maybe, maybe the ones who lowered it here shall own it. But he can't own it. He can't say that he will own it. You live on this good earth but for the grace of God. And that Kindly Spirit told us to look after this here, to take care of this earth and look after these creatures, so that we can take good care of these animals, and these birds, and the fish, and the lake, the trees, all of these things." He said that we've been told to be caretakers.

[29]   The people have been told now too how things are gathered up from the earth. One time this lake here, when I was about fifteen years old or maybe fourteen years old, I went around as a fishing guide and gave the white people whatever they would pay me for to teach them where the fish were at. Over there towards Neyaashiing I was told there were about fourteen of them [that] had moved. And we saw it from a ways off, as we eyed up those fish when they went along the shore. Now as I went over there you couldn't keep your eye on what was happening as they had made a terrible mess in the water that was just getting picked up. These white people—as they motorboat along it's that gasoline, they dump it there—they just put it there, those Big Knives as they're called.

[30]   Miinawaa-sh gegoo a'aw bezhig, a'aw anishinaabe, a'aw
       ogii-anooji'aan iko iniw ogozisensan. Ingii-paa-wiijiiwaa ko
       ji-baa-izhaad jiigibiig. Miish omaa gaa-ani-bimoseyaang
       jiigibiig. "Gayesh owidi inaabin," indig. Miish inaabiyaan
       iwidi jiigibiig akeyaa ani-izhaayaang. Omaa sa naa baawan
       aboonjiiyiwaad ingiw, ingiw dibishkoo go gegaa go ingiw
       gwiiwizensag ingiw gii-ayaawaad. Ingiw manidoonsag
       bemaashijig, mii gaye baagomojig omaa, gayesh ongow
       ikidong. "Mii ingiw, mii ingiw manidoonsag bemaashijig,"
       indinaa. "Gaawiin," ikido. "Gayesh owidi akeyaa o'ow
       akeyaa izhitaan," ikido. "Inaabin iwidi." Miinawaa-sh
       o-waabandamaan i'iw waasakonenjiganaaboo imaa angoodeg.
       Gayesh gaa-izhi-debibinaad onow okanan. "Gayesh weweni
       ganawaabam ingiw," indig. Mii sa weweni ganawaabamagwaa
       geget. Wa, oniisidoonaawaa ongow gwiiwizensag.
       "Ogaawag ingiw," ikido. "Mii dash ezhi-inaachigewaad ingiw
       chimookomaanag," ikido. "Mii i'iw waasakonenjiganaaboo
       ingiw bemibizojig. Gaye gaawiin gaye izhinaachigesiiwag ingiw.
       Mii akeyaa inga-wiinimbigoonaanig ingiw chimookomaanag
       o'ow gashkitooyaang o'ow gaa-ani-onigooyaang. Gegoo
       ongow chimookomaanag neko'aakwendamowaad wii-
       wewebanaabiiwaad gegoo, gegoo go o'ow da-izhi-
       dabaabendamowaad i'iw ezhinaagwak naamayi'ii. Gaawiin
       onizhishinzinoon ji-izhichigewaapan i'iw.

[31]   Mii o'ow iko mewinzha, mii i'iw gaa-izhi-mikamaang ko iniw
       waa-ani-ayaayaang. Mii imaa ko niising i'iw. Mii gaa-izhi-
       gashkidibeyaang iwidi aandi ezhi-debaabandamaang. Mii imaa
       gii-ayaawaad. Ingii-kwaamigoo gaa-izhi-mikawangid a'aw.
       Weweni gomaa ashi ningodwaaswi ko gii-tebinaagwak
       mewinzha ingiw giigoonyag ajina gomaa debinangidwaa
       biijisewaad gii-ayaawangidwaa ashi ningodwaaswi ingiw
       giigoonyag. Gegoo gaa-izhi-minosed mewinzha anishinaabe;
       weweni go gii-pimiwidood iniw. Mii gaa-izhi-michi-abwiiyaang
       iwidi gii-izhaawag. Gaawiin gaye, medwebanzigwaa
       ingiw isa. Mii zhooniyaamising ji-ayaamagadwaag a'aw, enh
       ji-maanensang ge-ani-aabajitoowaagin ani-baa-
       nininjii'igooyaan. Aanh, dibishkoo gaa-izhi-debinangidwaa
       ko giigoonyag. Gaye memwech chi-waasa, chi-waasa da-baa-
       izhaayaang o'ow gaa-anooji'igaang o'ow jiigibiig omaa gii-
       mikawangidwaa ingiw giigoonyag. Mii go gaa-izhi-
       gikendamaan i'iw wii-pi-wiindamawiwaad ingiw akiwenziiyag.

[30] And again this certain Indian, he used to bring his son
along in the boat. I used to hang around with him when
he went to the shore. "And look over here," he tells me. Then
I glanced over there at the shore in the direction we were
heading. There was something vaporizing in the air here
but they were kids, but it was like one could barely [see]
where those boys were. Those bugs were hovering, so they're
floating there, so that's what they say. "Those are bugs
sailing around," I tell him. "No," he says. "Over here, go over
that way," he says. "Look over there." And I went over and
looked at [what turned out to be] gasoline floating there [on
the water]. So he grabs [my arm] bones. "And take a good
look at them," he tells me. So I took a real good look at
them. Golly, those boys were lowering something. "Those
are walleye pike," he says. "That's how those white people
do things," he says. "The speedboaters [use] that gasoline.
But they don't do that in the [right] way. That's how those
white people are desecrating our waters so that we'll be
able to relinquish them. These white people want to have
everything so bad when they fish, they have a very low regard
for how things look underneath them. It just isn't right for
them to do that."

[31] It used be this way a long time ago, that is to say that we
used to find [what we needed] whatever we were at. It was
put there. We could make use of things over there wherever
we might happen to see them. That's how they were there.
I would not be refused when we found one of those [fish].
One time the catch was really good and there were sixteen
fish or [a] little bit less that we grabbed with our bare hands
as they swam up just fast and we had sixteen of those fish.
The Indian people had good fortune a long time ago; he
carried that with him in a proper way. When they went
somewhere, we paddled over there by hand. And they didn't
motor around. When there was no money to be had, they
found it disagreeable to use that which I had panhandled. It
was just like that when we used to catch some fish. And we
had to go a long, long way when we made sales of the fish we
[caught] at the shore there. That's how I knew about what
those old men wanted to tell me.

[32] "Gaye imaa baa-izhaayaan jiigibiig, baa-izhaayaan jiigibiig
waa-ako-baa-inaagwak," gii-ikidowag. "O'ow akina bizoyeg
omaa, gaawiin gaye omaa o'ow biiwaabikoons, gaawiin sa go
gaye o'ow gii-paangide'angodesinoon imaa. Daa-biinad.
Ogii-piini'aawaan sa go jiigibiig imaa gaye," a'aw akiwenzii
gaa-ikidod. "Ingoding igo, ingoding igo gaawiin daa-
nisidoo'anaagosinoon ezhiwebak o'ow, ezhinaagwak o'ow
aki," gii-ikido. "Mii go omaa ingiw chimookomaanag o'ow wii-
shiishiigiwaad imaa zaaga'iganiing." "Hey," ikido.
"Wiinichigewag owidi biboong," gii-ikido. "Mii gaye
ezhichigewaad. Mii dash inaa'itoowaad i'iw zaaga'igan.
Inga-miigaanigoonaanig ingiw chimookomaanag wii-
ayaamowaad. Wiin-sh wiinawaa dash odinaajitoonaawaa
o'ow zaaga'igan," gii-ikido.

[33] Mii i'iw akina Misi-zaaga'igan gaa-tazhindamowaad iko, akina
sa go. Akina go gegoo omaa neyaashiiwan gii-tazhindamowaad
ingiw akiwenziiyag. Gii-kikendaasowag ingiw akiwenziiyag
waa-ani-izhiwebak. Gegoo noongom igo, gegoo noongom igo
bangii-sh wii-izhaayaang, gaawiin igo noongom. Mii go
gashkitoosiwaang, nawaj anooj gii-igooyaan noongom.
Gaawiin igo, anooj gii-igooyaanin ezhi-dakone'iyangidwaa
ingiw chimookomaanag. Miinawaa dibendamowaad i'iw
zaaga'igan, gii-ikidowag. Gaawiin odibendanziinaawaa o'ow
zaaga'igan. Gizhe-manidoo debendang zaaga'igan, akina go
giigoonyan. Mii imaa gaa-asaad, gaawiin ji-asaad iniw
giigoonyan i'iw ji-ani-waabanji'aad a'aw anishinaabe awegwen
sa bemaadizid giigoonyan ji-izhi-bimaadizid sa go ji-amwaad
gaye. Mii gaa-inaakonigooyang. Gayesh noongom iniw ge-
izhi-inaajitood a'aw chimookomaan. Gegoo omaa miinawaa
gii-kashkading ingoji go apii a'aw manidoo-giizisoons besho
gii-kashkading. Mii go bizhishig iniw ko agomo iwidi ateg.
Namanj igo, mii akina ezhi-bi-meginamowaad iwidi
wiinitoowaad zaaga'igan. Ingoding igo oga-wanitoonaawaa
zaaga'igan. Mii sa go bangii azhigwa, azhigwa bangii
inga-wii-pagida'waanaanig. Inga-wiipazhibaawanaan. Mii
azhigwa ikidowaad, "gaawiin" ji-izhi-ind a'aw anishinaabe.
Ikidowag ingiw chimookomaanag gayesh wiinawaa ezhi-
inaachigewaad gegoo, gegoo minik debinangidwaa giigoonyag.
Aabiding niibing oga-bagida'waawaan. Gayesh wiinawaa
ingoding, ingo-giizhig minik nesaawaad niibowa anooj
wiinawaa onisaawaan, "Biizh iniw minik eni-nisangidwaa,"
ogabe-igoon.

[32]   "And I used to walk along the shore there, walking along
       [thinking about] how it used to look," they said. "This
       motoring around here didn't happen like that, and the tin
       cans and other junk wasn't left floating there. It should be
       clean. They cleaned them at the shore there too," that old
       man said. "One time, one time nothing will be disposed
       of on the earth as it happens [now] and how it is made
       to look," he said. "Right here those white people want to
       urinate in the lake there." "Hey," he says. "They're dirtying it
       over here in the winter," he said. "And that's what they
       do. That's what they're doing with that lake. Those white
       people are going to fight us for what they want to have. But
       that's what they say about this lake," he said.

[33]   They used to talk about the whole length and breadth
       of Mille Lacs Lake, all of it. Those old men talked about
       every one of these peninsulas here. Those old men were so
       knowledgeable about what was going to happen. Today,
       when we want to go somewhere, that's no longer the case. So
       we aren't able to do that, as I'm told more about a variety of
       other things presently. No, I must have been told variously
       that those white people have a confining hold on us. And
       they own the lake, they said. They do not own this lake. The
       Great Spirit owns this lake, and all the fish. He put them
       there, and those fish were not just put there, but shown to
       the Indian people alive at that time so that he could live and
       eat those fish. That decision was made for us. But today that
       white man is going to talk about it his way. And when the
       lake froze over here sometime in December it froze nearby.
       It was just an empty floating mass out there. I don't know,
       they always leave their [garbage] over there and dirty the
       lake. One time though they're going to lose the lake. It's a
       little bit right now, we just harvest those fish with nets a
       little bit now. But we are going to have [unfettered rights] to
       spear them. That's what they're saying now, as the Indian is
       told "No." But those white people themselves say that they
       want to do these things, to catch [more] fish. Some summer
       they're going to harvest fish with nets. But any time, any
       day whenever the [Indians] had killed many fish, killing all
       kinds of them, "Bring whatever you've killed," they're always
       told.

[34] Miish o'ow gii-kashkitoowaad o'ow ongow waadookawiyangijig
o'ow gaa-ina'oonigooyaang igo o'ow gii-nagishkawaawaad
ingiw akiwenziibaneg. Wa'aw Migizi gaa-inind a'aw aya'aa,
miinawaa aya'aa Zhaabaashkang gaa-ogimaawijig omaa.
Mii a'aw Migizi, a'aw nimishoomisiban miinawaa go,
miinawaa go gaye odedeyibanen a'aw aya'aa, miinawaa aya'aa
Zhaabaashkang gaa-inind. Mii gaye gaa-kashkitoojig o'ow
miinawaa go iwidi akeyaa niibowa gii-ayaawag ingiw iwidi
akeyaa. Bagone-giizhig gaa-izhinikaazod, mii gaye ingiw
waa-wiidookaazojig o'ow gii-miinigooyang akina o'ow aki gaye
dibishkoo sa go gii-makandweyang i'iw aki. Gaye o'ow gii-
ikidowag ingiw chimookomaanag, "Mii weweni, mii weweni
ongow anishinaabeg ge-bimiwidoowaad o'ow aki. Debinaak
o'ow ji-miigaanaasigwaa iniw chimookomaanan." Gegoo
a'aw Migizi gaa-inind, a'aw Bagone-giizhig gaawiin
ogii-kanoonaasiin anishinaaben dambeng igo dibi go
nisaadaaniking imaa chimookomaanag. Owidi biinish
go, biinish igo iwidi akeyaa Nisoogamaag miinawaa go
imaa akeyaa Oshki-oodenaang gii-izhinikaadeg, akina go
iwidi akeyaa gaa-tazhewaad ingiw chimookomaanag.
Mii i'iw gaa-poodaag gii-nisaad akina anishinaaben a'aw
chimookomaan. A'aw Bagone-giizhig wiidookawaapan. A'aw
Migizi gaa-inind omaa, "Gaawiin," ikido Migizi. "Gaawiin
niinawind nimiigaazosiimin." Miish i'iw gaa-izhi-inaatood a'aw
Bagone-giizhig. Miish i'iw weweni gaawiin wiikaa miinawaa
ji-miigaadising. Miish i'iw gii-miigwechiwi'ind a'aw Migizi
imaa gii-miigaazosig o'ow gii-miinindwaa o'ow aki. Miish
i'iw gaa-onji-ozhibii'igaadeg o'ow ji-dibendamang i'iw aki.
Aanawi go aanind gii-miigiwewag i'iw aki. Gaawiish wiin i'iw
gii-miigiwesiiwag i'iw, mitigoon, giigoonyan,
waawaashkeshiwan, miinawaa i'iw manoomin. Mii gaa-
kanawendamowaad anishinaabeg. Miish i'iw gaa-
kashkitoowaad imaa ongow Misi-zaaga'iganiing eyaajig sa go.
Mii i'iw ezhi-wiidookaazowaad gaye iwidi akeyaa, iwidi akeyaa
wendaabang, mii miinawaa gii-pakinaagewaad i'iw. Mii sa go
biinish igo gii-pakinawind a'aw chimookomaan. "Gaawiin
geyaabi," ge-izhi-ikidopan.

[34] But then these ones who've helped us, these old men who
      encountered those [whites] have been able to bestow a great
      gift upon us. That's this *Migizi* as he was called, and also that
      Zhaabaashkang who were chiefs here. That *Migizi*, he was my
      grandfather, and his father was the one called *Zhaabaashkang*
      as well. They're the ones who were able to do this even when
      there were so many [whites] over this way. And regarding that
      so-called *Bagone-giizhig*, it was because of the ones who
      wanted to help the [whites] that we were given this land just
      like the land had been taken away from us.* And those white
      people said this, "It is good, it is in a good way that the
      Indians shall take this land. They didn't want to foolishly
      fight the white man." The one called *Migizi*, *Bagone-giizhig* had
      not consulted him or any of the Indians anywhere about the
      killing of whites there. From over this way to up there, up to
      the edge of Nisswa and also over there by Brainerd as it was
      called, all the white people there were in an uproar. Those
      sentiments intensified as the white people [thought about]
      killing all the Indians. That *Bagone-giizhig* was just helping to
      make things worse. So the one called *Migizi* here, he says,
      "No. We are not fighting." Then *Bagone-giizhig* himself said
      the same thing about the situation. Then there was never any
      fighting again. *Migizi* was thanked there for not going to war,
      and they were given title to this land. That's why it was
      written down in the [treaty] that we own this here land.
      Some of them still made a land cession. But they never ceded
      this here, or the trees, fish, deer, and that rice. The Indians
      took care of those things. That how the ones at Mille Lacs
      have been able to [keep the land]. So they helped over that
      way, over there in the east, and they won there too.† Up until
      then the white people were getting beaten. "Not any longer,"
      he would say then.

      * The following passage refers to *Bagone-giizhig*, or Hole in the Day II
        of Gull Lake, Minnesota, who made overtures about drawing the
        Ojibwe into the U.S.–Dakota Conflict of 1862. The Mille Lacs leader-
        ship strongly opposed his efforts.
      † Here he refers to the Civil War.

MELVIN EAGLE

[35] Mii sa go gaye, mii go gaye gaa-izhi-waawiindamawiwaad ingiw
akiwenziiyag, mii i'iw. Moozhag go, moozhag go bimi-
mikwendamaan gaa-wiindamawiwaad i'iw weweni, weweni
ji-bimiwidooyang o'ow aki. Aanishinaa doodoosiwang i'iw aki
gaa-ina'oonigooyang. Gaawiin go wiin a'aw chimookomaan
gigii-ina'oonigoosiinaan. A'aw Gizhe-manidoo gaa-miininang,
mii sa go ji-baamendamang. Mii i'iw wenji-gashkitooyang
noongom. Gegoo wiidookawag inendaagoziyang igo weweni
ge-gashkitooyang i'iw gaa-ina'oonigooyang. Moozhag go,
moozhag go nimikwendaan iko gaa-izhi-mino-ayaad a'aw
akiing a'aw anishinaabe memwendang go giiyosed a'aw.

Gaa-nandawaabamag Waabooz

[36] Gegoo gii-maajawaasakwad. Iwidi akeyaa ingii-izhaamin.
Gaawiin aapiji go waasa iwidi akeyaa gii-paa-agoodooyaang
ingiw waaboozoog gii-nisangidwaa. Mii sa gaa-wedenimagiban
a'aw akiwenzii gii-kichiwag azhigwa a'aw akiwenzii. "Ambe,
ambe, ambe iwidi baa-agoodoodaa," indig. "Ingiw
waaboozoog." "Haaw," indinaa sa gii-maajiibatooyaang
mashkimodaasimoons madweyaang agaashiingobaans.
Maagizhaa gaye ingii-ashi-niiyo-biboonagiz babaamoseyaang
iwidi akeyaa. Akeyaa gichi-waabishkiki iwidi ayaamagad. "Haa,
michi-agoodooyang waabang giga-bi-naadagwiimin," indinaa.
"Gaawiin," ikido. "Gaawiin. Mii go baa-izhi-agoodoon gomaa
omaa go nisawiyan. Anooj igo baayendamogwen miikana,
waaboozoo-miikanensan," ikido. "Giga-gikinoo'amoon
ezhichigeyang. Gaawiin memwech gidaa-bi-izhi'iwesiimin
waabang," ikido. Mii sa, mii gii-michaag o'ow waabishkiki
gaa-agoodooyaang imaa akina go baa-agoodooyaang. "Haa,
ambe maajaan. Maajaan. Anooj igo iwidi akeyaa baa-izhaan
o'ow. Ambe. Izhaan omaa akeyaa," ikido gaye aya'aa.
"Zhooshkaan igo gaye bimoseyan igo," ikido. Miish
bi-dagoshinaan imaa wiin imbaabii'ig wiin niin. Niin
ingii-izhi-ig imaa ji-baamoseyaan iwidi bagijinaashkigeyaan. Mii
sa iidog. Gaawiin ingii-kikendanziin ji-bagidinaashkigeyaan.
Mii sa bi-dagoshinaan, "Aaniish wenji-izhi-wendig akeyaa
ji-baa-izhaayaan," indinaa. "Ambe," ikido omaa.

118

[35]   And that's what those old men told me about. Always, I will
always remember what they told me in this good way, how
we kept our hold on this land so well. Well we didn't do
[bad] things to this land when we migrated here on the
waterways. And the white people certainly didn't paddle us
over here. The Great Spirit gave it to us so that we could
take care of it. And that's why we are able to do so today. So I
help him with things since we have been considered in such
a wonderful way to be able to migrate [here]. Always, I
always remember how the people live so well on the earth,
how the Indian enjoys his life when he hunts.

My Rabbit Quest

[36]   Something happened [one time] way off in the tules. We
went over that way. Not too far over that way we had been
hanging up [snares] and killing those rabbits. I thought that
old man was acting silly in the things I did with that old man
at that time. "Come, come on, come on let's go snaring over
there," he tells me. "Those rabbits." "All right," I tell him
as we start running, making noise with the little sack and
backpack. And I must have been fourteen years old when we
went walking over that way. There's a huge swamp over that
way. "Boy, we'll hang these up by hand and then come after
our snares tomorrow," I tell him. "No," he says. "No. We'll
hang a certain amount here so you can make some kills.
Different things must be taken into consideration about the
trail, the rabbit trail," he says. "I'll teach you as we do this. It
won't be necessary for us to come after them tomorrow," he
said. So, this swamp was so gigantic that as we hung snares
there it [seemed like] we hung snares throughout the whole
thing. "Okay, come start out. Go on. You go over towards
that way. Come on. Go this way here," he says. "And then
slide the [snares into shape] while you are walking," he says.
So when I finally get over there he's waiting for me himself.
There he told me to walk along over where I had been placing
the [snares]. Confusion. I didn't know where I had put them
down. So when I got there, "How could it be possible for me
to backtrack that way," I tell him. "Come on," he says here.

[37]   "Omaa izhi'ishin ikidomagak." Wa! Gomaa apii wa, haa
dazhi-wiikwaji'o omaa waabooz. Omaa baskindibe'wag. Mii
sa omaa biindoomooyaan omaa mashkimodaang
bimoseyaang. Wa, miinawaa iwidi a'aw wii-ayaa,
"Ashkimoonaan!" Niibowa indizhi-bimiwinaanig ingiw
waaboozoog. Wiiyaa! Ashkimonaanigozibanewag. Tayaa!
"Ingaashkinaazig," indinaa. "Haa, inga-ani-bimiwindamoon,"
indig. Mii gaye gii-pi-izhi-bimoondang. Wayaa, indayekoz.
Waasa go gaye gaa-izhi-dibikadinaagwak gaa-ani-boodaajiged
ji-wanishinaang. "Daga aweshinimishinaam," indinaa.
"Gaawiin," ikido. "Gidamigoo gomaa besho-sh go omaa
endaayan wenji-wanishinang," indig. Gaye wii-pimoseyaang
o'ow isa gegapii indaniwin ayaag. "Endaayaan ate.
Wewiibitaan." "Gaawiin," ikido. "Moozhag maajaadaa go,"
ikido. "Wayaa indayekoz megwaa bimoseyaan o'ow isa anooj
igo ningodwaaso-jiigise. Apiitate bimoseyaang ingoji go ongow
waaboozoog o'ow isa megwaa ganabaj igo naa, ganabaj igo naa
ishwaaswi ingii-pimoomaag ingiw waaboozoog, waabishki-
waaboozoog ezhinikaazojig. Wa! Da-minwendamoog
ingitiziimag dagoshinowaad wiinawaa. Gaawiin gegoo. Apiichi-
gigizheb miinawaa geyaabi wii-poodaakwewaad. Wayaa! Gaye
niin inanjigeyaan gii-onaagoshi-wiisiniyaang ingiw waabishki-
waaboozoog. Mii miinawaa gigizhebaawagak, mii go miinawaa.
Aanishinaa gaawiin igo wiikaa gegoo aapiji ingii-ayaanziimin.
Dibishkoo ingii-inigaazimin sa go. Gaawiin dibishkoo wiikaa
ingii-ayanziimin. Gaawiin wiikaa ingii-miinigoosiimin i'iw
wiisiniwin. Booch igo.

[38]   Miinawaa giigoonyag, mii gaa-izhi-wewebanaabiiyaang. Mii
eta gaa-izhi-wiisiniyaang miinawaa niibing. Miinawaa
dagwaagig gaye manoomin niibowa ogii-ishkonaanaawaan
niij-niiyoshkinag o'ow gaa-kiizhiitoowaad. Mii gaa-
inanjigeyaang. Miinawaa go gii-kitigewag iniw opiniin.
Anooj igo gegoo gii-kitigewag. Mii eta go imaa naamayi'ii
naamakamig imaa ogii-ayaanaawaa naamayi'ii waakaa'iganing.
Mii eta go omaa gaa-tinowaad gegoo ge-miijiyaang. O'ow isa
gabe-biboon gii-wiisiniyaang gegoo, imaa ani-ziigwang, ani-
dagwaagig, mii go miinawaa gaa-izhichigeyaang
gii-ishkanangidwaag gegoo o'ow isa debiseg gaa-pabaa-
ayaayaang baa-nanda-agoodooyaang. Miinawaa go
waawaashkeshiwan babaa-nisaawaad gaye. Mii ko gegoo

[37] "Tell me what's to be said about this." Holy buckets! Golly, after a little while there was a rabbit trying to get free here. Then I killed him with a blow to the head. So I put him in the bag here as we walked along. Boy, again there was another one over there. "Put him in the bag." Thus, we ended up carrying a lot of those rabbits. Wow! They were all stuffed in the bag. Unreal! "The carrying is overwhelming me," I tell him. "Okay, I'll carry it for you," he tells me. Then he carried it. Boy, was I ever tired. It was completely dark way out there when he blew on his finger to see if we were lost. "Please get us out of here," I tell him. "No," he says. "You are so concerned with getting lost that you are oblivious to the fact that your house is so nearby," he tells me. And as we walked along, my house was right there. "My house is there. Hurry up." "No," he says. "Let's leave," he says. Golly was I tired while walking around [my house] about six times. Then our walking around was sufficient because these rabbits, while we were [doing that], I brought in eight more of those rabbits, white rabbits as they are called. Wow! My parents are going to be happy when they get back. Nothing. And it was still early in the morning when they built the cooking fire. Boy! As for myself, I had been eating those white rabbits when we had supper. And again in the morning, then too. Well we never had too much. We were quite poor. It was more like we never had enough. But we were never given that food. That's for sure.

[38] And regarding the fish, that's how we fished with poles. That's all we ate in the summer. And in the fall they saved up the rice, maybe four partners would finish it. That was our diet. They also planted potatoes. They planted a variety of things. They only kept things there in the cellar below, underneath the house. They only had certain kinds of things they could eat here. We would eat these things all winter, and in the spring there, and in the fall, we did that again to acquire a sufficient quantity of food wherever we would be and go snaring. And they killed deer too. The men were always leaving to go around hunting. Sometimes they would kill only one deer. So they all shared in that. Whatever amount they had was sufficient. So it is with all

maajaawaad wiinawaa ko ininiwag babaa-giiyosewaad.
Aaningodinong go bezhig eta onisaawaan waawaashkeshiwan.
Mii sa akina da-daashkonomidiwaad i'iw. Mii minik o'ow
debisewaad. Mii sa go akina go weweni go, weweni go gaa-
izhichigewaad anishinaabeg weweni go, weweni wii-
ashamaawaad iniw wiijanishinaabewaan bebangii go.
Mii debiseg gii-ayaawaad iko gaa-izhiwebiziwaad ko mewinzha
giiyosewaad. Miinawaa go waaboozoo-nagwaagan, waaboozoon
obiinaawaan. Mii ba-izhi-agoodoowaad igaye wiinawaa.

Gii-ina'oonind Anishinaabe

[39] Mii gaa-onji-gikendaasoyaan gaye niin gaa-izhiwebiziwaad
anishinaabebaneg. Mii sa wenji-gikendaasoyaan gaye niin o'ow
gii-pi-waawaabamagwaa gaa-pi-izhichigewaad miinawaa
gii-pabizindawagwaa gaye iwidi nimaamaa, nookomisag.
Biinish sa ingii-waawiindamaagoog gegoo gaa-izhi-
minosewaad ingiw anishinaabeg. Miish sa go gaye niin igo
ezhi-gashkitooyaan o'ow waawiindamoonaan igo nawaj igo
gegoo ge-ikidoyaan igo. Maagizhaa go gaye gabe-dibik o'ow
geyaabi go gidaa-waawiindamoon. Gigizheb o'ow giga-ayaa
omaa. Naa indaa-mooshkinadoonan iniw. Mii ezhi-
gikendaasoyaan akina gegoo. Mii sa wenda-minwendamaan
iko gaagiigidoyaan i'iw omaa niimi'idiing gegoo go ezhi-
mikwendamaan igo ezhi-gikinoo'amawagwaa ongow oshki-
ininiwag weshki-bimaadizijig i'iw bizindawiwaad ingiw
nesidotawijig. Miish ingoding, oga-ani-aabajitoonaawaan
gaye wiinawaa ji-ani-gikendaasowaad ingiw o'ow ezhi-
dazhimindwaa ingiw manidoog ge-ani-apiichi-nookwikamig
i'iw manidoo, manidoo bezhig o'ow isa. Niibowa waa-
ayaawaad manidoog gegoo akina gegoo omaa
o-ganawendweninangwaa ji-ganaweniminangwaa sa go gaye
ingiw manidoog. Aaningodinong iko, aaningodinong iko
niwenda-niizaanendam ko gaagiigidoyaan i'iw aaniin i'iw
wenji-ininendaagoziyaan i'iw. Miish igo naa mikwendamaan,
ingii-pi-wiindamaagoo ji-maada'ookiiyaan. Mii wenji-
gikenimid a'aw, mii sa go ji-wiidookawag inenimid a'aw
manidoo endazhimag. Moozhag go, moozhag go

good things, the Indians did things properly, and fed their
fellow Indians a little at a time. So it was enough with the
way they used to be, the way they used to behave when they
went hunting. And with the rabbit snaring, they would
bring a rabbit. Then they would all go snaring there
themselves.

The Indian Was Gifted

[39] This is how I became so knowledgeable myself about what
the Indians used to do. Then I became learned myself about
this which I saw them doing and listened to them too over
there, my mother, my grandmothers. They told me about
things like the Indian's good fortunes. Then I too became
able myself to tell you more about these things in what I
shall say. And I might be able to talk to you about this all
night long. In the morning you'll still be here. I could fill up
those [cassettes]. I have knowledge about everything. So
that's why I'm just happy talking about this here Drum
Ceremony and things I remember to teach these young men,
the young people who listen to me and understand me.
Then one time they will use these things themselves to
become knowledgeable about how the Spirits are spoken of
in a gentle way, and the one Spirit too. There will be a lot of
Spirits who look after us here, the Spirits who take care of
us. Sometimes it used to be, sometimes I used to be just
stingy when I used to be thought of to talk about this. Then
I remembered about how I was told to share. That's why he
knows me, so that I will help him when the Spirit I speak of
thinks of me. Always, I'm often asked this by different
people, "How come you know so much about this yourself?"
Intentionally, when I help these ones with such purpose, the
Spirits think of me in how those old men told me about
things long ago. Now I have since forgotten many things
that old man told me. And now I'm an elder. I'm a learned

ingagwejimigoog ingiw anooj igo awiiya go i'iw, "Aaniish
gaa-onji-gikendaman gaye giin o'ow?" Onjida, onjida ongow
go wiidookawagwaa, indinenimigoog manidoog o'ow gii-
pi-waawiindamawiwaad ingiw akiwenziibaneg mewinzha.
Gegoo niibowa go ingii-pi-wanendaan a'aw akiwenzii gii-
paa-wiindamawid azhigwa. Miinawaa azhigwa nichi-aya'aaw.
Nichi-aya'aaw gikendaasoyaan ezhinikaadeg gegoo. Mii
azhigwa ani-gikendamaan i'iw ge-izhi-minosed a'aw
niijanishinaabe azhigwa ge-izhi-gikendaasod igo awiiya.

[40] Mii gegoo, gegoo giin ge-izhi-waawiindamoonaan go gaye,
gegoo go wiindamoonaan iwidi niimi'idiing ko. Mii
ezhi-minwendamaan igo gegwejimid awiiya anishinaabe
moozag igo gagwejimid ezhi-gikendaasoyaan. Mii gaye niin
ji-ani-gikendaasoyaan, nawaj gikendaasod a'aw bezhig.
Miinawaa go ongow aanind ongow weshki-bimaadizijig gegoo
azhigwa midaaswi-ashi-ningodwaaso-biboonagiziwag azhigwa
gaye—gaawiin geyaabi indaa-izhi-agindanziin—maagizhaa gaye
midaaso-biboon, niishtana, namanj iidog. Miish i'iw wenji-
wiidookawag niijanishinaabe weshki-bimaadizid nesidootawid.
Mii ji-ani-gikendaasod gaye. Ingoding go naanimidana ashi
ingodwaaso-biboonagiziyaan, "Mii giin gikendaman o'ow
ji-mikwendaman o'ow gidizhitwaawininaan sa go gaye ge-
izhi-minoseyang sa go miinawaa go ge-izhi-minosewaad
giniijaanisinaanig, goozhishenyinaanig, giiji-ayaawaad, booch
eyaawaad goozhishenyinaanig. Ingoding gaye, mii moozhag
zhawendaagwak goozhishenyag ayaawaad imaa nawaj igo
gidaanikobijigaansag ayaawaad sa go ongow."

[41] Sa go ongow indaanikobijigaansag naaniwag azhigwa, bezhig
gwiiwizens miinawaa niiwin ikwezensag. Wayaa! Mii apiichi-
apiitenimagwaa. Mii gaawiin ge-inendaagoziwaanen ji-
daanikobijigeyaan. Niibowa wiin gaye noozhishenyag ayaawag.
Zhaangaswi ayaawag ingiw noozhishenyag. Miinawaa
naaniwag, ganabaj igo nising endaayaan. Indaa-bimaadiz ji-
daanikobijigeyaan. Maagizhaa gaye namanj ingikendaan.
Gaawiin sa go ingikendanziin minik weni-bimaadizid. Mii
go Gizhe-manidoo o'ow gii-pagaminang o'ow apii waa-ani-
ishkwaa-ayaayang sa go.

[42] Gegoo mewinzha ko, mewinzha ko gaye ingii-kagiibaadiz iko
mewinzha. Ingii-minikweshk gaye gegoo. Gegoo aangodinong
iko wii-minikweyaan, mii i'iw gaa-izhi-wanibiiyaan iko gaye.
Ingii-kiiwashkwebii sa go. Gaawiin ingikendanziin gegoo

elder as it's called. So now I do know about how the Indian has good fortune now and how one becomes knowledgeable about that.

[40] There's something, something I want to tell you too, tell you about how the Drum Ceremony used to be. This is why I am happy when someone often asks me about things I'm knowledgeable about. And I have come to be knowledgeable myself, although that one [elder] is more knowledgeable. And again some of these young people now are sixteen years of age—I can't count any more—maybe ten years, twenty, I don't know. That's why I help my fellow Indian, the young ones who understand. It's so that they'll become knowledgeable too. One time when I was fifty-six years old [I was told], "Since you know about this and remember our culture too and how we have good fortune as well, your children, grandchildren, companions will have good luck and your grandchildren wherever they're at. This time and always it will be a blessing wherever your grandchildren are at and your great-grandchildren are too."

[41] My great-grandchildren now number five, one boy and four girls. Wow! I have such strong feelings for them. I might or might not have been considered to have great-grandchildren. My grandchildren are numerous too. There are nine of my grandchildren. And the five [great-grandchildren], maybe three are at my house. I have been able to live to have great-grandchildren. But maybe I knew that. I didn't know how many would come into being. The Great Spirit has brought us here at this time until we will no longer exist.

[42] It used to be that a long time ago, a long time ago I used to misbehave. And I was [a] chronic drinker. Sometimes when I wanted to drink, I used to consume way too much [liquor]. I was a drunk. I didn't know when I arrived at my

dagoshinaan endaayaan gigizhebaawagak babaa-niibawiyaan,
"Aaniish gaa-izhi-dagoshinaan omaa?" Awiiya ingii-
kanawenimig. Inganawendaagoz. Gegoo ingii-kanawendaagoz.
Miish dash waa-kikendamaan gaa-onji-ganawinendaagoziyaan.
Mii i'iw wii-ani-wiidookawag a'aw niijanishinaabe, wii-
pimiwinagwaa dewe'iganag wiidookaazoyaan. Mii gaa-onji-
ganawinendaagoziyaan sa go gegoo. Dibishkoo go ongow
nimanidoomag inganawenimigoog. Enang, "Dibi go ezhaayan
booch igo giganawenimig gegoo, gegoo o'ow inaabiyan," indig.
"Akeyaa opime-ayi'ii gaye gegoo biijibideg, awenesh dabaziyan
awiiya. Giwii-nibaa gegoo wii-piizikaagooyan gaye. Gaye
giganawendaagoz. Ingiw gimanidoomag giganawenimigoog
o'ow wenji-gikendaasoyan, wenji-gikendaman sa go gegoo." Mii
i'iw gaye gaa-pi-izhiwaad ingiw akiwenziiyag. "Gegoo, gegoo go
gidoonji-ganawendaagoz," ingoding ingii-ig. "Gegoo ji-ani-
wiidookawad giijanishinaabe," ingii-igoog ingiw akiwenziiyag.

[43] Gayesh igo geget, mii go ezhi-waawiidookawag geshkitooyaan
gashkawewiziyaan ji-wiidookawag a'aw niijanishinaabe. Mii go
ezhi-miigwechiwi'ag izhi-inendamaan a'aw bi-gagwejimid
gegoo awiiya ji-waawiindamawag. Miish i'iw gegoo omaa, gegoo
omaa waawiindamoonaan o'ow eko-minwendamaan i'iw ji-
gikendaasod a'aw niijanishinaabe ji-wii-ani-bizindawid.
Gaye ingoding maagizhaa gaye ingoding o'ow gaawiin
imaa inga-ayaasiin ingoding ji-gikendaagwak i'iw wenji-
wiidookawag anishinaabe. Moozhag iko, moozhag iko o'ow
nimishoomisiban, ambesh go dino indayaamaambaan,
indinendam akina go gegoo gaa-pi-waawiindamawid. Mii
nawaj gikendaasoyaan, gaawiin dash memwech i'iw, memwech
i'iw. Ingoding go, ingoding go ezhi-mikwendamaan iko
gaa-pi-izhid gii-pi-gogiiyaan aangodinong go. Ingoding go
ingii-midaaso-biboonagiz i'iw. Ingii-ashi-niizho-biboonagiz
gii-pi-waawiindamawid a'aw akiwenzii, akiwenziiyag sa go,
miinawaa go mindimooyeyag. Mii go gaye wiinawaa ingiw
mindimooyeyag gaa-izhi-wiindamawiwaad iko i'iw. Mii go gaye
gaa-pi-izhiwebak, ge-ani-izhiwebak sa go gii-kikendaasowag sa
go ingiw akiwenziibaneg miinawaa mindimooyebaneg. Wii-
manidoowaadiziwag sa go ingiw akiwenziibaneg, gaawiin
miinawaa go o'ow, gaawiin go akina ongow. Moozhag go,
moozhag go nimikwenimaag ongow. Ingichi-miigwechiwi'aag
go ingiw akiwenziiyag gaa-wiindamawiwaad. Mii gaye niin

house, standing around in the morning, "How did I get here?" Someone watched over me. I am protected. I was protected in things. And then I wanted to know why I was being looked after. Then I wanted to help my fellow Indian, as I belonged on the Drums I helped. That's why I was protected in things. It was like my Spirits protected me. It was said, "Wherever you go you are certainly protected by the [Spirit], so you see these things," he tells me. "When something comes [at you], you dodge off to the side. When you want to sleep they will envelop you too. And you are protected. You are protected by those Spirits, that's why you are learned, why you know things." And that's what those old men told me. "You are protected for that reason," he told me one time. "You will help your fellow Indian," those old men told me.

[43] And truly, I do help him in what I am able to do to the full extent of my abilities to help my fellow Indian. Then I thank him as I think of how someone asked me to tell him these things. And then this here, what I'm telling you here is what I remember so that my fellow Indian becomes knowledgeable when he wants to listen to me. And one time, maybe I won't be there one time for it to be known why I help the Indian people. It always used to be like this with my grandfather, how I wish to have him with me as I would think about everything he told me. Now that I'm smarter, that's not so necessary. One time, I remember what he used to tell me sometimes when I was growing up. One time I was ten years old. Although I was twelve years old when that old man started talking to me, the elder men and the elder women. And those old ladies used to tell me things too. Those old men and old women were very knowledgeable about history and what was going to happen in the future. Those old men wanted to be spiritual people, although not all of them. Always, I will always remember them. I give my greatest thanks to those old men who told me about things. The reason I talk about this is because of what they told me. That's why they did that so that I would talk about this myself as I would become represented on the Drum over there far away and in all

wenji-waawiindamaageyaan i'iw gaa-pi-waawiindamawiwaad.
Mii gaa-onji-izhichigewaad i'iw ji-waawiindamaageyaan
gaye niin igo owidi go biinish waasa dibinendaagoziyaan
a'aw dewe'igan miinawaa go akina sa go gegoo, gegoo akina
go ji-wiidookawag inendaagozid, ji-wiidookawag a'aw
niijanishinaabe. Mii gaa-onji-asigooyaan gaye niin iidog omaa.
Inde-inendam sa go gegoo gaye giin. Mii go gaye giin gaa-
onji-asigooyan ji-ani-waawiidookawad ji-aaniikanootawad a'aw
bwaaniwitood ji-ojibwemowaad.

Inwewin Meshkawiziimagak

[44]   Mii eta go zhaaganaashiimowaad, eta go aanind igo gaye,
maagizhaa gaye ingoding go besho. Mewinzha ko gaawiin
igaye awiiya omaa, gaawiin gaye awiiya omaa gii-
shaaganaashiimosiin gaye, mii eta go. Mii gaye gii-pi-
agaashiinyiyaan igo eko-giiyaan igo iidog gaye niin gii-
anishinaabe-ganoozhiyaang ingitiziimag miinawaa go
akiwenziiyag. Gaawiin wiikaa gii-shaaganaashiimosiiwag
ongow akiwenziiyag. Gaawiin sa ogii-kikendanziinaawaa
ji-chimookomaani-gaagiigidowaad.
[45]   Gegoo giga-wiindamoon i'iw. Ingii-ingodwaaso-biboonagiz
omaa gii-maajiitaayaan ji-gikinoo'amaagooyaan. Gaawiin
gaye, gaawiin gaye ingii-kikendanziin i'iw chimookomaan
gaa-izhid. Gaawiin gegoo ingii-kikendanziin. Mii gaa-izhi-
bwaanawiziyaan awenesh ge-izhid a'aw indinendam. Miish
a'aw isa niitaawis gaa-wiijigimag o'ow dibishkoo. Mii a'aw
gaa-aaniikanootawid waawiindamawid. Jiigegaabaw gii-
izhinikaazo. Mii gaa-wiindamawid i'iw gaye ikidowin indig.
Aanish go ingii-kopaji'ig a'aw gwiiwizens, niijakiwenzii
dibishkoo go. Mii gaa-izhi-izhid ko ji-wiindamawag i'iw
gikinoo'amaagewinini. Ingii-wiinigiizhwe gomaa omaa gaye
ji-bazanjiiwid ko a'aw gikinoo'amaagewinini. Miish a'aw bezhig
igo miinawaa bezhig niitaawis gaa-pi-izhi-wiindamawid, "Gego
bizindawaaken Jiigegaabaw. Niin omaa bizindawishin gaye."
Mii a'aw weweni. "Gaawiin miinawaa inga-bizindawaasiin
wiikaa." Wewiib igo ingii-kikendaan igo i'iw wiinigizhweyaan
akina gaa-izhi-ikidoyaan gaye. "Eko-bi-wiijiiyan," ingii-ig gaye;
mii a'aw Jiigegaabaw gii-izhinikaazod. "Miinawaa go gibi-

things helping the [people] who are considered for it, helping my fellow Indian. That's why I have been seated [on the Drum] here myself. I've thought enough about this for you too. This is why you have been seated [on the Drum] to help [the people] and to translate for those who are unable to speak the Ojibwe language.

The Power of Language

[44] They only speak English, and only some [speak Indian], but maybe sometime soon [it will be different]. A long time ago there wasn't anyone here, nobody spoke English here. And when I was small too growing up myself, my parents and those old men talked to me in Indian. These old men never talked English. They didn't know how to talk American [English].

[45] I'm going to tell you something about that. I was six years old here when I started going to school. And I didn't know what the white people were telling me. I didn't know anything. I would be unable to process whatever he was telling me, I thought. Then there was my cousin that I accompanied. He was the one who translated for me what the [whites] told me. He was called *Jiigegaabaw*. He talked to me and told me a word. Well that boy would trick me, just like my fellow elder [today]. He told me to tell that [word] to the teacher. I swore and that teacher made me stand in the [corner]. Then another one of my cousins came and told me, "Don't listen to *Jiigegaabaw*. Just listen to me here." He was nice. "I'm never going to listen to him again." Quickly I learned about my swearing and everything I should say too. "You come with me," he had told me, that was that *Jiigegaabaw* as he was called. "I'll accompany you again," he tells me. "Sure," I tell him and all those young men. And no, well they didn't want to know how to talk Indian. They

wiijii'in," indig. "Enh," indinaa gaye wiin igo, ongow oshki-
ininiwag gaye miinawaa ingiw. Gaawiin gaye, aanish sa gaawiin
gaye owii-kikendanziinaawaa ji-anishinaabe-gaagiigidowaad.
Gaawiin ogii-kikendanziinaawaa. Miish i'iw gaa-izhid. "Gegoo
aanawewiziyan," indigoo. Gii-tagwaagig gii-maajii-
gikinoo'amaagooyaan, azhigwa ani-ziigwang, mii azhigwa
ani-izhi-gikendamaan i'iw chimookomaani-gaagiigidoyaan.
"Anishinaa go awenesh ge-bonezid," indinaag gwiiwizensag.
"Niizh ingikendaanan. Inga-ayetoonan," indinaag gaye.
Bizaaniyaawag. "Gaawiin imbaapi'igoosiin geyaabi.
Gaawiin geyaabi imbagosenimigoosiin," ingii-inaag,
baa-baapi'agwaa ingiw sa go weweni, weweni gii-kashkitooyaan
ji-gaganoonagwaa ingiw chimookomaanag dash.

[46] Gaawiin wiikaa, wiikaa dibi go baa-anokiiyaan—anooj igo
ingii-paa-anokii waasa iwidi akeyaa daga biizh ingiw
chimookomaanag gaa-wiidanokiimagak—gaa wiikaa gaye
ingii-wanendanziin i'iw anishinaabe-gaagiigidowin. Gegoo
azhigwa ginwenzh ingii-anokii iwidi Gakaabikaang. Ganabaj
igo nisimidana daso-biboon o'ow gaye ingii-anokii. Anooj
igo wii-tanakiiwagwaa ingiw chimookomaanag, gaawiin
wiikaa niwanendanziin i'iw indizhitwaawin. Gegoo
aaningodinong igo abinoojiinyag, mii gegoo noongom
igo ongow abinoojiinyag, mii dash gaawiin
ogikendanziinaawaa i'iw anishinaabe-izhitwaawin.
Ingikendaan igo. Gaawiin niibowa, niibowa o'ow gaye gichi-
aya'aag, gaawiin ogikendanziinaawaa i'iw anishinaabe-
izhitwaawin. Miinawaa ji-gaagiigidoyaan, mii eko-
maanendamaan i'iw bwaaniwitood anishinaabe ji-
anishinaabe-gaagiigidod iwidi gaa-ina'ooninijin ji-gaagiigidod.
Moozhag ko inendamaan maanendamaan ingiw waabamagwaa
niniijaanisag gegoo niniijaanisag, gaawiin ninisidootaagosiin
aano-gaganoonagwaa. Aanish igo gaye ganabaj igo gaye niin
igo, gaawiin niin ganabaj igo indizhichigesiin gegoo gii-pi-
agaashiinyiwaad weweni go bi-gaganoonagwaaban. Maagizhaa
gaye wiinawaa, mii ge-izhi-gikendamowaaban azhigwa go o'ow
apii. Gaawiish. Ingii-pi-aagonwetaan meta gii-
ojibwemotawagwaa, chimookomaani-gaagiigidoyaan gii-
agaashiinyiwaad gii-pi-gogiiwaad. Miinawaa gii-pizhishigwaa
anishinaabeg bi-gaganoonagwaaban gaa-pi-doodawiwaad
ingiw akiwenziiyag miinawaa go ongow ingitiziimag. Booch igo

didn't know how. That's what he told me. "You're
inadequate," I was told. It was fall when I started going to
school, but now, by the springtime, I already knew how to
talk like an American. "Well who is going to forget," I tell
the boys. "I know two [languages]. I'm going to use them,"
I told them too. They were quiet. I wasn't getting laughed
at any more. "I'm not getting wished for any more," I told
them, and I laughed at them in a good way, as I was able to
properly converse with the white people.

[46] Never ever in all my going around for work in different
places—and I worked all over, far away, working with the
white people—never did I forget the Indian way of talking.
I had worked over there in Minneapolis for a long time.
Maybe thirty years I worked there. I lived with those white
people, but I never forgot my religion. Sometimes children,
these kids now, they don't know the Indian religion. I know
it. Even a lot of them, a lot of the elders don't know about
the Indian religion. And when I talk, I feel quite bad about
how the Indian people are unable to manage speaking
Indian over there, to speak wherever they've migrated. Often
as I think about this I feel bad when I see my own children as
they do not understand when I speak to them in vain. Well
maybe there's nobody [to blame] but myself because I might
not have done things when they were small to talk to them
properly. And maybe them too, they know this now. But no.
I did not see the importance of speaking only Ojibwe to
them, as I spoke English when they were little and growing
up. And it is almost in vain that I talk to Indians now, how
the old men and my parents used to do things for me. It is
truly in a good way that I properly talk to my children, my
daughters, so they can understand and maybe know what
the Indian people have been given. Often, I always feel just
bad about my children not knowing that. But they certainly
know things like how to make a tobacco offering when
certain things will happen, when it is thundering they put
out tobacco. They know a certain amount about talking to

MELVIN EAGLE

weweni, weweni gaa-kaganoonagwaaban ingiw niniijaanisag,
indaanisag, nisidootamowaad, maagizhaa gaye odaa-
gikendaanaawaa i'iw anishinaabe gaa-izhi-miinind. Moozhag
go, moozhag go niwenda-maanendam niniijaanisag
gikendanzigwaa i'iw. Gegoo gaye booch igo gayesh
ogikendaanaawaa-sh igo wii-piindaakoojigewaad gegoo
wii-izhiwebak i'iw ge-animikiikaag gaye gegoo go
asemaan asaawaad. Ogikendaanaawaa ongow eniwek i'iw
gagwejimaawaad ingiw iwidi. Ingii-waabamaabaneg ingiw iwidi
gii-taayaang. Ongow ogikendaanaawaa ge-izhi-baayaashing gii-
izhinikaadeg ge-izhi-baayaashing ge-chi-nichiig wii-chigewaad
ingiw manidoog.

[47]   Ingoding owidi akeyaa iwidi bangishimog iwidi akeyaa
ingii-waabandaanan, mii iniw bi-naagwak akeyaa
biindaakoojigeyaan, a'aw mii dash ingozis imaa gaa-
wiijii-ayaad. "Hey. Ishpiming gaye inaabin," ikido
chimookomaani-gaganoonid. "Gayesh naa ongow, gayesh naa
wa'aw migizi," ikido. Gii-izhibaabasod a'aw sa omaa bi-
waabamag. Miinawaa ishpiming gaa-ani-izhi-izhaad
ishkwaa-bi-waabamangid a'aw migizi. Mii iwidi akina
gaa-ninikawag i'iw gii-ani-maajiidood a'aw migizi. Gaawiin
imaa gii-pangishinzinoon omaa, omaa anishinaabe-aki
akeyaa. Ingii-nakomigoo. Ingii-nakomewiz miinawaa gii-
piindaakoojigeyaan sa dash agaamed. Chimookomaanag
endaawaad, mii gii-ani-boonimaag gii-ani-bigishkaasijigewaad
iwidi manidoog iwidi agaamayi'ii miinawaa zaaga'iganiing.
Ingii-pizindaamin igo debaajimomaawag gii-ani-bangising.
Gaye gaawiin omaa gii-pagisinoon. Inashke, gaa-izhi-
gagwejimag a'aw bezhig Naawigiizisookwe miinawaa bezhig
a'aw Zhaawanaasang gaa-inind. "Eya'," ikido. "Aya'aa a'aw
binesi wayaabamad," ikido. "Ginookwezigemin imaa gii-
piindaakoojigeyan, awas oga-izhiwidoon akeyaa ishpiming
ge-izhi-baayaasing miinawaa booniimangiban imaa akina ge-
izhi-biishkaasigiban o'ow," ikido. Daaweshkesh igo eyaawaad
gidewe'iganag, gaawiin wiikaa booniimagasinoon eta noo o'ow.
Debwe gwek bi-izhaamagad miinawaa iwidi akeyaa miinawaa
ishpiming.

[48]   Mii ingiw dewe'iganag, gimishoomisinaanig begijigegig i'iw
weweni biindaakoonangwaa weweni bimiwinangwaa.
Weweni ongow, mii ingiw binesiwag i'iw genawenjigejig.

132

the [Spirits] over there. I've seen them over there where we lived. They know about when there will be a tornado as it was called, when tornadoes will form and the weather will turn really bad and the Spirits do certain things.

[47]   One time over there towards the west I saw them [thunderbirds], and since they looked that way I made a tobacco offering and my son was there with me. "Hey. Look up there," he says, talking to me in English. "Those ones and this bald eagle," he says. He was soaring here when I came to see him. He went up in the sky after we saw that eagle. Over that way I held out my hand to him and that eagle took [the offering] with him. It didn't touch down here, here on the Indian lands. I was answered. I was answered again when I made the offering and he traveled across the lake. Where the white people live, that's where they went to release [their fury] and the Spirits tore everything up over there on the other side of the lake. We listened as they told the story of its falling. Nothing came down here. You see, I asked that one *Naawigiizisookwe* and also that one *Zhaawanaasang* as he was called. "Yes," she said. "That's a thunderbird you saw," she said. "We burn medicine there when you make an offering, and he'll take it further up in the sky to sound out and leave us alone and not unleash himself here," she says. Wherever your Drums are at, nothing will be bothered. It truly turns right around and goes up there in the sky again.

[48]   It's those Drums, our grandfathers, where they make offerings, where we make offerings to them in a good way as we carry them. And properly, it is the thunderbirds who are

Ganawendaagozi sa go anishinaabe gegoo go, gegoo
zhawinendaagozid i'iw gagwedwed gagwejimaad
iniw manidoon o-biindaakoojiged. Mii i'iw wenji-
ganawinendaagozid a'aw anishinaabe gegoo. Mii go gaye
gaa-onji-gikendamaan. Mii go wenji-gikendamaan i'iw
akiwenziiyag gii-pi-waawiindamawiwaad gegoo.

Dibendaagoziwin

[49] Akina sa go wiindamoonaan, gaawiin gegoo
wiindamawisiiwaaban ingiw akiwenziiyag. Gaawiin
gaye gidaa-wiindamoosiinoon, gaawiin sa go gaye gidaa-
nagishkoosiinoon iwidi gii-pi-ganoonigooyaan ji-
wiidookawagwaa ingiw Gaa-waababiganikaag dewe'iganan
gii-pi-gagwejimiwaad. "Enh. Giga-wiidookooninim," ingii-
inaag. Miish i'iw bi-dagoshinowaad ingiw, ingiw gwiiwizensag
waa-pi-gagwejimiwaad. "Gidaa-wiidookooninim ji-
maajiishkaayaang iwidi dewe'igan iwidi ginwenzh gaa-abid
iwidi. Geget noongom ikidowag dash gii-wiindamawiwaad
i'iw gaa-izhiwebak o'ow gii-noondawind ko dewe'igan imaa
de-madwewed imaa gaye wiin. Gaawiin o'ow, gaawiin imaa
anami'ewigamigong daa-ayaasiin. Gaye gii-kashkendamoog
imaa ingiw manidoog, debendaagozijig gaa-onji-wiikwajiwaad
gimishoomisinaan ji-gowi'aawaad imaa. Mii sa geget gii-
kowi'aawaad iwidi. Miish i'iw gaa-izhi-wiindamawag. "Enh.
Giga-wiidookooninim," ingii-pi-inaag, mii ongow gwiiwizensag
o'ow isa ge-bimiwinaajig noongom iniw dewe'iganan. Ingiw
ogimaag gii-pi-gagwejimiwaad miinawaa go niigaani-niimiwed
gii-pi-gagwejimid. "Enh. Giga-wiidookooninim," indinaag.
"Iwidi o'ow gagwejimig a'aw nanaandawii'iwewinini a'aw.
Ogikenimaawaan onow dewe'iganan," ingii-igoog.
"Gaawiin," ikidowag. "Haaw. Mii sa gagwejimig a'aw
nanaandawii'iwewinini," ikidong. Mii sa gaye gii-
wiindamaagoowaad. "Naanig o'ow bi-zhoonig," iwidi
gii-igooyaan. Miish i'iw gii-wiindamaagooyaan i'iw
nanaandawii'iwewinini. Mii gaa-tinowaad o'ow iwidi
Neyaashiing eyaad. Mii a'aw bwaanzhii-dewe'igan gii-ikido
daga. Miish gii-pi-wiindamawiwaad. Haanh, miish gii-
ikido'amawagwaa ezhinaagwak miinawaa gii-atooyaang iniw

the protectors. The Indian people are protected in these things, he is blessed in what he asks, what requests he makes of the Spirits when he goes over to make an offering. That is why the Indian people are protected in these things. And that's how I came to know about it. That's why I know what the old men came to tell me about things.

Belonging

[49] Everything that I'm telling you, these things weren't just told to me by those elder men. I wouldn't be able to tell you, and I wouldn't even have been able to meet you if I hadn't been commissioned to help those [people] at White Earth when they came to ask me about the Drum. "Yes. I will help you," I told them. Then they came here, those boys who wanted to come ask me. "I can help you when you get started with that Drum which has been sitting over there for so long. They told me what had happened and what they say today about how the Drum used to be heard there sounding out there all by himself. The [Drum] should not, it cannot, be inside a church. And those Spirits were sad there, which is why the Drum members were trying to free our grandfather to enable him to leave there. Then they truly did enable him to leave over there. Then I told him that. "Yes. I will help you," I came to tell them, that's these boys who've come to carry that Drum today. Those chiefs came to ask me and again that head singer came to ask me. "Sure. I will help you," I tell them. "Go ask that medicine man over there about this. They know these Drums," the [elders] told me. "No," they say. "Well all right. Ask that medicine man," they say. So that's what they were told. "Get him and give him money," I was told. Then I was told that by the medicine man. There are many different kinds of [Drums] over there at Mille Lacs. But he said that was a Sioux Drum. That's what they told me. Well, then I explained to them how it was to look and again how we would put those songs on the [Drum]. Well I gave them certain things they would carry with [them] to this day. Right there, I got goose bumps on myself when you guys

nagamonan. Gegoo miinagwaa aanish noongom ge-awi-
bimiwidoowaad. Mii imaa, mii iko gaa-oozhendamaan i'iw gii-
maajiishkaayeg dewe'igan bimiwineg sa go gaye wii-
chawezhendamaan ji-minwendamaan sa go wii-ayaad a'aw
dewe'igan iwidi. Gaawiin daa-gii-inenaasiin a'aw. Gidaa-gii-
pimiwinaawaa igo. Ingiw gegoo gaa-izhichigewaad ingiw gaa-
pimiwinaajig, gii-azhe-asaawaad. Miinawaa imaa gaawiin da-
gijigesiiwag i'iw. Gaawiish gijigesiiwag o'ow isa gii-maajii-
bimiwinaawaad iniw.

[50] Mii sa go noongom i'iw, noongom igo wenji-
minwendaagozing iwidi. Mii sa go wenji-gikending a'aw
dewe'igan nagishkodaadiyang igo gaye ongow owidi
weshki-maajiitaayaang iwidi gii-kikinoo'amawagwaa
iniw nagamonan. I'iw nakweshkodaadi-nagamon ayaamagad
gaye, nakweshkodaadi-nagamon weshki-ayaawaad oshki-
nakweshkodaadiwaad igo. Mii a'aw akiwenzii ge-izhi-
gikinoo'amawid i'iw. Gaawiin igo aapiji indaa-izhi-
mikwendanziin igo. Naagaj igo inga-mikwendaan sa go i'iw.
Indaa-mikwendaan miinawaa, miish i'iw nakweshkodaadi-
nagamon ezhinikaadeg. Gaawiin igo indaa-izhi-mikwendanziin
azhigwa i'iw. Ayaa. Indayaan igo imaa. Niwenda-igoomin i'iw.
Gaawiin indaa-gikendanziin i'iw niin. Mii nitam iwidi, nitam
iwidi oshki-ayaad a'aw dewe'igan, oshki-maajiishkawangid
sa go.

[51] Mii o'ow apii i'iw gii-waabamaawaad ingiw gichi-aya'aag
iniw migiziwan niiwin gii-izhibaashkaanid imaa gii-
asangidwaa, gii-asangidwaa sa debendaagozijig o'ow omaa
dewe'iganing akina go. Mii imaa gii-waabamaawaad niiwin
iniw migiziwan gii-izhibaashkaanid imaa Gaa-
waababiganikaag zaaga'igan ezhinikaadeg. Mii imaa gaa-
tazhi-niimi'idiiyaang nitam gii-wiidookawagwaa sa. Niin
ingii-namadabi'aa a'aw niigaani-ogimaa booch ezhichigewaad
o'ow ge-namadabi'aawaad iniw. Mii ge-ishkwaa-namadabi'ag,
miish akina gaye gaa-paa-izhi-namadabi'aawaad gii-
kikinoo'amawangidwaa. Miish megwaa go baa-
gikinoo'amawagwaa baa-asaawaad iniw ge-dibendaagozinid
o'ow apii. Mii imaa gii-izhi-baabasowaad ingiw niiwin, ingiw
migiziwag. Gaye gii-shawendaagoziwag ongow anishinaabeg
iwidi eyaajig. Ingoding igo gaa-izhi-maamaajaawaad waasa
iwidi wending akeyaa izhaawag niiwin igo wending gaye

started that Drum you carry and I was just overwhelmed with happiness that there was going to be Drum over there. It couldn't be made up. You guys had to bring it [into being]. The ones who carried it did things that way, as they were reseated. They will never be removed from there again. They will never be removed as they have now started to carry that [Drum].

[50] It's that way today, that's why there are such good feelings over there now. That's why it is known that we've made our acquaintances at the Drum and that we have made a new start over there and I've been teaching about those songs. And there is a certain greeting song there, a greeting song for when they first come into being and they meet one another for the first time. That old man taught me that. A lot of the time I can't remember it. Later on I'll remember it. I can remember it again, that's that greeting song as it's called. But I can't remember it right now. It's there. I have it there. We were just told about it. I can't know of it myself. But for the first time over there, when the Drum was first [used] over there, we started it anew.

[51] Then at this time, those elders saw the four bald eagles circling there where we had placed them, where we placed the Drum members all here on the Drum. Then and there they saw those four bald eagles circling there at White Earth Lake as it's called. That's where we had Drum Ceremony the first time when I was helping them. I seated the first Drum chief although they certainly did things in seating the others. After I seated him, then they seated all of them as we gave the teachings to them. Then while I was teaching them, they seated those [who] would become Drum members at this time. Right there those four encircled the [Drum], those bald eagles. And these Indians who were over there were blessed. Then all at one time they started their departure in the far reaches of the winds over there; they went in the directions of the four winds and did so for this reason. And over there toward the east, the head Spirit is

gaa-onji-izhichigewaad. Gaye iwidi akeyaa wendaabang, mii
iwidi niigaani-manidoo eyaad, mii a'aw. Mii ingiw migiziwag,
mii iwidi dibishkoo go ingiw binesiwag, ingiw binesiwag. Mii
gii-paa-wiindamaagewaad; dewe'igan aandi eyaad. Mii gaa-onji-
maamaajaawaad i'iw manidoon iwidi gii-paa-
wiindamawaawaad dibishkoo go oshkaabewisag gii-paa-
wiindamaagewaad imaa gii-waabamaawaad iniw imaa gii-
oshki-bakite'wind a'aw dewe'igan; gegoo gaa-izhiwebak dash
iwidi sa gaa-chawaazhendamaan gii-chi-minwendamaan sa go
gii-maajiishkaayang a'aw dewe'igan gii-wiidookaazoyaan
ji-maajiishkaayang iwidi dewe'igan. Mii go noongom igo
gichi-apiitendamaan i'iw gii-wiidookawagwaa gwiiwizensag
sa go iwidi ji-maajiishkaawaad iniw dewe'iganan o'ow apii
jibwaa-giizhiikawangid giizhiikawaawaad iniw dewe'iganan.

[52] Ingii-pi-maakojii. Ingii-pi-maakowenan. Bezhig waakaa'igan
gii-ayaa. Mii imaa gii-pawaanag a'aw dewe'igan iwidi ezhi-abid
imaa niisidoowinigoowag, mii iwidi. Gaawiin igo onjida
indinaabandanziin i'iw dewe'igan i'iw ji-wiidookawagwaa
gaa-onji-inaabandamaan i'iw. Mii sa gaa-inendamaan i'iw.
Miinawaa noongom gaa-asangid a'aw noongom imaa
dewe'iganing a'aw ogichidaa gii-asangid noongom. "Gigii-
ayaa na imaa gii-asangid?" "Enh." "Ogichidaa?" Gaye ingii-
pawaanaa gaye a'aw oshki-inini. Ingii-tago-bawaanaan iniw
dewe'iganan bimi-wiidookaazod. Gaye ingii-inendaagoz
i'iw. Owii-inenimigoon iniw manidoon miinawaa iniw waa-
inaabishkawaajin i'iw ji-inaabandamaan i'iw weweni ji-bi-
bimiwinaad. Mii gaa-waawiindamawag a'aw oshki-inini. O'ow
isa naa gaye miigaadiwin gaye iwidi gii-ayaa. Gegoo gaye ingii-
wiindamawaa, "I'iw gijipizon onagamon, mii gaye ezhi-
niimikamowaad ingiw ogichidaag. Mii i'iw aanishinaa
ogichidaa-nagamon i'iw akina go." Mii i'iw gaa-izhi-
wiindamawag. "Gaawiin igo memwech i'iw eko-niizhing gidaa-
niimi'isiin," indinaa. "Mii i'iw akina ge-izhi-niimikaman binaa
go gijipizon," indinaa. "Gaye miinawaa go ingoji go gegoo
ingoji go dewe'igan a'aw bwaanzhii-dewe'igan madwewed
gikenimigooyan i'iw ogichidaawiyan, mii ezhi-wiidookaazoyan
dibi go." Mii gaa-izhi-wiindamawag a'aw oshki-inini weweni
ji-wiidookaazod i'iw jibwaa-migosig sa go i'iw gegoo go ingoji
aabadizid a'aw dewe'igan.

over there, that's one. These bald eagles, they are like those thunderbirds over there, the big birds. They went around telling the news; [this] is where the Drum was. That's why they started their departure, telling the Spirits over there, just like messengers they spread the news there that they had seen the Drum struck for the first time; and as these things happened over there I was so overwhelmed with happiness that we had started that Drum, that I was helping when we started that Drum over there. Today I have the highest regard for my helping those boys over there so that they could start that Drum at this time before we finished with him, before they finished with that Drum.

[52] And something happened with me. It happened to me with those things. There was a certain house there. Right there I dreamed about that Drum sitting over there as they were lowered into position, right over there. I didn't intentionally dream about the Drum that way, [it happened] so that I would help them, that's why I dreamed about it like that. This is how I saw it in my mind. Today again when we seated that veteran there at the Drum, we seated him that way today. "Were you there when we seated him?" "*Yes.*" "The veteran?" And I dreamed about that young man too. I dreamt about that Drum with him coming to help out. And I was thought of in that. He was to be considered by the Spirit who wanted him to represent him, so I saw that in my dream that he would come to be a good carrier. This is what I told that young man. And he was also over there during the war. And I told him things, "That belt song, those veterans dance for that too. Well, so it is with all veteran songs." I told him that. "You shouldn't dance just for that second one," I tell him. "You can dance for them all as well as the belt," I tell him. "And wherever it might be, wherever the Drum is at, when that Sioux Drum sounds his voice and you are known to be a veteran, wherever that is you shall help as well." And thus I told that young man to help in a proper way so as not to refuse his responsibilities wherever that Drum is used.

[53] Mii gegoo gaye, mii go gaye a'aw Medwe-ganoonind gaa-pi-
waawiindamawid i'iw. Mii i'iw. Gegoo gaye a'aw dewe'igan
opwaaganan odayaawaan. Gegoo akina ongow, akina ongow
akina go debendaagozijig, mii go ezhi-opwaaganiwaad.
Awegwen igo bemiwinaad, mii ge-izhi-bimiwinaad igo iwidi
opwaaganan. Mii i'iw. Akina go gidayaamin miinawaa go
opwaagan inashke izhi-ayaayang go opwaagan ingoji wii-
pimiwinad dibi go. Gaawiin gaye, booch igo weweni akawe
ji-giizhi'ad a'aw opwaagan i'iw ji-biindaakoonad gaye miinawaa
ji-ombaabasod gaye. Mii i'iw ezhi-aabaji'ind. Namanj igo gegoo
go ge-izhi-gagwejimad a'aw opwaagan ji-izhi-wiidookaak.
Mii go gaa-igooyaan i'iw, Medwe-ganoonind gaa-izhid. Mii i'iw
akina; mii i'iw wenji-gikendamaan gegoo sa i'iw. Gaawiin
go i'iw akina indaa-izhi-gikendanziin i'iw. Gegoo dewe'igan
moozhag niibowa ingikendaan. Ingiw dewe'iganag
ingikenimaag. Ingii-inendaagoz i'iw oshki-bi-wiindamawiwaad
ingiw akiwenziiyag o'ow weweni. Mii sa wenji-gikendaasoyaan
sa go.

[54] Gegoo gaye ongow ayaawag ogichidaag. Niigaani-ogichidaa,
mii i'iw dibishkoo a'aw gijipizon bemiwidood. Mii i'iw akina go
gaye ge-izhi-izhichiged imaa o'ow dewe'igan enangizod. Mii go
ezhi-ogichidaawid, mii go ezhi-oshkaabewisiwid, mii go gaye
niimi'iwewininiiwid akina sa go gaye gii-izhi-gaagiigidopan
gaye. Mii ingiw ogichidaag enangizowaad. Miinawaa-sh aanind
ongow ogichidaag ogii-pi-ani-asaawaan iniw bemaadizinijin.
Mii wenji-ogichidaawiwaad gii-shimaaganishiiwiwaad gaye. Mii
wenji-ogichidaawid o'ow a'aw anishinaabe omaa o'ow gaye.

[55] "Gigikendaan ina wiikaa i'iw bangisinjiged awiiya imaa de-bi-
izhichigeyang?" Bangisinjiged gaye maagizhaa gaye miigwan
bangishimod maagizhaa gegoo go bangisidooyan igo
imaa niimi'idiing, booch igo ji-gii'imod a'aw wiin a'aw
ogichidaa. Omamoon dash a'aw ogichidaa. Gaawiin gaye
obiinisigawadashamoosiin gegoo ogichidaa. Bangisidood
awiiya, awiiya gaawiin odaa-izhi-mamoosiin. Gaye imaa
azhemayishin ezhi-niimikang a'aw o'ow nagamon a'aw
ogichidaa. Namanj igo apii ogichidaa—niizhing, nising,
niiwing—namanj igo apii enangizod, maagizhaa gaye gijipizon
bemiwidood eyaad imaa. Miish i'iw ge-izhibaashimod imaa
dewe'iganing miinawaa-sh imaa gii-pangisijigaadeg. Mii
miinawaa ezhi-giizhibaashkang, niiwing ezhi-giizhibaashkang

[53] And regarding these things, it was that *Medwe-ganoonind* who told me about it. That's it. And that Drum also has a pipe. And all of these one, all of these Drum members, they are pipe carriers. Whoever is a carrier [of the Drum], shall also be carrier of the pipe over there. That's it. We are all there and all carry the pipe, like the pipe you carry wherever you go. But no, first in a truly good way you make that pipe so that you may give tobacco offerings with it and have them swirl upwards. That's how it is used. I'm not exactly sure, but you may ask that pipe to help you. This is what I've been told, what that *Medwe-ganoonind* told me. Thus it is with everything; that's why I know about those things. I can't know everything about that. But I've always known many things about the Drum. I know those Drums. I was considered that way when I was first told things by those old men in such a proper way. This is why I am knowledgeable.

[54] And there are these veterans. The head veteran, he is the same status as the one who carries the belt. And they all do things this way there whomever is counted among the Drum membership. He who serves as veteran, he who serves as messenger, and he who gives the Dance—they are all speakers. They are counted as veterans. And again some of these veterans seat the one who shall live. This is the reason they are warriors and served as soldiers. This is why the Indian becomes a veteran here.

[55] "Do you know what we do there when somebody ever drops things?" When someone drops something or maybe a feather falls or if you drop something there at the Drum Ceremony, truly it is the veteran himself who retrieves it. And that veteran takes it. And that veteran does not just dance in with something. If someone drops something, nobody can pick it up. And that veteran comes after it while he dances for the song. It doesn't matter which veteran—second, third, fourth—it doesn't matter which number, and maybe even the one who carries the belt if he's there. Then he dances there at the Drum and again there where it fell. Then again when he finished dancing for it, having finished dancing four times where the thing fell, then he goes to the

gaa-pangisijigaadeg, mii miinawaa ezhi-izhaad i'iw
dewe'iganing ezhi-mamood i'iw ezhi-izhaad ezhi-mamood i'iw
baaga'okwaan. Mii dash ezhi-mamood i'iw. Miish i'iw gegoo
ezhi-mamood. Miish i'iw baaga'okwaan ezhi-giishkizhang, mii
gegoo, akina gegoo. Miish ge-izhiwebak gegoo akina gaye gii-
mamood. Mii akina gegoo giishkizhang iwidi gii-maajii-
izhiwebak. Gii-maanzhii-izhiwebizid a'aw bengisijiged gegoo,
gegoo sa go ji-maanzhi-izhiwebizisig gegoo sa go zaagimijayi'ii
go ji-giishkizhang a'aw ogichidaa. Mii enangizod a'aw
ogichidaa. Mii ge-izhi-gaagiigidod gaye, namanj igo
gashkitood. Mii enangizowaad ingiw ogichidaag akina go,
mii ingiw maamawi dibishkoo a'aw naagaanizid ogichidaa.

[56]   Miinawaa go dibishkoo wiinawaa go gaye ingiw, ongow
oshkaabewisag, mii ingiw bemiwinaajig iniw asemaan.
Mii inag. Aanish naa mii a'aw anishinaabe maamawi-
niigaanizinid iniw asemaan. Mii a'aw naagaaned asemaa,
mii i'iw oshkaabewis bemiwinaad. Mii go gaye a'aw
oshkaabewis, awegwen sa go omaa ongow, awegwen igo
omaa debinendaagozid o'ow omaa, niimiwewininiwag
omaa, oshkaabewisag, ogichidaag, awegwen igo, mii go
abiigizigewininiwag, mii go opwaaganan ezhi-zaka'awaapan,
awegwen igo, gaawiin igo memwech opwaaganiiwinini, mii go
awegwen igo ezhi-gagwejimaad ayaasig a'aw opwaaganiiwinini,
awegwen igo. Mii go ezhi-bima'adoowaad. Miinawaa-sh weweni
obimiwinaan gaye onow opwaaganan.

Bizindamowin Miinawaa Gaagiigidowin

[57]   Ganabaj igo gigii-wiindamoon iko mewinzha aya'aa. Indaa-
inendam igo. Ganabaj gidaa-gii-wiindamoon. Gaawiin giishpin
gigii-wiindamoosiinoon gaye bijiinag go ji-gikendaman,
ji-gikendaman sa go o'ow wenji-atooyaan o'ow ji-inendaman
i'iw gegoo go. Ingoding igo bizindaman igo, mii ge-izhi-
gikendaman oshki-ayi'ii igo o'ow gegoo sa go booch igo, booch
igo dazhimag a'aw manidoo gegoo omaa gaagiigidoyaan o'ow
gaa-pi-izhiwebak, gaa-izhiwebiziyaan, gaa-pi-izhiwebiziwaad
ingiw ingitiziimag, ingiw akiwenziiyag, akina sa go. Ingoding
igo inga-waawiidookaagoo ji-minji-mikwendamaan igo o'ow
ezhi-waawiidookawid a'aw giijanishinaabem. Mii wenji-

Drum to fetch something, he goes and retrieves that
Drumstick. Then he takes it. Then he grabs it. Then with
the Drumstick he makes a cutting motion, that's for the
thing [which has fallen], everything. Then as this happens
he grabs everything [which had fallen]. He cuts everything
over there as this starts to happen. The one who drops
things might have bad things happen to him but won't
have anything bad happen to him when the veteran cuts
underneath it. That's whichever numbered veteran. And
he shall make a speech, whatever he might be able to do.
All of those veterans count the same, together they are just
like the head veteran.

[56]   And again things are the same with these messengers; it is
they who carry the tobacco. So I tell him. Well it is all the
Indian people's tobacco that is combined for the most
important use. And it is this important tobacco which the
messenger carries. And so that messenger, or whomever is
here, whichever Drum member is here, the dance givers
here, messengers, veterans, whomever, the Drum warmers,
they thusly light the pipe, not necessarily the pipe man, it is
whomever he asks when the pipe man is not present,
whomever. They carry it. And also in a proper way he may
carry the pipe.

Listening and Speaking

[57]   Perhaps I used to tell you this a long time ago. I should
think so. Maybe I did tell you. But if I didn't tell you, then
this will be your first opportunity to know this, to know
what I am putting [on tape] here so you can think about
these things. And one time when you are listening to this, so
shall you know it for the first time and for certain how I
speak to the Spirit about things here, how I give speeches
about history, what happened with me, how things were
with my parents, those old men and everything. One time
I will be helped to remember and will thusly be told so by
your fellow Indian. This is the reason I see in my mind for

inendamaan i'iw ji-wiidookawag inendaagozid a'aw
anishinaabe. Miinawaa go ongow, weweni ongow, weweni
ongow ji-wiidookawadwaa gaye giin giijanishinaabeg gegoo
o'ow gagwejimikwaa gikendaman gaye wenji-gikendaasoyan sa
go. Mii wenji-waawiindamoonaan o'ow gegoo go. Ingoding
gegoo giga-wiindamoon. Mewinzha go gigii-wiindamoon i'iw,
gigii-wiindamoon giin igo ji-gaagiigidoyan gashkitooyan. Gigii-
wiindamoon igo i'iw booch igo. Gaye aaningodinong gaye
gaawiin indaa-gashkitoosiin ji-izhaayaan iwidi Gaa-
waababiganikaag. Gaawiin gegoo, gegoo sa go imaa, gaawiin
gegoo gidaa-gikendanziimin igo. Inga-ikid ji-izhaayaan iwidi
naano-giizhigak. Maagizhaa gaye gaawiin indaa-izhaasiin.
Maagizhaa gaye da-biigodaabaane. Namanj iidog. Gigikendaan
ina? Booch igo, booch igo ji-gashkitooyan ji-bimiwidooyan
o'ow akina go gaagiigidoyan miinawaa go ezhichigeyan akina
go ezhi-gikendaman i'iw. Mii wenji-waawiindamoonaan i'iw
gaye. Giin eta go gaye gidaa-gii-nisidotaan. Miinawaa i'iw
weweni gigaagiigid. Mii gaa-onji-minwendamaan i'iw gii-
ikidoyan i'iw ji-gaagiigidoyang o'ow dibi gegoo ekidoyaan.

[58]   Maagizhaa gaye geyaabi go omaa gaasiidibeyang indayaan
waa-kaagiigidoyaan. Miinawaa niin nimooshkinadoon igo
naanan, ningodwaaswi gaye. Gaye inendamaan azhigwa i'iw
gegoo, gegoo i'iw akiwenzii ikidoyaan apiish ayaamaambaan
i'iw dinowa. Gayesh, mii azhigwa omaa gikendaagwak
omaa i'iw ji-gashkitooyaan omaa gaagiigidoyaan omaa
ji-bizindawiyan, ji-bizindawiwaad sa go ingiw awegwen igo
ongow anishinaabeg ji-ani-gikendaasowaad gaye. Gaye
gizaagi'igoomin. Gizaagi'igoomin i'iw wenji-gashkitooyaan
o'ow ji-gaagiigidoyaan omaa sa. Obi-ani-wiidookaagoon igo
gegoo go waawiindamoonaan sa go apane.

[59]   Mii gaye weweni gaa-izhid a'aw akiwenzii gaye. "Gaye gaawiin
imaa. Awi-gikendan igo omaa wiindamoonaan. Mikwendan
igo weweni go. Gego naa gaye wiikaa wanendangen," ikido.
Gaawiin igo apane omaa indaa-ani-ayaasiin, mii ji-ayezhinood.
Gaawiin wiikaa apane omaa indaa-ani-ayaasiin. Booch igo giin
omaa ji-ani-gikendaman i'iw. Mii wenji-waawiindamoonaan
giin. Gego-sh wiikaa wanendangen. Gego wiikaa ani-
wanendangen ji-wiidookawad a'aw giijanishinaabe awegonen
igo gagwejimigooyan. Gego naa wiikaa zhaagwenimoken,
gaawiin wiikaa, gaawiin ji-inad o'ow. Gegoo sa go ji-

me to help the Indian people when they are considered for it. And also when you help your fellow Indians yourself, and when they ask you about the things you know, this will be the reason you are so knowledgeable. So this is why I am telling about these things. Sometime I'll tell you more things. A long time ago I told about this, I told you to speak yourself as you've become able. I really did tell you that. And sometimes I will not be able to make it over there to White Earth. We can't know everything that [will happen]. I'll say I'm going to go over there on Friday. But maybe I won't be able to go. Perhaps my car will break down. I don't know. Do you know? Truly, certainly you will be able to carry all of this and to speak and do all these things you've thusly come to know about. And this is why I'm telling you this. You are the only one who can understand it. And you speak well. This is why I was so happy that you said that we would speak about that which I am saying.

[58] I have more that I want to talk about but maybe we'll be erasing [over what's already been said]. And I might fill up five or six [tapes]. And now that I think about things, things about the elder men, there are [many] different things I have to say. And also, it is now known here that I am able to speak about them for you to listen to me as well as whomever else of these Indians, so that they can become learned too. And we are loved. We are loved and that's why I am able to speak here. The [Spirit] helps the [people] with what I am always telling you.

[59] And that's what that old man told me in a good way as well. "Not there. Learn what I am telling you here. Remember it well. And never forget it," he says. "I won't be here forever," that's how he addressed the matter. I won't be here forever [either]. It is up to you to know this here. So this is why I'm telling you. And don't ever forget it. Don't forget to help your fellow Indian in whatever is asked of you. Never be shy, never, to talk to him about this. And so I help [the people] in the things for which they are considered. And always, all the time I express my thanks that my fellow Indians listen to me

wiidookawag inendaagozid. Moozhag gaye, moozhag
gaye nimiigwechiwitaagoz i'iw bizindawiwaad
ingiw niijanishinaabeg o'ow gegoo o'ow omaa gegoo ezhi-
bizaaniyaawaad iko imaa niimi'idiing ingiw anishinaabeg
bizindawiwaad. Mii go bizindawaawaad sa go iniw
gayaagiigidonijin. Mii gaye wenji-gikendaasowaad imaa ingiw
akiwenziiyag. Mii go gaye niin wenji-akiwenziiwiyaan. Miish
i'iw wenji-gikendaasoyaan i'iw bizindawagwaa ingiw
akiwenziiyag gegoo, a'aw Naawigiizis, miinawaa Gimiwan
bizindawagwaa. Mii ani-izhi-gikendamaan. Akina sa go imbi-
gikendaan igo bebizindawagwaa ingiw gaagiigidoyaan.
Miinawaa go bezhig akiwenzii gii-pizindawag iko Eshpan gaa-
inind. Mii gaye gaa-pizindawag iko miinawaa go Niibaa-giizhig
akina sa go. Mii i'iw akina maamawi-inendaagwak omaa gii-pi-
bizindawagwaa igo ayi'ii inendamaan igo gegoo gaa-izhid a'aw
akiwenzii bezhig miinawaa awedi bezhig. Mii i'iw akina imaa—
akina imaa ani-gikendaasoyaan gegoo wenji-gikendaasoyaan
igo. Gaawiin igo biizikamaan indizhi-gikendaasosiin i'iw.
Weweni go ingii-pi-wiidookawaag, inendaagozid o'ow
ji-gikendamaan gegoo. Onjida sa go gii-inendaagoziwag ingiw
akiwenziiyag i'iw, o'ow ji-bi-miizhiwaad o'ow ge-ani-ikidoyaan.

[60] Miish i'iw, gego wiikaa wanendangen o'ow. Booch igo ingoding
giga-ani-gikendaan i'iw. Gemaa maagizhaa gaye waabang,
awaswaabang, giin onjibaayan gegoo bakaan, baa-anokiiyan,
maagizhaa gaye gaawiin gidaa-mikwendanziin. Ingoding sa go
eyaayan, mii go ge-izhi-gikendaman biinish igo anooj igo ezhi-
gaganooninaan.

[61] Mii sa ganabaj igo minik i'iw ge-izhi-waawiindamoonaan.
Maagizhaa gaye ingoding miinawaa giga-aadizookoon
ingoding miinawa gashkitooyaan. Aaningodinong ingikendaan
i'iw aadizookaan, booch igo ge-izhi-mikwendamaan i'iw akawe,
akawe weweni. Gaawiin gaye iniw bakaan, anooj gigii-animoon.
I'iw aadizookaan baamaash weweni sa go ayizhising go
niizhinoon i'iw aadizookaan. Mii i'iw Makoozid ezhinikaadeg.
Niizhinoon i'iw. Gaye nitam i'iw gaa-izhi-gashkitood
a'aw Makoozid gii-makandwed o'ow aki. Miinawaa-sh
ogii-wiidigemaan iniw chi-ogimaan odaanisan. Mii miinawaa
imaa aanji-andaadizookeng. Miinawaa bakaan i'iw weweni
gii-ani-izhi-ayaawaad niizhing. Ingikendaan. Gaawiin igo
ingikendanziin i'iw eko-niizhing. Bezhig eta go weweni

about these things and are customarily so quiet there at
the Drum Ceremonies so the Indians listen to me. They
listen to the speakers. That's why those old men are so
knowledgeable there. This is why I am an old man myself.
And this is why I am so knowledgeable, by listening to
those old men, like that *Naawigiizis* and *Gimiwan* to whom
I listened. This is how I've come to know things. I've come
to know everything about my speaking by listening to them.
And there was another certain old man I used to listen to
named *Eshpan*. Then I also used to listen to *Niibaa-giizhig*
about everything. That's everything being thought of in
unison here, how I came to listen to them and think about
things I was told by that one old man and that other one
over there. This is how it is with everything—everything of
which I have knowledge there, that's why I'm knowledgeable
about it. I am thusly not knowledgeable about everything
with which I've come into contact. But for those who are
thought of, I help them in a proper way with everything I
know. Those old men were considered in these things for a
reason, so that they could give me that which I would come
to say.

[60] So then, never forget this. Some time you will definitely
come to know this. Maybe tomorrow, or the day after, as
you are from a different place, you go around working, and
maybe you won't remember it. But one time when you are
there, you will know about these things I'm telling you.

[61] So maybe that's the extent of what I'm going to tell you.
Maybe again another time I will tell you legends, another
time when I'm up to it. Sometimes I know that legend, I'll
remember the first part, the first part well. Not the different
parents, but you can pick up different parts. And later on,
that legend comes in two parts. It is called *Makoozid*. It is in
two parts. In the first that *Makoozid* stole the earth. And he
married the great chief's daughter. And there the story
changes again. Again it is different in the second part when
they lived well. I know it. But I don't know the second part.
But it was only the first that I used to know so well. I always
listened to them. *Makoozid* as he was called, when the great
chief urinated there, that's how he came to have the foot of

ingii-kikendaan iko. Moozhag go ingii-pizindawaag ingiw. Makoozid gaa-inind a'aw chi-ogimaan gii-shiishiiginid imaa, mii ani-makoozid. Ingoding sa go giga-aadizookoon. Gaawiin igo aapiji gidaadizookaasiinoon i'iw. Ingoji go maagizhaa gaye ingo-diba'igan imaa awashiime. Namanj iidog.

[62]   Mii i'iw.

[63]   *Ho, miigwech.*

[64]   Ahaaw.

a bear. Some time I'll tell you the legend. I don't tell you legends too much. It might be an hour long there or more. I'm not sure.

[62]   That's it.
[63]   Ho, *thank you.*
[64]   Okay.

Gaa-waababiganikaag
White Earth

JOE AUGINAUSH

JOE AUGINAUSH (1922–2000), whose Anishinaabe name was *Giniw-aanakwad*, was a man of remarkable wisdom. He both watched and participated in incredible changes for Ojibwe people during his years on earth. Those experiences, his intelligence, and time combined to develop his inspiring world view.

Joe Maude, as friends often called him, was one of the last Anishinaabe from the White Earth Reservation to have been born in a *wiigiwaam* or *nisawa'ogaan*. His family followed the seasonal rounds of traditional Ojibwe life at the large and vibrant Ojibwe village called Gaa-jiikajiwegamaag on the south shore of Roy Lake, where Joe spent the first several years of his life, in the *wiigiwaam* his parents maintained for their entire family. They built a *nisawa'ogaan* near Gaa-niizhogamaag (Naytahwaush, Minnesota) for maple sugaring in the spring and a new *wiigiwaam* for ricing at Manoominiganzhikaaning (Rice Lake, Minnesota) in the fall, but Gaa-jiikajiwegamaag was home.

The seasonal lifestyle was a happy one for Joe, who remembered with special fondness the now-deserted village at Gaa-jiikajiwegamaag and the large rice camps at Manoominiganzhikaaning, where people from all over White Earth and even the neighboring reservations came for the harvest. It is widely believed that Manoominiganzhikaaning offered one of the largest and finest wild rice beds in the state of Minnesota. Soil erosion, flooding, and chemical run-off from nearby chicken farms and cattle ranches have recently damaged the rice beds there, but during Joe's childhood the site was truly remarkable, with hundreds of Ojibwe camped out, harvesting and processing wild rice all day and singing and playing moccasin games all night. Joe Maude once remarked to me that he couldn't understand how so many people got by with so little sleep, as the camp was buzzing day and night.

Joe Maude's father eventually built a log house on Auginaush Creek, not far from the main village at Gaa-jiikajiiwegamaag, where the family lived for several more years. However, as the tribal housing project at Rice Lake expanded, the village was abandoned, and most families moved to Rice Lake or Naytahwaush for the luxury of modern homes and easier access to developed roads and the towns of Bagley, Detroit Lakes, and Bemidji.

Adolescence was difficult for Joe Maude, as he was taken away from his family and sent to a Bureau of Indian Affairs residential boarding school at Wahpeton, North Dakota. The school was strictly regimented, and Joe remembered with great anger that he was beaten for speaking the only language he knew—Ojibwe. He recalled that he and other children would gather to secretly converse in Ojibwe and sing pow-wow songs. He got his share of beatings, but he never forgot who he was, socially, culturally, and linguistically.

His parents and grandparents weren't any happier with Joe's boarding school experience than he was. They stubbornly fought for permission for him to attend the local day school in Bagley. They eventually succeeded; however, day school in Bagley wasn't much better, as Joe felt isolated from and unsupported by both staff and students. At the age of seventeen, he left the reservation and traveled around the United States and Canada, working in Montana and elsewhere, earning enough money to eat and to travel to pow-wows.

In 1942, he enlisted in the United States Army and spent the next three years in the European theater. After World War II, he returned to the United States and again traveled to look for work. For several years he migrated from job to job, but he eventually returned to White Earth. There he lived out the remainder of his life, together with his wife Gertrude, raising their children and making himself available as a community resource. He traveled frequently to speak at schools, pow-wows, and educational forums, always using Ojibwe and speaking about the importance of the language and bicultural living.

He impressed upon me the nature of the struggle for the Ojibwe language—how the language survives and remains intact but is losing speakers. He also inspired many with his wise words about the importance of language. Joe was dedicated to his family, people, and language. He was a true leader—not by command, position, or power, but by his peerless example of genuine goodness.

Gaawiin Giwanitoosiimin Gidinwewininaan

[1] "Haa ganabaj giwanitoomin," ikidong. "Anishininaabe-
izhichigeng giwanitoomin." Gaawiin ganabaj—i'iw
anishinaabemowin geyaabi ayaamagad. Mii go giinawind eta
go; giwanishinimin, akina gegoo giwanitoomin. Anishinaabe-
izhichigewinan miinawaa go anishinaabe gaa-pi-izhichigewaad
mewinzha, geyaabi imaa ayaamagad. *Like I heard one old gentleman say, "We're not losing our language, the language is losing us."*

Gaa-jiikajiwegamaag Ingii-tazhi-ondaadiz Wiigiwaaming

[1] Ahaaw sa naa ingii-odaapinaa sa go asemaa, iidog wa'aw isa
inini gaa-miizhid iidog, nawaj igo wii-kikenimid miinawaa go
ezhichigeyaan omaa sa gaye niin akiing ayaayaan. Nashke o'ow,
gimanidoominaan ingagwejimaa gaye niin ji-wiidookawid
omaa sa noongom waa-ani-ayikidoyaan.

[2] Nashke ojibwe-izhinikaazoyaan, Giniw-aanakwad indizhinikaaz.
Miinawaa dash o'ow chimookomaanikaazoyaan *Joe Auginaush*,
indizhi-gikenimigoo.

[3] Owidi dash gii-ondaadiziyaan, mii go omaa besho zhaawanong
omaa Gaa-jiikajiwegamaag ezhinikaadeg, agaamiing iwidi
Gaa-jiikajiwegamaag ezhinikaadeg. Mii iwidi gaa-tazhi-
ondaadiziyaan. Iskigamiziganing ingii-tazhi-ondaadiz; *1922*
ingii-ondaadiz. Mii dash igo eko-gikendamaan; mii go gii-
ayaayaang omaa sa iskigamiziganing. Idash indede iidog gii-
ozhige owidi *Auginaush Creek* ezhinikaadeg, mii iwidi ozhiged.

[4] Mii dash igo apane gii-ayaayaang maagizhaa go ingoji
go. Gaawiin ingikendanziin aapiji agindaasoyaan sa
ojibwemowining, ingoding gii-inaakonigewaad inga-
zhaaganaashiim. Maagizhaa go ingoji go ishwaasobiboonagiziyaan ingii-apiitiz apii gikendamaan i'iw isa
gikendamaan sa akina gegoo gaa-pi-izhiwebak miinawaa
go gaa-pi-izhiwebiziyaang. Apane ko ingii-wiijiwaag sa
ingitiziimag miinawaa go nookomisag anooj gii-izhaayaang
gii-paa-niimi'idiiyaang, miinawaa midewining gii-izhaayaang.

[5] Biinish igo apii ingoji go midaaso-biboonagiziyaan gii-
apiitiziyaan; mii apii gaa-maajaayaan gikinoo'amaadiiwigamigong, gii-izhaayaan. Gaawiin ingii-kikendanziin i'iw

We're Not Losing Our Language

[1] "Well, maybe we are losing it," they say. "We are losing the Indian culture." But maybe not—the Indian language is still here. It is only us: we are lost, and [therefore] losing everything. Indian traditions and what the Indian came to do long ago, it's still there. Like I heard one old gentleman say, "We're not losing our language, the language is losing us."

I Was Born in a Wiigiwaam at Gaa-jiikajiwegamaag

[1] All right, I've accepted the tobacco given to me by this man who wants to know me better as well as the things I do while I am here on earth myself. See this, I am asking myself for our Great Spirit to help me here today in what I am going to say.

[2] As for my Ojibwe name, I am called *Giniw-aanakwad*. But then again this white man's name, Joe Auginaush, is how I am known.

[3] And I was born over here, that's here near the south end of Roy Lake as it's called, over there on the other side of Roy Lake as it's called. It's over there that I was born. I was born in the sugar bush; I was born in 1922. And that's what I've come to know of it; we were here in the sugar camp. And my dad he built a house over here at Auginaush Creek as it's called, he built the house over there.

[4] Then we were always someplace [around there]. I don't know the extent to which I studied in Ojibwe, but one time they decided I'm going to speak English. Maybe when I was somewhere around eight years old; I was that age when I knew everything I know of what happened and how things were with us. I always accompanied my parents and grandmothers wherever we went to pow-wow together and when we went to the medicine dance.

[5] That was until I was around ten years of age; then at that time I left, departing for the boarding school. I didn't know English when I left. And we were taken over there to

zhaaganaashiimowin apii gaa-maajaayaan. Iwidi dash *Wahpeton,*
North Dakota ingii-izhiwinigoomin gikinoo'amaagooyaang.
Owidi apii gaa-izhi-dagoshinaang, aanish naa gaawiin ingii-
kikendanziin i'iw zhaaganaashiimowin. Ingii-kagwaadagitoo
ko ingoji go; ingo-biboon ingii-kagwaadagitoon
zhaaganaashiimoyaan.

[6]   Inashke iwidi gaa-izhaayaang, gaawiin igo ingii-
pagidinigoosiimin ji-ojibwemoyaang. Gaawiin gaye ingii-
pagidinigoosiimin gegoo ji-nagamoyaang waa-ani-
niimi'idiiyaang. Booch dash igo ingii-izhichigemin. Imaa
dash *Wahpeton* ingoji go ingii-ayaa, *1937* ishkwaaj imaa
gii-ayaayaan. Ishkwe go weweni gii-shaaganaashiimoyaan,
miinawaa gaye eighth grade ingii-kiizhiitaa.

[7]   Mii dash gaa-pi-izhi-giiweyaan, omaa dash indaa-ani-
wiiji'izhinizhaawigoo owidi Mashkimodaang ezhinikaadeg,
miinawaa go ji-gikinoo'amaagooyaan. Gaawiin dash ingii-
minwendanziin, miinawaa gegaa go ingii-inendam, "Imaa niin
eta, imaa indayaa." Noongom ezhi-gikendamaan ganabaj niin
eta ingii-anishinaabew imaa. Gaawesh, gaawiin dash ingii-
inendanziin gii-izhaayaan baanimaa sa wayaabishkiiwed akeyaa
ginwaabamaawizod. Inashke dash, gaawiin ingii-izhaasii. Ingii-
izhi-naanaagadawendam i'iw biboon i'iw endaayaang gii-
ayaayaan. Inashke ingitiziimag imaa go nookomisag miinawaa
ganabaj igo gii-izhichigewaad anishinaabewin, booch gaye niin
daniziyaan. Anooj gegoo indani-gikinoo'amaagoog.

[8]   Mii dash gegapii gaa-izhi-ayaayaan ji-maadanokiiyaan imaa
gichimookomaaning akeyaa. Naa booch iidog gii-anokiiyaan,
mii dash gii-maadanokiiyaan, *1939* ingii-maajaa. Anooj dash igo
ingii-paa-izhaa ji-baa-anokiiyaan. *Montana* gaye ingii-paa-izhaa
gii-paa-anokiiyaan, anooj igo i'iw gii-izhichigeyaan biinish igo
apii gaa-nandamigooyaan ji-o-miigaazoyaan iwidi sa chi-
agaamiing gii-kichi-miigaadiing.

[9]   *World War Two* gii-izhinikaade. Mii dash apii gaa-maajaayaan
gaye niin; ingoji go imaa *1942* ingii-maajaa. Sa naa chi-
agaamiing ingii-paa-ayaa iwidi akeyaa *Europe* ezhinikaadeg.
Mii iwidi gaa-paa-izhaayaan gii-miigaazoyaan gaye niin
wiidookaazoyaan. Ingoji go niso-biboon ashi aabita ingii-ayaa
imaa miigaadiing.

[10] Inashke dash miinawaa owidi gii-pi-azhegiiweyaan, gaawiin igo
omaa gaa-tanakiiyaan, ingii-pi-izhaasii igo. Ingii-paa-ayaa

Wahpeton, North Dakota, as students. When we arrived over there, well I didn't know that English language. We had a hard time; for one year I had a hard time speaking English.

[6] You see over there where we went, we were not permitted to speak the Ojibwe language. And we were not permitted to sing anything when we wanted to pow-wow. But we certainly did that anyway. And I was somewhere around Wahpeton, after 1937 that's where I was. And after a while I spoke English very well, and in the eighth grade I was done.

[7] Then I came home, and here we were sent along over to Bagley as it's called, and again I was a student. But I didn't like it, and I almost thought, "It's just me, I am the only one there." Now I know I was perhaps the only one who was Indian there. But no, no I didn't think about it that way when I went later on, the way the white man looks at himself. In fact I didn't even go. I was there at our home in the winter reflecting. You see, my parents and maybe my grandmothers, they did things the Indian way, and that's right where I belonged. They could teach me all kinds of things.

[8] Then around the time I was there [at home] I started to work in the white man's way. I must have worked hard, when I started working. I left in 1939. And I went all over the place to work. And I went around Montana working, doing all kinds of things up until the time I was enlisted to go over and fight in Europe during the big war.

[9] It was called World War Two. And then I left there myself; sometime in 1942 I left. I was overseas over there in Europe as it's called. Over there I went all over the place, fighting and helping out. I was in the war there for three and a half years.

[10] And when I returned over here again, I didn't come back here to live. I was all over the place again, going over to

miinawaa owidi *Montana* miinawaa ingii-paa-izhaa. Ingoji go,
oon ingoji go gegaa midaaso-biboon gaawiin omaa ingii-
ayaasii, omaa gaa-onji-ondaadiziyaan omaa.

[11] Mii dash gaa-pi-azhegiiweyaan. Mii dash miinawaa gii-
maajiitaayaan dash indanishinaabewin, anishinaabewin—
niimi'idiing miinawaa go anooj ingii-izhaa ji-baa-giigidoyaan.
Miinawaa go ingii-naaniim. Miinawaa ingii-nagam.

[12] Inashke gaye gaa-ishkwaa-miigaazoyaan, ingii-nagishkawaa sa
niitaa, *Scott Headbird*. Miish igo apane besho ingii-ayaamin.
Besho ingii-wiiji'idimin, biinish igo apii gaa-ishkwaa-ayaad.

[13] Inashke gaye anooj igo ingii-izhichige. Ingiw chimookomaanag
gaye ingii-kagwejimigoo gaye wiinawaa iidog ji-
wiidookawagwaa miinawaa go eyaabojiiwaad sa gaye
wiinawaa izhichigewaad. Haa anooj gegoo ingii-izhichige
imaa akeyaa chimookomaaning.

[14] Gaawiin dash go wiikaa ingii-nagadoosiin i'iw isa
anishinaabewin. Inashke dash omaa noongom, aanish naa, mii
azhigwa gaa-ako-niizhwaasimidana-ashi-nisobiboonagak
indapiitiz. Gegaa go imbwaana'ow. Mii dash noongom eta go
izhichigeyaan anooj izhaayaan niimi'idiing gaye niin baa-
wiidookaazoyaan sa ojibwemoyaan gaagiigidoyaan sa
dibishkoo go wiidookawagwaa niijanishinaabemag. Inashke
gaye, anooj gaye indizhaa baa-wiidookaazoyaan o'ow isa
anishinaabe-nagamong, miinawaa go anishinaabe-anami'aang.
Gaawiin awenen igo midewin-sh geyaabi indizhitwaasiin. Mii
eta go apane dibaajimag a'aw isa gimanidoominaan miinawaa
go akina iniw aadizookaanan.

[15] Inashke gaye noongom anooj indizhaa gaye imaa
gikinoo'amaadiiwigamigong ganoonigooyaan sa iidog gaye
niin ji-wiindamawagwaa sa ongow oshki-anishinaabeg
miinawaa oshki-chimookomaanag mewinzha gaa-pi-izhichiged
sa a'aw anishinaabe. Naaniibowa niwiindamaagoog sa ji-
ojibwemoyaan. Gaawiin dash onisidotanziinaawaa. Booch
igo indizhichige.

[16] Inashke gaye owe noongom akina chi-anishinaabe geyaabi
eyaad, indigoo. Niizhobimaadizi go indawaaj, indaa-ikid.
Gegaa go, aanish naa zanagad wii-anishinaabewi miinawaa
wii-gichimookomaaniwiwag gaye wiinawaa. Booch gaye
ji-gii-izhichigeyan chimookomaan-izhichigeyan gaye niinawind
dash ji-anishinaabewiyaang akeyaa ji-izhitwaayaang. Haa ingod

Montana again. Just about, oh, nearly ten years I wasn't
here, here where I was born.

[11]   Then I returned home. Then once again I started my Indian
ways, the Indian way—pow-wow and again going around
speaking. Once again I danced. And I sang.

[12]   And after I fought, I met my brother-in-law, Scott Headbird.
And we were always close. We were good friends up until the
time he was no longer here.

[13]   You see I did all kinds of things. I was asked by those white
men themselves to help them out and advance their understanding too in what they did. I did all kinds of things in the
white man's way.

[14]   But I never abandoned the Indian way. You see here today,
well, now I'm seventy-three years old. I'm almost feeble.
And today I only do certain things when I go to pow-wows
and go around helping out, speaking Ojibwe, talking and
helping out my fellow Indians. And you see, I go all over
helping out with this Indian singing, and also with the
Indian praying. I no longer practice the medicine dance.
I only speak to our Great Spirit and all of his fellow
spirits.

[15]   And now I go to different schools too, being spoken to
about helping these young Indians and young white kids,
about what the Indian did long ago. A lot of them tell me
to speak Ojibwe. But they don't understand. But I certainly
do it.

[16]   You see this here today among all of the older generation
that's still here, I am told. They might as well lead a dual life,
I should say. Almost, well it is difficult being Indian as well
as wanting to be white people themselves. Certainly you had
to do certain things, doing them in the white man's way, but
we are still Indians and believe that way. Oh it's truly

geget sa zanagad, maagizhaa go indaa-ikid miinawaa
zhaaganaashiimong, *"You try to lead a double lifestyle."*

[17] Inashke go, ingoji go inashke go naa niin. Haa mewinzha
ingii-maajiitaa naaniimiyaan. Owidi go ingoji go gaa-
ishwaasobiboonagiziyaan, mii gaa-maajiitaayaan niimiyaan,
biinish igo 1968 ishkwaaj gii-niimiyaan. Mii dash apii
gaa-ani-bwaana'owiyaan miinawaa ji-niimiyaan niin.

[18] Haa namanj iidog geyaabi ge-ikidowaambaanen. Haaw iidog
i'iw ganabaj minik.

Gii-pakitejii'iged Wenabozho

[1] Ahaaw akawe bangii niwii-tibaajimaa a'aw isa Wenabozho.
Inashke Wenabozho iidog anooj gii-izhichige. Anooj gegoo
ogii-kashkitoon. Akina gegoo ogii-kikendaan iidog.

[2] Inashke dash aabiding iidog, inamadabid imaa—imaa sa
endaad iidog. Mii sa gaa-chi-inendang, "Haa ganabaj apane
inga-babaamose." Mii iidog maajaad babaamosed. Maagizhaa
imaa aandi eyaad iidog wa haa bakitejii'igewag. Miish iidog
omaa ezhi-biindiged imaa bakitejii'igewaad. Miish imaa
bezhig iidog gaa-izhi-nandomigod, "Hey Wenabozh! Giwii-
pakitejii'ige na?" "Haaw isa geget." Wa, mii sa iidog odaminod
bakitejii'iged.

[3] Maagizhaa mii sa iidog wiin nitam iwidi obakite'aan i'iw
bikwaakwad. Wa, hay' niibawid aazhaa gaa-izhi-bakite'ang. Wa
apane iidog i'iw bikwaakwad iwidi chi-waasa iwidi ogii-ani-
ganaandaan. Miish iidog imaa gii-ipitood imaa ji-gizhiibatood
iidog anishinaabeg gaa-izhi-noondaagoziwaad aaniin igo
anishinaabeg, "Haa Wenabozh! *Home run. Home run,*" inaa
iidog. Haa mii sa go Wenabozho iidog, mii sa go apane
gii-kiiwebatood." Haa mii sa i'iw.

difficult, so maybe I should say it again in English, "You try to lead a double lifestyle."

[17] You see, that's how things are with me. A long time ago, I started pow-wow dancing. When I was about eight years old over here, I started dancing, dancing up until 1968. Then at that time I became too feeble to dance myself.

[18] Well, I don't know if I'm going to say anymore. That must be enough.

When Wenabozho Played Baseball

[1] All right, first of all I want to tell a little story about that Wenabozho. You see Wenabozho must have been up to something. He was always trying to do something. He must have known everything too.

[2] One time he was sitting there—there where he lived. He was really thinking hard, "Maybe I'll walk around." Then he left walking around. Maybe there where he must have been they were playing baseball. Then he went in there where they were playing ball. Then one person there must have invited him [to play], "Hey Wenabozh! Do you want to play baseball?" "You bet." So he must have played, playing baseball.

[3] So maybe during his turn he hits that ball way over there. He just stands there after he already hit it. But he smacked that ball way far over there. Then as he was running there, running just fast, the Indians made a ruckus. "*Haa* Wenabozh! Home run. Home run," he must have been told. So Wenabozho ran home. That's it.

Miskwaagamiiwi-zaaga'igan
Red Lake

COLLINS OAKGROVE

COLLINS OAKGROVE (b. 1944), whose Indian name is *Zhaawanoowinini* (Man of the South), is one of Red Lake Reservation's strongest Ojibwe language advocates. He was born in a house at the reservation community of Redby and spent most of his formative years in the Redby-Ponemah area. Similar to the experience of most of his peers, Collins's parents and grandparents spoke Ojibwe to him from birth, and that was his first language. In his teens, Collins went to school for a time in Santa Fe and in Minneapolis. His experiences in these locations gave him an early understanding of the special gifts he had received through his traditional upbringing at Red Lake. They also inspired him to spend most of his adult life involved in efforts to revitalize the Ojibwe language.

Collins was drawn to Minneapolis in his early adulthood because he felt his best job prospects lay in the city. He knew that a significant percentage of the Red Lake Indian population lived there as well, and he had something to offer them and all Anishinaabe people. He worked for nearly fifteen years in the Minneapolis school districts, teaching Ojibwe language, culture, and history. Eventually, he was persuaded to accept a position at the University of Minnesota and to apply his talents and knowledge to the education of adults, which he did for another fifteen years. During those thirty years in Minneapolis, Collins acquired many friends and had hundreds of students pass through his classrooms. His reputation as a fine teacher and comedic storyteller strengthened with each successive wave of students.

Collins loved his work and his growing family in the city, but other passions attracted him as well. He longed for the woods of his childhood and the sense of cultural solidarity at Red Lake. He had given thirty years to Ojibwe language and community work for Indians in Minneapolis, and he realized that his knowledge could also be well applied at Red Lake. In 1996 he returned to the reservation and took a job at the neighboring town of Bemidji, again teaching Ojibwe language. In addition to teaching, he tutored and coached the American Indian Knowledge Bowl team. This recently developed competition has achieved great popularity among many Minnesotan schools with significant native populations. Students compete in knowledge of Ojibwe language, American Indian history, and geography. Collins's team won two consecutive Knowledge Bowls, in large part on the strength of their knowledge of Ojibwe words and phrases.

Collins eventually left Bemidji to work more directly with reservation youth in the Red Lake School System. There, too, he has continued to promote Ojibwe language education and to stress the importance of bilingual learning and living. He has most recently been active in efforts to acquire funds for the construction and operation of a charter school on the reservation, a school that would function with a strong focus on bilingual education. Despite the many years Collins has devoted to Ojibwe language education efforts, he shows no signs of slowing down. According to Collins, "There is just too much work to be done."

Zhaawanoowinini Indizhinikaaz

[1] Zhaawanoowinini indizhinikaaz, miinawaa dash a'aw ogiishkimanisii indoodem. Imaa wenjibaayaan, imaa Miskwaagamiwi-zaaga'iganiing, mii wenjiiwaad ingitiziimag apane. Miinawaa dash a'aw nimaamaayiban, onow odoodeman migiziwan. Ganabaj a'aw nimishoomisiban Zhaaganaashiiwakiing gii-onjibaa. Gii-pi-izhaa omaa. Aabiding igo ogii-mawidisaan onow ikwewan imaa Obaashiing. Mii gaa-ikidowaad ingitiziimag apane.

[2] Aan noongom niwii-aadizooke. Geyaabi biboonagad gomaa noongom. Mii dash noongom, mii wenji-izhichigewaad anishinaabegoban. Anishinaabeg aadizookewag megwaa biboonong, megwaa biboong.

Bijiinag Anishinaabe Gaa-waabamaad Chimookomaanan

[1] Aabiding giiwenh wayeshkad gii-pi-izhaawaad omaa chimookomaanag, imaa ingiwedog, gaawiin wiikaa ogii-waabamaasiiwaawaan chimookomaanan, anishinaabeg gaa-ayaawaad omaa.

[2] Mii dash aabiding a'aw inini ogii-inaan owiiwan, "Megwaa dagwaagig." Ogii-inaan owiiwan, "Gizhenaab, niwii-kiiyose noongom. Mii imaa ningaabi'anong keyaa niwii-izhaa." "Haaw," ikido a'aw, "Aaniish apii waa-pi-azhegiiweyan?" "Ajina sa go inga-ayaa imaa megwekob."

[3] Gaa-izhi-maajaad a'aw inini babaa-giiyosed. Megwaa ayaad imaa ogii-noondawaan awiiya biidaasamosed. Mii dash, ogii-paabi'aan ji-dagoshininid onow—maagizhaa gaye gii-inendam, waawaashkeshiwan. Wa, gaa-izhi-noogised ji-baabi'aad imaa, noomag igo gii-ayaa imaa. Miinawaa dash a'aw gaa-pi-izhaad imaa. Ho wa, wii-waabamaad onow chimookomaanan imaa chi-goshko'igod onow a'aw. Gaawiin wiikaa ogii-waabamaasiin chimookomaanan ji-bi-izhaang imaa.

[4] "Hey," a'aw chimookomaan gii-piibaagid, "You see anything today?" Ho wa, maagizhaa gaye a'aw anishinaabe, ganabaj ogii-kosaan iniw chimookomaanan. "Ho, aaniish enendamaan ji-izhichigeyaan," inendam wa'aw anishinaabe. "Mino-giizhigad noongom, eh," gaa-izhi-inaad. Mii dash ezhi-ikidod a'aw

My Name Is Zhaawanoowinini

[1] My name is *Zhaawanoowinini,* and my clan is the Kingfisher. Where I am from, there at Red Lake, that's where my parents were from. And my late mother, she was of the Bald Eagle Clan. My grandfather may have been from Canada. He came here. One time he visited this woman there at Ponema. That's what my parents always said.

[2] And today I'm going to tell legends. It's still winter today. And that's how the Indians did things. Indians tell legends while it's winter, in the midst of the winter.

The First Time an Indian Saw the White Man

[1] Once when the white people first came here, these ones there, the Indians around here, they had never seen white men.

[2] Then one time that man told his wife, "It's the middle of autumn." He told his wife, "Dear, I going to go hunting today. I am going to go there towards the west." "All right," she says, "When will you come back?" "I'll be there in the bush for just a little while."

[3] So that man left to go around hunting. While he was out there, he heard someone approaching. Then, he waited for him to show up—maybe, he thought, a deer. *Wa,* he stopped to wait for him there, hanging around there for a spell. And then he came there. *Ho wa,* he was going to see that white man, as that [Indian] guy was shocked by him. He had never seen a white man come there.

[4] "Hey," that white man yelled, "You see anything today?" *Ho wa,* and maybe that Indian, perhaps he was afraid of that white man. "Ho, what can I think of to do," thinks this Indian. "It's a nice day today, eh," he told him. Then that white man says, "Jeez, it's a nice day out." "Yup," says that

chimookomaan, *"Jeez, it's a nice day out."* *"Eya',"* ikido a'aw anishinaabe. Ogii-waabandaan dakonang baashkizigan. Gaawiin wiikaa ogii-waabandanziin i'iw baashkizigan. "Awegonen o'ow gii-takonaman," gaa-izhi-gagwejimaad wa'aw anishinaabe. Ogii-kagwejimaan onow chimookomaanan. *"Ya, it's a good day,"* ikido a'aw chimookomaan. Mii dash i'iw, booch igo abwezowag anishinaabe miinawaa a'aw chimookomaan.

[5]   Miinawaa dash a'aw anishinaabe ogii-poodaan o'ow ojaanzhan imaa akiing i'iw, bingwiing imaa. Ishkwaa-izhichiged, miinawaa dash o'ow chimookomaan gaa-izhichiged— omoshwens ogii-poodaan o'ow jaanzhan imaa.

[6]   Noomaya go ogii-inaan anishinaabe, *"Hey,"* ogii-inaan, "Akina gegoo ogoshkanaan a'aw chimookomaan," odinaan.

Wenji-nibwaakaad Nenabozho

[1]   Aabiding giiwenh o'ow babaamaazhagaamed a'aw Nenabozho enind, ogii-waabamaan biidaasamosed wiijanishinaaben. Mii dash o'ow, ogii-naazikaagoon iniw anishinaaben. "Nenabozho," ikido anishinaabe, "Giwii-kagwejimin gegoo." "Ahaaw," Nenabozho gaa-izhi-nakwetawaad. "Aaniin wenji-nibwaakaayan," ogii-kagwejimigoon iniw anishinaaben, wiijanishinaaben.

[2]   "Haaw." Nenabozho gaa-izhi-inendang wii-inaad iniw anishinaaben, wiijanishinaaben. "Apane sa niin niijii nimiijinan nibwaakaaminensan." "Oon, dagish waabanda'ishin wendinaman onow nibwaakaaminensan. Gaye niin niwii-nibwaakaa." "Haaw," Nenabozho gaa-izhi-inaad, "Daga wiijiwishin. Giga-waabanda'in wendinamaan onow nibwaakaaminensan."

[3]   Mii dash megwekob gii-izhi-izhaawaad imaa. Megwaa bimosewaad, Nenabozho gaa-mikang o'ow waaboozoo-miikanens. "Mii imaa wendinamaan nibwaakaaminensan," ikido Nenabozho imaa miiginaad onow nibwaakaaminensan gaa-izhi-miinaad bezhig owiijanishinaaben—a'aw waa-kikinoo'amawind. "Daga zhakamon abezhig," ikido Nenabozho. "Ahaaw." Owiijanishinaaben gaa-izhi-zhakamod bezhig. "Ishte," ikido owiijanishinaaben, "Gaawiin aawaasinoon nibwaakaaminensan. Waaboozoo-moowensan gosha." "Enh. Enh," ikido Nenabozho, "Miish o'ow gaye giin nibwaakaayan."

Indian. He saw him holding a gun. He had never seen a gun. "What's this you're holding," this Indian asks him. He asked that white man. "Ya, it's a good day," says that white guy. By then, they are really sweating—the Indian and that white guy.

[5] And then that Indian blew his nose there on the earth, in the sand there. After he does this, then that white man does this—he blew his nose there in his handkerchief.

[6] Soon thereafter the Indian says to him, "Hey," he tells him, "The white man keeps everything," he says to him.

Why Nenabozho Is So Smart

[1] This one time as that guy called Nenabozho was walking along the shore, he saw a fellow Indian walking towards him. Then he was approached by that Indian. "Nenabozho," the Indian says, "I want to ask you something." "All right," Nenabozho replies to him. "Why are you so smart," he was asked by that Indian, his fellow Indian.

[2] "All right." Nenabozho was thinking of what he wanted to tell that Indian, his fellow Indian. "As for me, my friend, I always eat smart berries." "Oh, please show me where you get these smart berries. I would like to be intelligent myself." "Okay," Nenabozho told him, "You come with me. I'll show you where I get these smart berries."

[3] Then they went off there in the bush. While they were walking along, Nenabozho finds this rabbit trail. "I get the smart berries right there," Nenabozho says there as he gives away the smart berries, giving one to his fellow Indian—the one who was going to be taught a lesson. "Put one in your mouth," says Nenabozho. "Okay." His fellow Indian put one his mouth. "*Ishte*," says his fellow Indian, "These aren't smart berries. These are damned rabbit turds." "Yes. Yes," says Nenabozho, "Then you're getting smart yourself."

Bebaamosed Miinawaa Gawigoshko'iweshiinh

[1] Apane babaamosed a'aw Nenabozho gii-pabaamose gii-ayaad omaa. Mii dash o'ow ani-babaamosed gaa-izhi-miikawaad onow binesiwan, onow gii-naganaawaad omaamaayiwaa omaa. Gaa-izhi-gagwejimaad, "Aaniish giinawaa ezhinikaazoyeg," ogii-kagwejimaan a'aw Nenabozho. Mii dash, ogii-nisidotaagoon i'iw ayaawid. Mii dash, gaawiin ogii-nakwetawaasiigoon onow binewan. "Gaawiin giwii-pooni'isiinooninim. Aaniish ezhinikaazoyeg?" Mii dash binesiwag gaa-izhi-inaawaad, "Bine indizhinikaazomin." "Oon. Inashke niin niizhing indizhinikaaz. Mii i'iw bezhig, Nenabozho indizhinikaaz. Miinawaa dash Bebaamosed gaye indizhinikaaz." "Oon." Gaawiin ogii-nakwetawaasiigoonaan Nenabozho. "Wiindamawishin ezhinikaazoyan. Niizhing akina awiiya adayaanaawaan izhinikaazowinan," ogii-inaan Nenabozho. Mii dash iniw binewan, "Gawigoshko'iweshiinh indizhinikaazomin gaye niinawind," gii-ikidowag.

[2] "Sate! Gaawiin giin. Onzaam sa go gibi-wiiji'ininim," gii-ikido a'aw Nenabozho. Mii gaa-izhi-zhaagode'enid gaa-izhi-miiziinaad onow sa binesiwan. Mii dash gaa-izhi-maajaad a'aw Bebaamosed.

[3] Megwaa, bimised a'aw ikwe-bine, gaa-izhi-booniid imaa. "Wish," ikido a'aw, "Awenesh gaa-toodooneg owe gii-miiziinegwaa?" "Nenabozho," gii-ikidowag oniijaanisan. "Wha. Inashke niin ge-doodawag. Aaniish wenji-izhichiged?" "Ingii-kagwejimigoonaan iwe ezhinikaazoyaang. Mii dash, ingii-inaanaan, ingii-wiindamawaanaan ezhinikaazoyaang— Bine miinawaa Gawigoshko'iweshiinh." "Oon." "Mii dash, ingii-miiziinigoonaan omaa." "Haaw. Inga-izhaa imaa. Aaniish akeyaa gaa-izhaad imaa Nenabozho?" "Mii akeyaa imaa, ningaabi'anong gii-izhaa." "Oon." Mii dash a'aw ikwe-bine gaa-izhi-biini'aad oniijaanisan.

[4] Megwaa biini'aad onow, Bebaamosed—enind Nenabozho—megwaa bimosed a'aw gaa-izhi-waabamaad imaa iniw akiwenziiyan imaa namadabinid. Odaanan dash owiidabimigoon imaa. "Aaniish wenji-namadabiyeg," ogii-kagwejimaan Nenabozho. Mii dash gaa-izhi-inaabid imaa giishkaabikokaaning imaa chi-waasa imaa enaabid. Mii dash akiwenzii gaa-izhi-inaad Nenabozhon, "Mii awiiya ge-giishkitood ji-azhe-gwaashkwanid, mii awe ge-wiidigemaad onow indaanisan omaa." Owaabamaan odaanan. "Mii owe

Bebaamosed *and* Gawigoshko'iweshiinh

[1] That Nenabozho walked all over when he was here, always walking around. Then as he was walking around, he found these birds that had been left by their mother here. So he asks them, "What are your names," that Nenabozho asked them. Then, he was understood by them in his being [there]. But he wasn't answered by those birds. "I'm not going to leave you alone. What are your names?" Then those birds told him, "We are called *Bine*." "Oh. Look, I have two names myself. For the first one, I am called Nenabozho. And I am also called *Bebaamosed*." "Oh." They didn't answer Nenabozho. "Tell me what you are called. Everyone has two names," Nenabozho told them. Then those partridges said, "We are also called *Gawigoshko'iweshiinh*."*

[2] "*Sate!* Not you. I've been hanging around with you too long," said that Nenabozho. Those birds were frightened as he crapped all over them. Then that *Bebaamosed* took off.

[3] In the meantime, that hen flew up and perched there. "*Wish*," she says, "Who did this to you, crapping all over you?" " Nenabozho," her kids said. "*Wha*. Just look at what I am going to do to him. Why did he do this?" "We were asked what our names were. Then, we told him, we told him what our names are—*Bine* and *Gawigoshko'iweshiinh*." "Oh." "Then he crapped all over us here." "All right. I am going there. Which way did Nenabozho go there?" "That way there, he went towards the west." "Oh." Then that hen cleaned up her children.

[4] While she was cleaning them, *Bebaamosed*—the one called Nenabozho—while he was walking he saw an old man sitting there. And his daughter was sitting with him there. "Why are you sitting," Nenabozho asked them. Then he glanced at the cliff there, looking a long way there [to the bottom]. Then that old man told Nenabozho, "Whoever shall be able to jump, he's the one who will marry my

* *Gawigoshko'iweshiinh* means "the little scary bird."

ge-izhichigeyaan," gii-inendam Nenabozho gaa-izhi-
wiindamawaad onow akiwenziiyan, "Niin sa go inga-
wiidigemaa gidaanis. Inga-azhe-gwaashkwan owe omaa
giishkaabikokaaning."

[5] Mii dash ishkwe gaa-izhi-bimosed, noomag gii-niibawid imaa
waabandang giishkaabikokaaning imaa gaa-izhi-chi-
bimibatood imaa. Jiigayi'ii imaa gaa-izhi-chi-noogised. Gegaa
sa go gii-pangishin imaa biinjayi'ii imaa. Wa hiyaa, gaa-izhi-
waabamaad miinawaa odaanan. "Niin sa go inga-wiidigemaa."
Ishkweyaang go gaa-izhi-bimosed naanaagadawendang o'ow
ge-izhichiged gaa-izhi-chi-bimibatood imaa miinawaa. Jiigayi'ii
gaye gaa-izhi-chi-noogised gayesh. Gegaa go gii-pangishin
imaa. "Hiyaa," ikido Nenabozho, "Niin sa go inga-wiidigemaa
gidaanis," ogii-inaan akiwenziiyan gaa-izhi-azhe-bimibatood.
Gii-chi-inendam o'ow. "Inga-izhichige. Gaye niin sa go
inga-giishkitoon ahe-gwaashkwaniwaanen," gii-inendam a'aw
Nenabozho.

[6] Jibwaa-ani-bimibatood, gaa-izhi-booniinid ikwe-binewan imaa
jiigayi'ii giishkaabikokaaning. Mii gii-inendang a'aw ikwe-bine,
"Inga-goshko'aa a'aw Nenabozho jibwaa-ani-gwaashkwanid
imaa."

[7] Mii dash a'aw Nenabozho gaa-izhi-chi-bimibatood imaa.
Jiigayi'ii gaa-izhi-chi-noogised; mii dash onow ikwe-binewan
gaa-izhi-bazigwiinid, "Papapapa." Gaa-izhi-goshko'aad onow
Nenabozhon. Hay'! Mii sa go. Gii-pangishin imaa biinjayi'ii.

daughter here." He sees the daughter. "That's what I shall do," Nenabozho thought as he told that old man, "I shall marry your daughter myself. I am going to jump over this here precipice."

[5] Then he walked back, standing for a little while there, looking at the cliff there, he ran really hard there. He came to an abrupt stop right at the edge. He almost fell over there. *Wa hiyaa*, he looked at [the old man's] daughter again. "I am going to marry her myself." Afterwards as he walked [away from the edge] reflecting on what he would do, he sprinted there again. And he came to a stop right at the edge too. He almost fell there. "*Hiyaa*," says Nenabozho, "I'm going to marry your daughter myself," he told that old man as he ran back. He was really thinking hard. "I am going to do this. I must be able to jump off myself," that Nenabozho thought.

[6] Just before he ran, that hen perched there near the edge of the precipice. That hen thought, "I'm going to scare that Nenabozho before he jumps there."

[7] Then that Nenabozho really took a run for it there. Right at the edge he came to a halt; but that hen flew up like this, "*Papapapa.*" She scared that Nenabozho. *Hai'!* He fell right over the edge there.

Gaa-zagaskwaajimekaag
Leech Lake

EMMA FISHER

EMMA FISHER (1911–1996), whose Indian name was *Manidoo-binesiikwe* (Spirit Bird Woman), exemplified the experience of her generation in many ways. She was born in a *wiigiwaam* near the Leech Lake Reservation community of Boy River and given the name Emma Bugg. (Fisher was her married name.) Her mother died shortly after childbirth and Emma was raised by her grandparents in the village. She played in the woods and at the beach with her cousins and dogs under the lax but loving care of her extended family.

Emma recalled vividly the many changes her generation experienced—from the construction of the first log homes and tarpaper shacks at Boy River to the more pernicious assault on culture through Bureau of Indians Affairs (BIA) Circular 1665 and boarding schools. BIA Circular 1665 actively suppressed tribal dances, ceremonies, and giveaways throughout the United States until 1933, and Emma remembered clearly this environment of religious persecution. Even more influential on her life and upbringing, however, was the BIA boarding school she was forced to attend in Tomah, Wisconsin.

Emma described boarding school life as harsh and unpleasant: she recalled marching to and from class, beatings for speaking Ojibwe, and little love or support in the rigid confines of school life. She ran away from Tomah with some of her girlfriends and eventually started day school near Boy River. Many effects of the schooling she received, however, were permanent. She never lost her language, but she also did not try to teach it to her children, fearing that they might endure similar hardships for their knowledge of Ojibwe. By the time the boarding school era came to a close, her children had already grown up immersed in English. The threat was gone, but the opportunity was lost.

Emma responded poorly to her experiences in Tomah and was a rebellious and difficult teenager, running away at least twice and eventually eloping with her future husband, an Ojibwe from Mille Lacs. She did finally settle down, raising five children of her own. Parenting would be an emotional trauma for her, however, as four of her five children died in early adulthood.

Emma eventually moved from Mille Lacs back to Boy River and then to Cass Lake, where she lived the last several years of her life in the elder housing unit run by the Leech Lake Reservation. She loved her pet dog and cat and the company of her many visitors, some of whom she adopted as children and grandchildren.

Gii-agaashiinyiyaan

[1] *Emma Fisher* indizhinikaaz. Mii gaa-ondaadiziyaan, ingii-maajig imaa Gwiiwizensiwi-ziibing. Mii i'iw wendaadiziyaan biindig anishinaabe-wiigiwaaming, wanagekogamig waawiyeyaakwak. Nimaamaa gii-nibo ishkwaa-ondaadiziyaan. Miish i'iw apii nitaawigi'idwaa nookomis, nimishomis igaye. Mii dash gii-anishinaabewinikaanagwaa imbaabaa, nimaamaa gaye. Mii ezhi-maajigiyaan, ingii-aanjigozimin imaa Gwiiwizensiwi-zaaga'iganing, gaa-ayaawaad indinawemaaganinaanig. Noongom ayaamagad gaa-tazhishinikaag imaa gaa-danakiiyaang.

[2] Debaasige gii-akiwenziiwi i'iw apii wendaadiziyaan. Miish ezhi-owiiyawe'enyid. Ingii-wiinig a'aw akiwenziiban. Gii-piibiiyaan, ingii-sagaswe'idimin ji-anishinaabe-izhinikaanigooyaan. Mii nising ezhi-wiinzoyaan. Apiitendaagwad ji-wiinzod anishinaabe ji-mashkawiziid obimaadiziwining.

Indayag

[1] Gwanaajiwan gii-agaashiinyaan. Mii go apane ko wayaabamagwaa animoshag gaa-odaminoyaan imaa mitigokaag, ingii-animiwinaag, bimiwinagwaa imaa endaayaan. Mii dash igo gii-ayaawagwaa midaaswi animoshag ingoji go, bimaadiziyaan imaa noopiming. Mii go gii-kanawenimiwaad gaa-pabaa-odaminoyaan, ezhi-zegi'aad awesiinyan migoshkaaji'iwinid.

[2] Ingii-tanakiimin imaa megwaayaak, besho Gwiiwizensiwi-zaaga'iganiing, endaawaad niibowa anishinaabeg. Aangodinong ingii-izhaamin imaa ji-mawadishiweyaang, gii-misawendamaan ji-dazhitaayaan gaa-ayaawaad abinoojiinyag. Mii dash igo gii-saaga'amaan ji-bimoseyaan imaa mitigokaag wiiji-ayaawagwaa indayag. Ingii-nisaanaanig akakojiishag ji-amwigod iniw animoshan. Aapiji go gii-minwendaagwad. Gii-pabaaminizha'waad waawaashkeshiwan, miinawaa go gaye ingii-akwaandawe imaa mitigong.

[3] Nookomis ogii-ayaanan biizikiiganan ji-biizikamaan gii-pabaa-odaminoyaan agwajiing. Mii dash igo ko gii-minwendamaan

When I Was Little

[1] My name is Emma Fisher. When I was born, I grew up there at Boy River. I was born inside an Indian lodge, the round dome-shaped kind. My mother died [shortly] after I was born. And from that time on I was raised by my grandmother and my grandfather. But I called them mother and father in Indian. When I got bigger, we moved there to Boy Lake, where our relatives were [living]. Now there's a cemetery there where we used to live.

[2] *Debaasige* was an old man at the time of my birth. And he was a name giver. That old man named me. When I was a baby, we had a pipe ceremony for me to get my Indian names. I was named three times. It is very important for the Indian to be named so he can be strong in his life.

My Dogs

[1] My childhood was beautiful. Whenever I saw dogs as I played there in the woods, I carried them away, bringing them there to my house. And I always had about ten dogs when I was living there in the forest. They looked after me when I went around playing, as they scared the wild animals off, pestering them.

[2] We lived there in the woods, near Boy Lake, where a lot of the Indians lived. Sometimes we went there to visit, when I wanted to play where the other kids were. Then I would go outside to go walking there in the forest with my dogs. We killed woodchucks so my dogs could eat them. It was so much fun. They chased deer around there and I climbed trees.

[3] My grandmother had clothes for me to put on when I played outside. Then I was usually happy to go barefoot.

ji-zhaashaaginizideyaan. Apane ko ingii-bimaazhagaame, bakobiigwaashkwaniyaan imaa zaaga'iganiing gemaa gaye imaa ziibing. Mii sa go gii-pimaadagaawaad indayag igaye. Ingii-izhi-anishinaabe-wiinaag akina indayag. Aanind odayaanaawaan zhaaganaashiimo-wiinzowinan, mii dash igo anishinaabe-inwemagak, dibishkoo go Jaanish, wiindeg Jaan zhaaganaashiimong. Bezhig gii-izhinikaazo Mazina'ige.

[4]   Oon, gagiibaadadoon akina owiinzowiniwaan, aanind zhaaganashiimong, aanind anishinaabemong.

[5]   Nimikwendaan gii-agaashiinyaan, naanaagadawendamaan gaa-izhichigeyaan i'iw apii. Apane ingii-izhaa imaa megwaayaak ji-odaminotawagwaa indayag. Apane ko ingii-wiindamawaag ingiw i'iw isa gaa-wiindamawangidwaa ko anishinaabe-animoshag—"mawinazh!" Miigaazowag igaye.

[6]   Aabiding ninzhishenyiban ingii-waabamig imaa noopiming. Miinawaa go gaye gii-ayaayaan imaa mitigong.

[7]   Mii sa indayag gii-ayaawaad imaa ogidakamig, miish igo ayaayaan mitigong. Ninzhishenh gii-noogishkaa imaa gaa-odaminoyaan gaa-izhi-bimosed imaa noopiming. Gii-miishidaamikamban, dibishkoo go aanind anishinaabeg. Mii go apane ezhi-debibinid, ingii-miishi-zinigonig indengwayang, mii go gaye wiisagendamaan. Ingii-paazagobinaa, miigaanag. Miish ezhi-ikidod a'aw, "Giga-wiidigemin netaawigiyan. Inga-webinaa niwiiw." Ingii-tebwetaag. Ingii-maw, miigaazoyaan igaye, wiikobidooyaan odiinisizisan miinawaa go gaye baazagobinag.

[8]   Bezhig giizhig ingii-tebibinig ninzhishenh ishpi-ayaayaan mitigong, ezhi-ikidod, "Inga-akwaandawe imaa ji-wiiji-ayaawinaan, ji-wiidabiminaan. Giwii-wiidigemin niin sa mitigong." "Gaawiin igo," ingii-ikid. Miish ezhi-gagwejimid, "Aaniin danaa?" "Mawinazh!" gaa-inagwaa indayag.

[9]   Mii dash ezhi-ikidod, "Enh, gaawiin inzegizisii ji-miigaanagwaa gidayag." Ingii-anoonaag indayag maajii-naazikawaawaad mitigong. Akina indayag ozhiitaawag ji-mawinanaad. Gaawiin daa-gii-kiimiisii ninzhishenh; miziwe gaa-ayaawaad indayag. Gaawiin idash owii-mawinanaasiiwaawaan biinish anoonaasiwagwaa.

[10]   Endaso-mamaazikaad, gii-niikimowag, waabanda'aad odiibidaniwaan. Miish apii bezhig animosh gii-tebibinaad

I always walked along the shore, diving into the lake there or maybe there in the river. And my dogs would go swimming too. I gave all my dogs Indian names. Some had English names, but they sounded like Indian, like *Jaanish*, that was John in English. One was named *Mazina'ige*.

[4] Oh, all their names were crazy, some in English and some in Indian.

[5] I remember when I was little, thinking about what I did back then. I always went in the forest to play with my dogs. I always told them what we tell Indian dogs—"attack!" And they fought too.

[6] One time my uncle saw me there in the forest. And [I] was up there in a tree.

[7] My dogs were there on the ground, but I was up in the tree. My uncle stopped there where I was playing as he walked along there in the forest. He had a mustache, [you know] how some Indians [had]. Then he would get a hold of me, and give me a whisker rub on my face, and that hurt. I used to scratch him, fighting him. Then he said, "I'm going to marry you when you grow up. I'm going to divorce my wife." I believed him. I cried, fighting him too, pulling his hair and scratching him.

[8] One day my uncle got ahold of me when I was up in that tree, saying, "I'm going to climb up there to keep you company, to sit with you. I'm going to marry you myself in that tree." "No way," I said. Then he asks me, "Why?" "Attack!" I told my dogs.

[9] Then he says, "Yeah, I'm not scared to fight your dogs." I ordered my dogs to start surrounding him at the tree. All my dogs were ready to attack him. My uncle couldn't escape; my dogs were everywhere. But they wouldn't attack until I ordered them [to do so].

[10] Every time he moved, they growled, showing him their teeth. Then one got ahold of his pants. Then he screams,

ogiboodiyegwaazonan. Miish ezhi-aazhikwed, "Tayaa! Geget
igo indakwamigoog ingiw." "Geget oganawenimaawaan ingiw
animoshag eyaad," baanimaa owiindamawaawaan
indinawemaaganinaanig.

[11] Ninzhishenh noonde-bi-wiidookawaa. Nimishoomisiban
gii-pi-naagozi, zaagajiwed ji-bimaaji'aad ninzhishenyan.
Gaawiin igo ingii-wii-wiidookawaasii. Ingii-shazhiibitam.
"Anoozh gidayag ji-booni-mawinanidwaa," indig ninzhishenh
anishinaabemong, "Wiindamaw gidayishag." "Gaawiin,"
indinaa. Ingii-wenda-majiw. "Mawinazh!" Ingii-ikid.
Gii-niikimowag, naazikaagewaad besho, ezhi-dakwangewaad.

[12] "Aaniin," madwe-ikido nimishoomis. Mii dash igo ezhi-ikidod
ninzhishenh, "Bi-naadamawishin." Gii-saagajiwe nimishoomis,
biidood zaka'on, mii go gaye zegi'aad, oshaakawaad iniw.
Ishkwaakamigak baanimaa ingii-noondawaa wiindamawaad
nookomisiban, "Gego babaamendangen apane mitigokaag
nazhike-baa-ayaad."

Gii-kinjiba'iweyaan

[1] Aabiding ingii-kinjiba'aa nookomis. Gii-nichiiwad,
animikiikaamagak, wawaasesemagak igaye maajii-
mikwamiwang. Mii maamakaaj ji-izhiwebak niibing.
Ingii-amwaa a'aw mikwam. Nookomis ingii-wiindamaag
maazhipogozinid. Gaawiin idash ingii-pizindanziin ekidod.
Ingii-kinjiba'iwe, ezhi-amwag a'aw mikwam. Mii dash igo
nisayenh gii-saaga'ang, nisaabaawed, ji-biindigenaazhikawid
izhidaabaanid imaa biindig.

[2] Aabiding baanimaa miinawaa go gaye ingii-kinjiba'iwe,
aabajitooyaan i'iw isa azheboyi-jiimaan. Nookomis
ingii-piibaagimig, mawimid imaa agamiing.
Gii-chiigeweyaazhagaame nookomis, ezhi-ekidod,
"Madaabiin. Omaa bi-izhaan!" "Gaawiin," ingii-ikid,
ezhi-azheboyeyaan imaa Gwiiwizensiwi-zaaga'iganiing.
Naaningim ingii-maji-izhiwebiz.

"*Tayaa!* They are really biting me." "Those dogs really do watch over her wherever she's at," he later told our relatives.

[11]   My uncle needed help. Then my grandfather showed himself, coming around the hill to save my uncle's life. I didn't want to help him. I was stubborn. "Tell your dogs to quit attacking me," my uncle tells me in Indian, "Tell your dogs." "No," I say to him. I was really bad. "Attack!" I said. They growled, closing in on him, [and] biting him.

[12]   "Hello," my grandfather's voice is heard. Then my uncle says, "Come help me." My grandpa came over the hill, bringing his cane, and scared [the dogs], frightening them off. After it was all over I heard him tell my grandmother, "You don't have to worry about her going off in the woods by herself all the time."

When I Ran Away

[1]   One time I ran away from my grandmother. It was stormy: thundering, lightning flashing, and starting to hail. It's strange to have that kind of weather in the summer. I ate ice. Grandma told me it tasted bad. But I didn't listen to what she said. I ran away, eating that ice. Then my older [step]brother came outside, getting wet to chase me inside, dragging me inside there.

[2]   And one time later on I ran away again, using that rowboat. My grandmother yelled at me, crying for me there on the shore. My grandma walked along the shore, saying, "Come to shore. Come here!" "No," I said, as I rowed away there at Boy Lake. Often times I misbehaved.

Gii-kikinoo'amaagoziyaan

[1] Ingii-ozhigaagoonaanig ingiw odaake-ogimaag. Mii gaa-ozhitoowaad iko mitigo-waakaa'iganan i'iw apii. Apane ko ingii-anishinaabemomin gaganoonidiyaang. Nawaj sa gii-kikendamaan anishinaabemowin i'iw apii awashiime gikendamaan noongom. Mii gaa-kagwe-gimoodimiwaad enweyaan ingiw chi-mookomaanag gii-kikinoo'amaagoziyaan. Ingii-izhinaazhikaagoo imaa, wiindamawidwaa odaake-ogimaag giiwiziyaan. Gaawiin ingii-kiiwizisii. Gaawiin nandawendanziiwag ji-maajaayaan nimishoomis, nookomis igaye. Mii dash wiin gii-animiwinigooyaan.

[2] Oon ingii-izhaamin imaa Washashkoonsing ji-gikinoo'amaagoziyaang. Mii dibishkoo go gii-ayaamagak miigaadiwini-gikinoo'amaadii-wigamig. Wayeshkad aapiji go gii-sanagad ji-ayaayaan imaa. Gii-apiitendaagwad ji-gwayako-inoseyaang bebezhig. Ingii-pakite'wigoomin giishpin wanichigeyaang. Akina anishinaabe-gaawizijig gii-kikinoo'amaagoziwag imaa, mii sa ingiw Wiinibiigoog, Ojibweg, Manoominiig igaye imaa Wazhashkoonsing. Ingii-ishwaaso-biboonagiz i'iw apii.

[3] Gii-ayaamagadoon gwiiwizensiwi-waakaa'iganan dibishkoo gabe-gikendaasowigamigong. Gwiiwizensiwi-waakaa'iganan gii-ayaamagadoon opime-ayi'ii i'iw gikinoo'amaagewigamigong, dibishkookamig ayaamagak iniw ikwezensiwi-waakaa'iganan. Ingii-danakii imaa giiwizigamigong, wiiji-ayaawagwaa gaawizijig. Ingii-gikinoo'amaagoo imaa jibwaa-apiitiziyaan ji-anokiiyaan. Gii-ayaawag ogimaakweg, ogimaag igaye.

[4] Ingii-kinjiba'iwe. Ingii-ashi-niso-biboonigiz i'iw apii ginjiba'iweyaang, niin igaye aanind ikwezensag. Nookomis, nimishoomis ingii-kanawenimigoog ishkwaa-azhegiiweyaan imaa Gwiiwizensiwi-ziibiing. Ingii-kina'amaagoog ji-azhegiiweyaan imaa Wazhashkoonsing. Mii sa go maajii-gikinoo'amaagoziyaan imaa Gwiiwizensiwi-ziibiing, gikinoo'amaagewigamigoonsing. Ingiw chimookomaani-getigejig ogii-ayaanaawaa waakaa'igaans besho Gwiiwizensiwi-ziibiing. Ogii-nanaa'itoonaawaa ji-ayaamagak gikinoo'amaagewigamig.

When I Went to School

[1] Those government officials were building houses for us. They always made log houses at that time. We were always speaking Indian when we talked to each other. I knew the Indian language better at that time than I know it now. The white people tried to steal my language when I [was sent] to school. I was sent there, told by those government officials that I was an orphan. I wasn't an orphan. My grandfather and grandmother didn't want me to leave. But I was taken away.

[2] We went there to Tomah [Wisconsin] to go to school. It was just like a military academy. At first it was really hard for me to be there. It was important that we march in single file. We were beaten if we made mistakes. All the Indian orphans were sent to school there at Tomah, that is the Winnebago, Ojibwe, and Menomini. I was eight years old at that time.

[3] There were boys dormitories just like in college. The boys dorms were off to the side of the school, and a similar building was there for the girls dormitories. I lived in the orphan hall, in the company of the orphans. I studied there before I was old enough to work. There were matrons and bosses too.

[4] I ran away. I was thirteen at the time we ran away, me and some other girls. My grandmother and grandfather looked after me after I returned home there at Boy River. They forbade me to go back there to Tomah. So, I started going to school there at Boy River, in the little schoolhouse. Those white farmers had a building near Boy River. They fixed it up to function as a school.

[5] Mii i'iw gaa-inakamigak i'iw apii gaa-gikinoo'amaagoziyaan. Ingii-poonitoomin giisphin misawendamaang. Ingii-azhe-izhiwijigaaz Wazhashkoonsing ishkwaa-boonitooyaan gikinoo'amaagoziyaan imaa Gwiiwizensiwi-ziibiing. Mii go miinawaa go gaye gii-kinjiba'iweyaan, izhaayaan imaa Misi-zaaga'iganing. Miish imaa nakweshkawag ninaabem. Ingii-wiidigendimin. Mii dash gii-nagadamaan niwaakaa'igan imaa Gwiiwizensiwi-zaaga'iganiing ji-danakiiyaan imaa Misi-zaaga'iganiing. Naaning ingii-ondaadiziike, gii-niigi'agwaa naanan abinoojiinyag. Niwani'aag niiwin; bezhig eta zhaabwiid.

Indinawemaaganag

[1] Noongom ayaamagad gaa-tazhishinikaag imaa gaa-odaminoyaan iko gii-agaashiinyaan. Ingii-mamakii'igoomin imaa, nimiseban gaye niin sa. Ingii-ayaawaa bezhig nimise, mii dash igo nitaawigid omaa Gaa-miskwaawaakokaag, gii-nitaawigi'aad odinawemaaganan *Emma Bear*. Gii-webinidiwag ingitiziimag. Imbaabaaban gii-nagazhiwe, naganaad nimaamaayan. Gaawiin moozhag ingii-waabamaasii imbaabaaban, aanawenimag wayaabamag. Ingii-wiindamawaa nookomis, "Gaawiin niminwenimaasii a'aw." "Aaniin dash?" ezhi-gagwejimid nookomisiban. "Gidede gosha naa aawi." Ingii-wiindamawaa, "Gaawiin niminwenimaasii, booch igo gaawiin."

[2] Mii dash aapiji zhawendiyaang nookomis, nimishomis igaye niin sa. Miish igo aanind ninzhishenyag nonde-nitaawigi'iwaad. Ingii-panaaji'ig nookomis; mii go gaa-inendamowaad ninzhishenyag. Gaawiin ingii-tibendaagozisii, mii gaa-inendamowaad. Gaawiin dash ingii-misawendanziin ji-danakiiyaan gaa-ayaawaad niibowa abinoojiinyag. Ingii-minwendam ji-danakiiyaan iwidi endaad nookomis.

[3] Ingii-ayaawaag niiwin ninzhishenyag igo gaye bezhig nisayenh. Akina gii-ojaanisiwag, mii ezhi-ayaawaad niibowa abinoojinyag. Ninzhishenyag ingii-wiindamaagoog, "Eshkam igo gibanaadiz. Gidaa-ganawenjigaaz weweni. Gidaa-dibendaagoz." Apane ko ingii-miigaanaag odabinoojinyag, mii ishkwaaj gii-apa'iweyaan

[5]   That's what happened when I went to school. We quit if we
      really wanted to. But I was sent back to Tomah after I quit
      going to school there at Boy River. So once again I ran away,
      going there to Mille Lacs. And there I met my husband. We
      were married. Then I abandoned my house at Boy Lake to
      live there at Mille Lacs. I gave birth five times, bearing five
      children. I lost four; only one is left.

My Relatives

[1]   Now there's a cemetery where I used to play when I was
      small. We were given allotments there, my older sister and
      I. I had one sister, but she grew up here in Cass Lake, as she
      was raised with her relative, Emma Bear. My parents were
      divorced. My father left, abandoning my mother. I didn't
      see my father much, and I didn't have a high opinion of
      him when I did see him. I told my grandmother, "I don't
      like him." "Why?" my grandmother asked me. "He's your
      dad." I told her, "I don't like him, definitely not."

[2]   But my grandmother, grandfather, and I really loved each
      other a lot. Then some of my uncles wanted to raise me.
      My grandmother spoiled me; at least that's what my uncles
      thought. I didn't belong there, that's what they thought.
      But I didn't want to live where there were a lot of other
      children. I was happy living over there at my grandmother's
      house.

[3]   I had four maternal uncles and one elder brother. They were
      all family people, and they had a lot of kids. My uncles told
      me, "You're getting more and more spoiled. You should be
      cared for properly. You should be a part [of our family]." I
      always fought his kids, and afterwards I would run away to

ji-gaazootawagwaa ingiw iwidi endaanid nookomisibaniin.
Aanish mii sa go gaa-izhi-maajigiwaad indaangoshenyag,
eshkam igo mashkawiziiwaad, ingii-aangwaamiz. Ingii-
ayaawaag niibowa indinawemaaganag, mii dibishkoo go ingiw
Mitchells mii go gaye *Cummingses*—gwiiwizensag, ikwezensag,
egaashiinjig, mendidojig, bekaakadozojig, waaninojig,
gegwaanisagizijig. Mii gaa-mindidowaad ingiw gwiiwizensag,
gaawiin ingii-miigaanaasiig. Nawaj gii-mashkawiziiwag,
gagwaanisagiziwaad gaye awashiime niin. Mii i'iw apii
gii-miigaanagwaa ikwezensag. Mii i'iw.

hide from them over there at my grandmother's house. Well then as my cousins grew up, they got stronger, and I had to be careful. I had many relatives, like the Mitchells and the Cummingses—boys, girls, little ones, big ones, skinny ones, fat ones, mean ones. As those boys got big, I didn't fight them. They got stronger, and they got meaner than me. Then I fought the girls. That's it.

SCOTT HEADBIRD

SCOTT HEADBIRD (1927–1996), whose Indian names were *Ba-gwekabiitang* (Turns Towards the Sound) and *Niigani-bines* (Head Bird), was a gifted storyteller. Although the single story included in this book is too short to fully display his talent, it gives an excellent taste of Scott's oratory. I visited with him on several occasions when he told incredibly animated stories, stories so funny that Scott would literally slap his own knees as he laughed at the punch lines.

Scott, like all Ojibwe people of his generation, grew up immersed in his language and culture. As a member of Leech Lake's Mission Community, west of Cass Lake, Minnesota, he lived the seasonal life of all Ojibwe people in the area. His family's allotments, scattered between lakes Andrusia and Cass from the Mississippi River to Big Lake, contained some of the best hunting, trapping, and fishing grounds on the Leech Lake Reservation. Scott's family lived by using and selling what they acquired from the land. Scott ate so much fish as a child that he actually lost the taste for it in his later years, preferring red meats if given a choice.

Scott attended the mission day school until his teens. He completed high school in nearby Cass Lake. The benefits of living at home, rather than attending residential boarding school like many of his contemporaries, were great. Scott never lost his language or had it beaten out of him, and that sustained knowledge made him truly wise about many things—language, Ojibwe plants and medicines, and traditional lifeways.

Scott made his way in the world by retaining the skills he learned as a child. Throughout his lifetime, Scott made and set nets, snared rabbits, and gathered berries and pine cones for sale. He augmented the income from such endeavors by working many years as a logger and a carpenter. He acquired passions in the culture of European settlers as well. Scott was a talented pool player, and in his younger years he frequented bars and local tournaments in pursuit of worthy opponents. He joined the Ojibwe Hymnal Singers and was one of their loudest vocalists and most ardent supporters. Scott also enjoyed playing bingo and was a regular at the Leech Lake Bingo Palace and Casino in the 1980s and 1990s.

Scott truly treasured his family. He rarely went further than the grocery store without his wife, Susie. Even more arduous endeavors such as netting fish involved his family. He frequently spoke about the future of the Ojibwe language with great trepidation and hoped that his grandchildren would master it. His impact, however, reached far beyond his substantial family network. To a great many people, myself included, Scott offered fresh inspiration to care for the language he so artfully used for the entertainment and teaching of all Ojibwe people.

Waawaabiganoojiish

[1] Aabiding gii-ayaawag ingodwewaan anishinaabeg gaa-
onjibaawaad i'iw isa Miskwaagamiiwi-zaaga'igan
ishkoniganing. Obaashiing izhinikaade i'iw oodena
gii-tanakiiwaad. Mii apane go gii-minikwewaad imaa sa
gete-anishishinaabe-waakaa'iganishing. Moozhag
gii-kiiwashkwebiiwag ingiw niizh.

[2] Aabiding ezhi-minobiiwaad, baapinikamigiziwaad, bezhig inini
ogii-waabamaan waawaabiganoojiinyan ipitoonid imaa sa
michisag. Geget igo gii-onzaamibiiwag ingiw anishinaabeg.
Bezhig ogii-gaganoonaan wiijiiyan, wiindamawaad, "Oon
ingashkendam ji-waabamag a'aw waawaabiganoojiinsh.
Bakadenaagozi, giishkaabaagwenaagozi igaye. Niijii, miizh a'aw
waawaabiganoojiinsh bangii o'ow isa ishkodewaaboo."
"Ahaaw," ikido. Mii dash gii-mamood gaanda'igwaason,
mooshkinebadood, aabajitood i'iw ishkodewaaboo. Miish apii
gii-atood i'iw ishkodewaaboo imaa michisag.

[3] A'aw waawaabiganoojiinh ogii-waabandaan i'iw
gaanda'igwaason atemagak imaa michisag ezhi-ipitood.
Ogii-nandomaandaan i'iw. Mii dash geget igo gii-minikwed,
ziikaapidang akina. "Inashke," gii-ikido a'aw inini gii-
wiindamawaad wiijiiyan ji-miinaad ishkodewaaboo, "Geget
igo noonde-minikwe." "Aabiding miinawa miizh a'aw
waawaabiganoojiinsh ishkodewaaboo. Gidinawemaaganinaan
noonde-minikwe." "Ahaaw," ikido. Miinawaa ogii-siiginaan
ishkodewaaboo biindig i'iw gaanda'igwaasoning. Geget idash
miinawaa ogii-minikwen a'aw waawaabiganoojiinh. Nising
ogii-miinigoon ishkodewaaboo.

[4] Agaashiinyiwag waawaabiganoojiinyag. Mii i'iw gaa-onji-
gichi-giiwashkwebiid a'aw waawaabiganoojiinh. Gii-
kiiwashkwebitoo a'aw waawaabiganoojiinh ezhi-gagwe-
baamibatood. Eshkam igo gii-kiiwashkwebii. Eshkam
igo gaye gii-soongide'e. Mii apii gii-ikwanagwenid a'aw
waawaabiganoojiinh. Mii dash ezhi-ikidod, "Aandi ayaad
a'aw gaazhagens?"

That Old Mouse

[1] One time there was a pair of Indians from the Red Lake Indian reservation. The town where they lived was called Obaashiing. And they were always drinking there in one of those tarpaper shacks. Those two were always drunk.

[2] One time as they had a good buzz going, having a real brou-ha-ha, one guy saw a mouse running there on the floor. Those Indians had really been drinking too much. The one talked to his friend, telling him, "Oh I feel so bad to see that mouse. He looks hungry and thirsty. Friend, give that mouse some of this here whiskey." "All right," he says. Then he took a thimble and filled it up, using that whiskey. Then he put that whiskey there on the floor.

[3] That mouse saw that whiskey put there on the floor as he was scurrying by. He sniffed at it. Then he really drank, slurping down everything. "Look," said that guy who had told his friend to give him the whiskey, "He really needs a drink." "Give that old mouse the whiskey once again. Our relative needs a drink." "All right," he says. And he poured another shot of whiskey into that thimble. And that old mouse really drank it again. He was given whiskey three times.

[4] Mice are small. That's why that mouse got so drunk. That mouse was staggering all over when he tried to run. He was getting ever more inebriated. And he was getting increasingly brave. At that time, that mouse rolled up his shirtsleeves. Then he said, "Where's that cat?"

SUSAN JACKSON

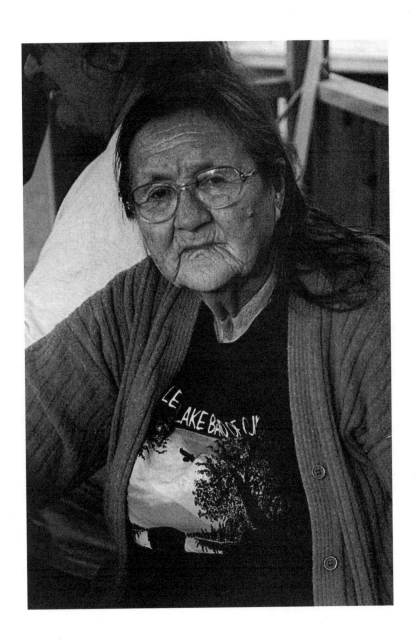

SUSAN JACKSON (b. 1925) is a perfect example of the positive effects of traditional Ojibwe living. *"Niwajebaadiz,"* she often says, in reference to this indisputable fact. *Wajebaadizi* means to be spry, peppy, and full of life. Most people don't believe her when she tells them that she is well over seventy years old. Her body is strong, her wits are sharp, and she rarely complains of any physical condition.

Susan's parents and grandparents taught her the value of hard work and a positive demeanor through their excellent examples of good character. As a small child, Susan chopped wood, hauled water, and shoveled snow. Even today she continues in these activities because, in her opinion, daily labors are good for the mind and body alike.

Susan grew up in and around the Leech Lake Reservation community of Chi-achaabaaning (Inger, Minnesota). Although there wasn't much money in her early days, her father worked hard at several jobs and the whole family hunted ducks, snared rabbits, and harvested wild rice. The entire community was heavily involved in traditional Ojibwe religious ceremonies, and the culture united her family and community in many fundamental ways.

Chi-achaabaaning has been home to Susan for most of her life, from childhood to the present day. Currently she spends much of her time watching grandchildren and traveling to support her ever-growing extended family. Frequently, she is asked to lend her skills and knowledge of the Ojibwe language to assist in the instruction of reservation youth at language camps and in other forums. The second of her stories in this anthology is a recording of one of her sessions, designed to teach reservation youth about the art of snaring rabbits—from dressing for a walk in the woods to eating the victuals after harvest.

With an easy laugh and a positive outlook, Susan is great company. *Wajebaadiziwin*, however, is only one of her endearing qualities. Humble, reserved, honest, and wise, she manifests the fruits of traditional culture and lifeways. As her knowledge of Ojibwe language and culture and her example of traditional virtue are increasingly recognized, Susan has come to be highly valued as a cultural resource for her family, community, reservation, and people.

Chi-achaabaan Naanaagadawendamaan

[1] *Inger* ingii-tazhi-ondaadiz, Chi-achaabaaning ezhinikaadeg.
Mii iwidi nimaamaa, miinawaa nimbaabaa gii-ayaawaad. Mii
iwidi ondakaaneziwaad, gaa-onji-gikendamaan akina gegoo
gii-pizindawagwaa nimaamaa miinawaa nookomis, gaye
gegoo gii-kagwejimagwaa gegoo waa-izhi-gikendamaan
gii-izhichigeyaan gii-ani-mindidoyaan. Miish onow namanj
gii-kikendamaan gegoo i'iw.
[2] Miinawaa go ingii-kagiibaadiz gii-agaashiinyiyaan iidog.
Gaawiin gegoo dibishkoo go ingii-pizikendanziin ji-wii-
kikendamaan. Baamaash naagaj i'iwe maagizhaa gaye
niizhwaasobiboonagiziyaan, miish o'ow dibishkoo gii-
naanaagadawendamaan ji-bizindawagwaa gegoo ekidowaad
miinawaa go gegoo gikinoo'amaagooyaan ji-ani-gikendamaan.
[3] Gaawiish wiin ingii-kikinoo'amaagoosii gegoo ji-gikendamaan
gegoo, akina gegoo. Ingii-wiidookawaa gaa-maamaayaan
aseked gaye. Mii imaa gii-kanawaabamag gii-wiidookawag.
Mii imaa gaa-onji-gikendamaan i'iw waa-izhichigeyaan.
Akina gegoo ingii-wiidookawaa nimaamaa. Gaawiin wiikaa
gegoo gii-anokiisii nimaamaa. Mii eta go gii-chiibaakwed.
[4] Akina gegoo niinawind ingii-nisimin ingiw niiwiijaan,
indinawemaag gayesh. Mii imaa ayaad bezhig nimisenh gaye
niin dash mii gaa-nisayeyaan. Mii minik gaa-ishkonewaad,
gaa-ishkoneyaang i'iw minik.
[5] Akinash gegoo ingii-wiidookawaanaan nimaamaa. Gaawiin
gegoo gichi-anokiisii. Miinawaa akina gegoo ingii-
izhichigemin. Imaa gaye nimbaabaa gii-anokiid, niinawind
akina gegoo ingii-izhichigemin. Ingii-kiishkiboojigemin,
biindigenising bigishkiga'iseyaang gaye, akina gegoo
bi-naadiyaang gaye akina gegoo. Mii eta go gii-pagidinised a'aw
nimaamaa jiibaakwed akina gegoo. Mii izhi-wiidookawag
nimaamaayiban gii-pimaadizid. Akina gegoo, gaawiin
ingii-pagidinaasiiwaanaan ge-gichi-anokiid gegoo.
[6] Mii eta go gii-anokiid nimbaabaam. Azhigwa nenitaawigid
indinawemaa, mii ezhi-wiijiwaad onow nimbaabaayan
gaa-anokiinid. Miish i'iw booch dagoshinowaad, mii booch,
maagizhaa go onaagoshig, miish i'iw akina gegoo anokiiyaang.
Mii gaa-izhi-wiidookawangid nimaamaa, miinawaa
nimbaabaayinaan.

SUSAN JACKSON

When I Think About Chi-achaabaan

[1] I was born in Inger, *Chi-achaabaaning* as it's called. My mother and father were over there. That's where they come from, where I got my knowledge of everything from, listening to my mother and grandmother and asking them what I wanted to know in what I did as I got bigger. That must be how I learned these things.

[2] And I must have been foolish when I was little. It was just like I didn't pay attention to the things I wanted to know. Then maybe after I was seven years old, then I started to reflect on things like this to listen to them in the things they said and the things I was taught to know.

[3] I wasn't just taught things to know them however, not everything. I helped my mother when she tanned hides. And there I would observe her as I helped her. That's how I knew what I wanted to do. I helped my mother with everything. My mother never took any kind of job. She only cooked.

[4] It was always the three of us, my siblings, and my relatives. There was my one older sister and myself and my older brother. That was how many of them survived, just that many of us survived.

[5] And we helped my mother with everything. She didn't work very hard. And we did everything. And my dad worked there, and we did everything [at home]. We sawed wood, chopping it into kindling as it was brought inside and everything; we hauled in everything. And my mother only hauled in wood and cooked everything. That's how I helped my mom when she was alive. In all things, we never let her work too hard.

[6] My dad was the only one who worked. Now as my [older brother] grew up, then he accompanied my father when he worked. Then when they arrived, maybe sometime in the evening, then we did all the work. That's how we helped my mother and my father.

[7] Gayesh nimaamaa gii-ishkwaa-ayaad, mii dibishkoo gaawiin aapiji nimaanendanziin gii-wani'ag nimaamaa. Imaa sa akina gegoo ingii-wiidookawaa. Mii gaa-onji-maanendanziwaan aapiji gii-wani'agin nimaamaa. Mii go gaye nimbaabaa gii-ayaadog, noomag gii-ani-bimaadizi niizhwaasimidana ashi niizh ganabaj gii-wani'angid nimbaabaa, mii i'iw. Gaawiin igaye ingii-maanendanziin iye gii-ishkwaa-ayaad nimbaabaa. Akina gegoo ingii-wiidookawaa. Ingii-wiidookawaa gii-pimaadizid. Nizhawenimaa sa go nimbaabaa gii-ayaad.

[8] Mii go noongom bimaadiziwaad miinawaa, gaawiin niin indaa-asaasiig imaa endazhi-ganawenimindwaa gichi-aya'aag. Niin igo indaa-bami'aag. Mii i'iw akiwenzii gaa-ayaawangid, Bezhigoogaabaw gii-izhinikaazo. Niin ingii-kanawenimaa gii-ani-gichi-aya'aawid. Gaye dash gaawiin ingii-pi-maanendanziin apii ishkwaa-ayaad akiwenzii. Mii gii-shawenimag gii-omishoomisinaan akiwenzii. Ingodwaak awashiime gii-taso-biboonagizid gii-nibod. Mii gaa-izhi-zhawenimag; zhawenimag sa go gichi-aya'aa.

[9] Gaawiin gegoo booch igo maajaayaan igo gegoo wiidookawag. Onow gaye niin niizhwaasimidana indaso-biboonagiz. "Gaawiin," indigoo dash wiin igo. Gaawiin indebwenimigoosii gaye. Niwiindamawaa endaso-biboonagiziyaan. Indaa-wiindamawaa, "Niwajebaadiz giiwenh o'owe."

[10] Mii sa ganabaj i'iw.

Aabadak Waaboozoo-nagwaaganeyaab

[1] Mii o'owe ayi'ii wii-agoodooyan, miinawaa akina gegoo ge-aabajitooyan—babiinzikawaagan, gimakizinan, giminjikaawanag, miinawaa ginagwaaganeyaab, mashkimod miinawaa aagimag. Mii imaa onow gaye ge-ozhiitaayan wii-agoodooyan. Miish imaa akina onow gaa-aabajitooyan.

[2] Miinawaa imaa azhigwa maajaayan, noopiming ezhaayan, nandawaabandaman iniw waaboozoo-miikanan, mii imaa ji-agoodooyan miikaman i'iw waaboozoo-miikanens. Miish imaa azhigwa gii-maamawising ginagwaaganeyaab. Mii imaa mitigoons ezhi-atooyan miikanens ayaamagak. Mii imaa ge-izhi-agoodooyan ginagwaagan. Miinawaa gii-kiizhiikaman imaa iye ginagwaagan gii-agoodeman imaa, maajaayan miinawaa geyaabi indawaaj nandawaabandaman.

[7] And then after my mother was gone, it was like I didn't feel bad about having lost my mom. I had always helped her there with everything. That's why I didn't feel overly sorrowful when I lost my mother. And my father must have been, he must have lived just a little past seventy-two perhaps when we lost my dad. And I didn't feel bad about it after my dad was gone either. I had helped him with everything. I had helped him while he was alive. I loved my dad while he was [here].

[8] And the ones still living today, I can't put them in a nursing home. I can only take care of them myself. There was one old man, he was called *Bezhigoogaabaw*. I looked after him myself as he became an elder. Then too I didn't feel bad about that old man's passing. I loved that old man as he was like a grandfather to me. He was over one hundred years old when he died. That's how much I loved him; I loved that old guy.

[9] And it's not [time] for me to leave as I'm helping him. And I'm seventy years old too. But I'm told, "No." And they don't believe me. I tell them how old I am. I should tell them, "I'm [still] spry."

[10] That must be it.

Using a Rabbit Snare Wire

[1] When you want to go snaring, this here is everything you will need to use—a coat, your moccasins, your mittens, and your snare wire, a rucksack, and snowshoes. And you have to get these things ready when you want to go snaring. That's everything you use.

[2] And there now when you leave, you go into the deep forest, looking for rabbit trails, and where you find that rabbit path, that's where you set your snare wire. And there you put your snare wire together. And you place sticks where the trail is. Then you hang your snare there. And when you've finished hanging your snare there, you leave again looking for more.

[3] Gaye a'aw gookooko'oo imaa nemadabid, mii a'aw waa-
kimoodimik iniw giwaabooziman imaa nagwaanad.
Waaboozoo-gimoodishki a'aw gookooko'oo.

[4] Miinawaa dash maajaayan imaa nawaj nandawaabandaman
iniw miikanensan, iniw ajina waa-agoodooyan. Mii go minik
ge-miikaman miikanensan.

[5] Mii miinawaa gii-nagwaanadwaa ingiw waaboozoog, mii ge-
izhi-dazhiikawadwaa. Gii-kiizhiikawadwaa ingiw waaboozoog,
miish imaa azhigwa ji-giizizwadwaa, da-atooyan nibi, imaa
ji-atooyan miinawaa awegonen go imaa waa-tagonaman
zhiiwitaagan, wiisagad igaye. Miish azhigwa ji-onji-giizizwad,
mii imaa gii-kiizizwad dash a'aw waabooz miinawaa awegonen
imaa waa-tagonaman, miinawaa go imaa ji-atooyan imaa nawaj
wiisiniyeg imaa adoopowin. Onaaganan imaa atewan,
emikwaanensan gaye badaka'igan. Mii imaa wii-wiisiniyeg. Mii
azhigwa waabooz gii-amweg imaa awegonen imaa
gaa-tagoziyeg, opiniig igaye.

[6] Mii dash gii-ishkwaa-wiisiniyan, mii i'iw ge-izhinaagwak o'ow
gimisad onzaam niibowa wiisiniyan gaa-piikojiiyan. Mii i'iw
ge-izhi-aanizhiitaman wii-wiisiniyan.

[7] Mii go gaye wii-kiiyoseyan gaye, mii go omaa gaye naasaab igo
ge-biizikonayeyan gaa-piizikaman wii-kiiyoseyan wii-izhi-
babaa-nandawaabamad a'aw waawaashkeshi. Mii mewinzha
gaa-izhichiged anishinaabe gii-maajaad wii-wiisinid, giiyosed.
Mii go gaye naasaab iniwe giigoonyan wii-amwaad; miish igo
maajaad o-bagida'waad imaa, jiimaaning boozid. Mii imaa gaye
gaa-ondinang mewinzha anishinaabe gii-wiisinid.

[3] And [maybe] that owl's sitting there, wanting to steal
the rabbits you snare. That owl is a chronic rabbit thief.

[4] And again you leave, looking for more of those rabbit trails,
as that's where you want to set snares. Then that's as many
trails as you'll find.

[5] And those rabbits you snared, they must be dressed out.
When you finish those rabbits, now then you cook them,
putting in water, and you put in there whatever you want to
mix in there, salt and pepper. Now that's how you cook him,
and you cook that rabbit there and whatever you want to
add in with it, and you put it there on the table so you all
can eat well. Plates are put there, spoons and a fork. That's
where you all will eat. And now you all eat that rabbit there
and whatever you all added in, potatoes too.

[6] Then after you eat, this is how that belly of yours will look,
from overeating; you got a potbelly. That's how you finish
your meal when you're going to eat.

[7] And when you want to go hunting too, here it's the same
thing too, as you shall get dressed [and,] having donned
what you'll go hunting with, you'll go around searching for
that deer. That's how the Indian did things when he left for
what he wanted to eat, hunting. And it's the same if he
wanted to eat fish; then he left, going over and setting net
there, embarking in a canoe. Long ago the Indian got what
he ate from there too.

HARTLEY WHITE

HARTLEY WHITE (b. 1925), whose Indian name is *Zhaawanose* (Walks from the South), is a conspicuous figure in language revitalization efforts at the Leech Lake Reservation. A highly principled man, he advocates issues he believes in loudly and passionately, without regard for the obstacles that sometimes block his path.

Hartley was raised at Sugar Point on the Leech Lake Indian Reservation, an area steeped in the history of Ojibwe struggle for land and lifeways. The entire area of Bear Island and the surrounding mainland lakeshore was a hub of commerce, politics, and religious ceremony for the reservation throughout the nineteenth and early twentieth centuries. The last battle between the United States Army and Indians occurred at Sugar Point in 1898, as soldiers came to arrest the local chief *Bagone-giizhig*. A shoot-out ensued in which the Ojibwe emerged victorious, killing a policeman and a handful of soldiers without casualties on their side. The moment is remembered with great pride by Hartley, whose grandfather participated in that event, eventually being captured by army troops and interrogated about his role.

Hartley grew up immersed in the oral history, legend, and language of his forefathers at Sugar Point. He learned a great deal not only about history, but also about the prophecies many Ojibwe elders spoke of during his youth. All of that information was ingrained in him, and, especially in recent years, Hartley has shared that wisdom and knowledge with others interested in Ojibwe language, history, and prophecy.

Hartley's teenage years and early adulthood were difficult. He struggled with addiction to alcohol and the problems it caused. Hartley eventually realized that alcoholism was a pernicious disease tearing at his family, friends, and people. As an adult, Hartley began a healing process that brought renewed faith, happiness, and humor to his entire family. That endeavor would convince Hartley of the importance of sobriety, family, and connection to community for the long-term healing of all Ojibwe people. Since that time he has been active in efforts to teach reservation youth about traditional lifeways, Ojibwe language, and sobriety. He served on the Leech Lake Tribal Council and, more recently, on the school board for the Bug-O-Nay-Geshig School, which serves Indian youth throughout the region. He frequently volunteers his time at language camps and at educational forums. He also raises his grandchildren and in all endeavors strives to keep the Ojibwe language, history, and prophecy alive for all people.

Onizhishin o'ow Bimaadiziwin

[1] Boozhoo anishinaabeg, indinawemaaganidog. O'ow isa gagwejimigooyaan ji-gaagiigidoyaan ji-nisidotamoonagwaag sa go abinoojiinyag noongom niibowa gegwaadagitoojig, gagwaadagii'igoowaad o'ow isa gaye niin gaa-kagwaadagii'igooyaan.

[2] Akawe go niwanendaan igo ojibwewi-izhinikaazoyaan. Zhaawanose indizhinikaaz. Mii gaa-miizhid niyawe'enh nitam gaa-tazhi-izhinikaanid gii-igooyaan. Nookomis miinawaa nimishoomis ingii-nitaawigi'igoo o'ow wayeshkad o'ow gii-ondaadiziyaan. Mii imaa gii-makandwewaad niiyawish. Geget gii-sanagad o'ow gii-pi-abinoojiinyiwiyaan igo. Niibowa ingii-noondawaag chi-aya'aag dazhindamowaad ezhi-zanagak akina gegoo gii-noojichigaadeg gaye miijim. Noongom idash, mii eta go adaawewigamigong izhaang adaawed. Gaawiin mewinzha—gii-kiiyosewag ininiwag. Ikwewag idash weweni gii-chiibaakwewaad gii-paamenimaawaad abinoojiinyan.

[3] Miish o'ow waa-tazhindamaan dawaaj igo gaye niin gaa-kagwaadagii'igooyaan, mii i'iw minikwewin maanaadak. Giniijaanisinaanig niibowa anishaa ji-gii'igoowaad, nisidiwaad, maagizhaa gaye wiinawaa nisidizowaad. Ashi niswi indaso-biboonagiz apii maajiitaayaan gaye niin gii-oshki-minikweyaan o'ow zhoominaaboo, mii i'iw. Mii imaa gaye niin gaa-maajiikamaan i'iw minikwewin. Bijiinag-sh niimidana endaso-biboonagiziyaan, mii bijiinag maagizhaa indaa-ikid gii-aabaakawiziyaan, gaa-aabaakawiziyaan o'ow isa, anishinaa ji-gii'igooyaan o'ow gaye minikwewin, mii i'iw. Ingii-wiidige igaye. Niizhwaaswi abinoojiinyag—naanan ikwezensag, niizh gwiiwizensag ingiw—ingii-nitaawigi'aanaanig. Mii ongow gaa-inigaa'agig o'ow isa minikwewin apane gii-tazhiikamaan.

[4] Gaawiin. Gaawiin wiikaa gaye nimikwenimaasii awenen a'aw manidoo. Ongow nimishoomis, nookomis gaa-izhi-gikenimaawaad weweni bamenimag a'aw manidoo. Ingii-wani'aa dash a'aw. Ingii-wanendaan. Mii i'iw minikwewin maji-manidoo ezhichigemagak.

[5] Noongom idash moozhag indazhindaan bijiinag gaa-ayendamaan i'iw minikwewin zhawenimagwaa sa ongow waasookangig eni-gaa'idizowaad eni-gaa'aawaad gaye wiinawaa odabinoojiinyiimiwaan. Apegish gegoo, inga-

This Is a Good Way of Life

[1] Hello Indians, my relatives. I have been asked to speak so that the children can understand me, the many who are having difficulties today, suffering through things as I suffered myself.

[2] First of all I forget my Indian name. My name is *Zhaawanose*. It was given to me by my first namesake who named me I've been told. I was raised by my grandmother and my grandfather at first when I was born. So I was taken there. Things were really hard when I was a child. I heard a lot of elders talking about how tough everything was, even getting food. Today they only go to the supermarket to buy things. But not a long time ago—the men hunted. The women were good cooks and took care of the children.

[3] I want to talk about how I was made to suffer through alcoholism. Many of our children are told about this in vain, as they kill one another and maybe even kill themselves. I was thirteen years old when I first started drinking wine, that's all. I starting my drinking habit right there. I was forty years old when I first said I would sober up and get well, and be talked to about drinking. I got married too. Seven children—five girls, two boys—we raised. They were the ones I made suffer through the drinking I was always involved in.

[4] No. I never remember the Spirit, whichever one. My grandmother and grandfather knew him so well and took care of that Spirit. But I've lost him. I forgot it. That drinking is the devil's work.

[5] But today I always talk about when I first started to disapprove of that drinking because I feel for the abusers of alcohol who punish themselves and inflict such pain on their children. My hope is this, I'll say. I hope I'll be able to

ikid. Apegish gashkitooyaan ji-daanginangiban ji-izhi-
inigoondebinagiban a'aw bemaadizid ji-booniikang o'ow isa
gegwaadagitoowaad gegwaadagii'igoowaad gaye wiinawaa sa
ji-nandawaabandamowaad aandi o'ow dibendaagoziwaad o'ow
dibishkoo omaa akiing. Niitaa, akina endaso-bezhigooyang
ingii-miinigoomin, ingii-pagidinigoomin gaye giinawind.
Gaawiin igo gidayaasiimin gegoo gomaa. Ayaamagad gigii-
izhi-miinig a'aw manidoo gaye giin ge-bima'adooyan ge-
ani-waabanda'ad sa anishinaabe bemaadizid miinawaa a'aw
wiijabinoojiinyiimag. Miish i'iw apane, gaawiin
noondawidwaa bizindawagwaa weweni ongow chi-
anishinaabeg, chi-aya'aag gaagiigidowaad. Mii go
gaye wiinawaa ge-izhi-inaaboo'iwewaaban ongow.

[6] Endaso-giizhig akina gegoo bakaan gigii-kikendaan,
mii i'iw endaso-giizhig apane gikendaasowin. Mii i'iw akeyaa
bimaadiziyan. Mii gomaa ji-naazikaman ji-noondaman ji-
waabandaman. Miinawaa maada'ookii a'aw manidoo. Mii i'iw
akeyaa nandawaabandaman wenizhishing. Mii gaawiin wii-
ani-maanaadak. Gegoo bizindawiyaang omaa zhebaa a'aw
bezhig chi-aya'aa mindimooyenh gaagiigidoyaang i'iw gomaa
anooj gii-ikidowaad ongow anishinaabeg wiijii'idiwaad,
anooj ikidowaad o'ow gaa-injinawetaadiziwaad chi-
baabaapiwaad. Noongom idash gaawiin nitaa-izhichigesii.
Mii go onzaamakamig ji-niiwani'wigoowaaban o'ow awiiya
bisoomak. Gaawiin dash, mii i'iw anishinaabe bemiwidood
baapiwin miinawaa menwendang menwaanigozid.
Miish giishpin dazhiikaman o'ow maji-ayaawish o'ow gaye
zegaswaajigaadeg anooj endoodaagooyang anishinaabewiyang.

[7] Mii o'ow ge-ani-gaa'igoowing giishpin wii-
kikinoo'amawaasiwangidwaa ongow gidabinoo
jiinyiiminaanig weweni gikinoo'amaadiiwigamigong
ji-izhaawaad ji-gabe-gikendaasowaad sa gaye wiinawaa
weweni sa ji-ani-bimaadiziwaad ji-gikendamowaad sa
weweni gaye obimaadiziwiniwaa weweni go ji-anokiiwaad.
Gaawiin wiin, imaa ge-dazhi-inigaaziwaad.

[8] Miish o'ow akeyaa endaso-giizhig goshkoziwaanen go
mikwenimagig ge-inigaazojig abinoojiinyag. Mii o'ow
minikwewin wenjishkaamagak gii-inigaa'aawaad onow.
Niibowa ongow ayaawag ongow mindimooyenyag,
akiwenziiyag zhewendaagoziwaad sa go inenimaawaad

reach them to convince the people to start over, to abstain
from this suffering, from that which makes them suffer,
and they will look for their real place of belonging here on
earth. *Niitaa*, we've all been gifted, every one of us, and we've
been put here ourselves. We're not here for very long. But
there is something that Spirit gave you to carry with you
so you can show the living Indians and their children.
Although not all the time, they do hear me, just as I listened
to these elders in a good way when the old people spoke.
And they will echo those thoughts themselves.

[6]   Every day you learn something different, every day a new
piece of knowledge. That's the way you live your life. Then
you approach those things a little more to hear them, to see
them. And the Spirit shares. That's how you search for the
good things. Nothing bad will come of it. You were listening to us here this morning, that one elder woman and I,
speaking about the different things Indians said when
they were together, saying all kinds of things, teasing and
laughing so hard. But today he's not so good at doing that.
When somebody wants to beat someone up it's usually an
overreaction because of a misunderstanding. But no, the
Indian has a sense of humor and likes to have a good
time. But if you are involved with bad things like smoking
marijuana, those of us who are Indian do [bad] things to
one another.

[7]   We are going to be very pitiful if we don't teach these
children of ours to go to school in a good way, and to get
good college educations for themselves too, so that they can
lead good lives, so they can learn things in their lifetimes to
acquire good jobs. If not, they are going to be poor and
pitiful.

[8]   Every day when I get up I remember the kids who are going
to have a hard time. It's the start of this drinking that has
made them so pitiful. There are lots of these old women and
these old men who are blessed when they think about their
children all the time, when they talk [to them]. We don't like

onow odabinoojiinyiimiwaan apane gaagiigidowaad.
Mii go ezhi-zhingitaagoziyaang. Aaningodinong
ingiikaamigoonaanig abinoojiinyag. Indabinoojiinyiiminaanig
gaawiin onisidotanziinaawaan. Bijiinag maagizhaa gaye
wiinawaa da-goshkoziwag, da-aabaakawiziwag. Mii sa o'ow gaa-
tibaajimang, gaa-tazhindang wa'aw mindimooyenh miinawaa
akiwenzii o'ow ji-izhiwebak. Mii o'ow waa-waabandamaan
noongom. Mewinzha ko gii-kaagiigidod a'aw nimishoomis
a'aw gaye nookomis o'ow ge-bi-izhiwebak.

[9] Enh indanishinaabensidog! Mii noongom waabandamaan
endaso-giizhig o'ow isa gaa-tazhindamowaad ongow chi-
anishinaabeg. Gegoo noongom geyaabi noongom
odazhindaanaawaa. Zhawendaagoziwag zhawenimigoowaad
go anishinaabeg sa i'iw. Maagizhaa ogii-igoon o'ow.
Enaanimiziwaad abinoojiinyag ongow gaye anishinaabensag.
"Odinigayendaanaawaan. Nizhingenimigoog.
Indinigayenimigoog," mii ekidowaad. Gaawiin giishpin
inigayenimigwaapinood nimishoomis i'iw a'aw, nookomis.
Gaawiin da-gaagiigidosiiwag. Mii go apane enda-
zhawenimaawaad wii-kagwe-giikimaawaad, ji-ani-
gikendamowaad awenen o'ow isa mino-bimaadiziwin
eyaamagak omaa.

[10] Mii i'iw apane ji-dazhindamaan gabe-ayi'ii. Ingii-
kagwaadagii'igoo, ingii-kitimaagii'igoo iniw minikwewinish
i'iw. Noongom idash ezhi-minwaanendamaan miinawaa
minwaagoziyaan waabamagwaa niijanishinaabeg,
indinawemaaganag chi-baabaapiyaang. Gayesh indazhimigoo
apane gii-kiiwashkwebiiyaan. Ingii-inigaayenimigoog. Aaniish
naa, gaawiin maanoo niin ingii-toodaaz. Gaawiin awiiya
bakaan.

[11] Apegish, mii sa i'iw noongom apegish awegwen o'ow ge-
bizindamogwen o'ow gaagiigidoyaan sa ongow abinoojiinyag
weshki-bimaadizijig gaye gii-pizindamowaad sa go gaa-izhi-
gagwaadagii'igoowaad sa o'ow endazhindamaan. Geget,
geget indabinoojiinyiimidog! Onizhishin. Onizhishin o'ow
bimaadiziwin. Giishpin weweni geget wii-inaazikameg
wendinameg gidaa-nandawaabandaanaawaa—gego wiin
onow ziiginigewigamigong, gego gaye nandawaabandameg
o'ow gaye zagaswaadameg. Mii o'ow gaye gii-inaazikaagooyeg.

to use that [alcohol]. Sometimes the children argue with us. Our own children don't understand these things. Maybe when they first get up they're just sobering up. We lectured like that old woman and that old man talk about what will happen in the future. This is what I want to see today. A long time ago my grandfather used to talk, and my grandmother too, about what was going to happen.

[9]   Yes young Indians! Now I used to see these elders talk about this every day. And now today they are still talking about it. The Indians are blessed and loved. Maybe they were told this. But these young Indians are intimidated. "They disapprove of them. They dislike me. They disapprove of me," that's what they say. But my grandfather never expressed disapproval or my grandmother. They wouldn't say such things. They just love them so much that they want to preach to them so that they'll know about the good life that is right here.

[10]   This is what I'm talking about all the time. I really suffered and I was so pitiful with that alcoholism. But today I am able to have a good time and laugh with my fellow Indians and relatives while maintaining a clear mind. And I still get talked about from when I was a drunk. Some people disliked me. Well, I let myself do those things. Nobody else did.

[11]   I wish, that is, today I hope that whomever would happen to hear what I'm saying here, like these kids and young ones, will listen to what I'm saying about their current state of suffering. Really, truly my children! It is good. This way of life is good. If you pick it up in a good way you will find everything you are searching for—not in these bars, and not if you are looking for it in a haze of smoke. But it will come to you.

[12] Miish i'iw minik eta go noongom. Apegish geget bizindawiyeg bizindawegwaa sa gaye ongow chi-anishinaabeg baa-gaagiigidowaad. Maanoo ji-bizindameg gegoo imaa gigii-ondinaawaa. Apegish gagwejimagiban Gizhe-manidoo, Manidoo zhawenimineg maanoo. Miigwech.

Ishkwaakiiwan

[1] Ahaaw sa. Ninaanaagadawendam onow. Moozhag igo nimikwendaan iko gaa-pi-izhi-gagiikimiwaad ingiw a'aw nimishoomis gaa-nitaawigi'id gaa-namadabiwaad ingiw gaagiigidowaad. Mii baanimaa mawadisidiwaad, mii sa i'iw gaa-tazhindamowaad iko niibowa waa-ani-izhiwebak gaagiigidowaad iko. Miish wiin noongom naanaagadawendamaan i'iw gaa-izhi-dazhiikwewaad gaa-izhi-gaagiigidowaad o'ow apii gii-maajii-dazhindamowaad ishkwaakiiwang. Gaawiin wiikaa o'ow noondawaasii i'iw gaa-tazhindang. Wiinawaa dash ongow gegaa go apane go owii-tazhindaanaawaa. Maagizhaa gaye wiinawaa miinawaa. Namanj iidog.

[2] Aaniish naa, nimishoomis gaa-nitaawigi'id ingii-peshwa'aa a'aw apane, namanj igo ezhaad dino wiin. Miish igo gaa-tazhindamowaad—ongow chimookomaanag akina gegoo omaa mamoowaad o'ow akii—miskwaabik, ashkikomaan, baashkizwaabik, awegodogwen igo dino akina gegoo. Gaawiin gegoo omaa odazhi-atoosiinaawaa. Miish igo akiwenziiyag, ikidowag, "Aaniin dana? Ingoding maagizhaa da-naangan o'ow aki. Mii iwidi ge-apizoyang. Hey mii sa anishinaabedog, mii iwidi ge-o-naangiziyang." Aaniish gaa-izhi-gikendamowaad iwidi ji-izhidebining. Aanawi dazhimindwaa. Gaawiin gegoo ogii-kikendanziinaawaan. Gaye niin, mii iko gaa-wanendamaan o'ow jibwaa-ani-atenig. Namanj ikidoyaan. Gaa gegoo ogii-kikendanziinaawaa. Namanj ezhiwebak.

[3] Anooj noongom izhiwebad. Miinawaa bezhig gaa-tazhindamowaad, mii sa gii-ishkwaakiiwang a'aw bezhig akiwenzii. Anooj gegoo da-izhiwebad. Anooj gaye ongow awesiinyag gaye izhinaagoziwag. Miinawaa go anooj bakaan igo da-izhichigewag ongow awesiinyag, mii go gaye makwag,

[12]   And that's all for today. I truly hope that you listen to me
       and listen to these elders in what they say. Let yourselves
       listen and you will get [a good life] from there. In this wish
       I ask the Great Spirit [for a favor], that the Spirit may bless
       you all. Thank you.

The Apocalypse

[1]   All right. I reflect about these things. I always remember
      what they used to preach to me about, the people who sat
      around and talked [with] my grandfather who had raised
      me. After they visited one another they used to talk a lot
      about what would happen in the future as they conversed.
      Today I think about how they preached there, talking
      this way as they began to address the issue of apocalypse.
      Nobody is ever heard of who talked about that. But these
      people wanted to talk about that almost constantly. Maybe
      there [are] others. I don't know.

[2]   Well, I was always near my grandfather who had raised me,
      wherever he might go. That's what they talked about—
      how the white people were taking everything from this
      earth here—copper bouillon, lead, uranium, anything and
      everything. They never put anything [back in] here. Then
      the old men, they said, "What does this portend? Sometime
      maybe this earth will become light in weight. Then we'll just
      go flying off [into space] over there. Hey Indians, then
      we'll be weightless over there." How did they know about
      the condition of the ozone way over there? [People] were
      made aware of this though. They didn't know anything [for
      certain]. Me too, I used to forget about this before it came
      o be so. I'm unsure of what to say. [People] didn't know
      anything [for certain]. Events are uncertain.
[3]   Now many things are happening. And that one old man was
      talking [with] them about the apocalypse. Many things shall
      come to be. And these animals will look [different] too. And
      these animals will come to do many things differently, the
      bear, and the deer—all kinds. It must be four years now that

waawaashkeshiwag—anooj igo. Miish i'iw noongom maagizhaa
niiyo-biboon waabamagwaa ongow bineshiinyag. Ganabaj
ingii-tibaajim i'iw awasonaago gii-waabamagwaa ingiw
bineshiinyag. Gaawiin wiikaa niwaabamaasiig. Wayaa akina
onizhishiwag, mii ganawaabaminaagoziwaad.

[4]   Miinawaa a'aw nigig. Gaawiin wiikaa niwaabamaasii
ji-gwaashkwanid a'aw. Mii eta go niizhing waabamag
gwaashkwanid. Mii eta go bimoodedood dibishkoo o'ow.
Mii anooj. Miish i'iw mekwendamaan iko i'iw. Mii ganabaj
igo beshowang.

[5]   Miish azhigwa ekidowaad, "Haa noozis. Ozhiitaan. Ozhiitaan
weweni. Ozhiitaan. Gaawiin gigikendanziin apii ge-maajaayan."
Gaawiin ingii-nisidotawaasiin. "Maajaayan," ingii-inendam iko.
"Giwii-ikonaazhikaw. Niwii-saagidinaash. Ogimaa wiijaan."
Mii gaa-inendamaan. "Gaawiin gonaa. Omaa ozhiitaan.
Mii dawaaj ji-gaganoonad a'aw manidoo. Mii go gaye wii-
pizindanziwan, gaawiin giga-izhibaadizisii." Ingii-tebinig a'aw
nimishoomis.

[6]   Ingii-izhinaajitoon i'iw nimbimaadiziwin. Mii o'ow
minikwewinish. Noongom eyaag niibowa ezhinaajiigwang
miinawaa go zagaswaajigaadeng. Mii gaye gaa-
tazhindamowaad. Aandiish gaa-ondinamowaad i'iw
gaa-kikendamowaad o'ow akina? Miish noongom
waabandamaan i'iw.

[7]   Inzegiz iko aaningodinong aaniish ge-izhichigeyaan
inandomag a'aw manidoo. Mii gaye omaa bi-dagoshinaan
niwaabamaa maajaayaan biindaakoojigeyaan gii-miizhid
i'iw naanaagadawendamowin. "Weweni giga-ganoonig
a'aw giijanishinaabe." Mii go gaye ji-gikinootawid
igo ji-wiidookawag a'aw. Wii-nibwaakaa a'aw wiin gii-
kwayakosidamawid i'iw wanigiizhweyaan gegoo i'iw
da-biimendang.

[8]   Miish i'iw. Ate go noongom o'ow. Ogikendaanaawaadog anooj
o'ow akiing. Ganabaj gii-pimisemagad, amanj igo. Inashke
iwidi zhaawanong zoogipog. Gisinaamagad. Gaawiin wiikaa
gii-izhiwebasinoon. Mii eta omaa gaa-tazhi-gisinaamagak.
Miish noongom o'ow. Gemaa gichi-aabawaa go inashke go
biboong. Ishkwaa-aabawaag, gaawiin aapiji gisinaasinoon. Mii
iwidi gii-kisinaag i'iw zhaawanong. Mii iw.

I've been [closely] observing these birds. Maybe I talked about that the day before yesterday, about my observations of those birds. I never see them. They're all so beautiful when they are viewed.

[4]   And that otter. I never see him jumping [as usual]. Only twice have I seen him jump. He just hobbles along like this. It's a variety of things. Then that's what I used to remember about it. So maybe [their predictions] are near [fulfillment].

[5]   So then they say, "Grandchild. Prepare. Prepare properly. Get ready. You don't know when the time will come for you to leave." I didn't understand him. "When you leave," I used to think. "You want to chase me off. I'm going to be evicted. The chief's son." That's what I thought. "Not at all. Make preparations here. It is best for you to talk to the Spirit. And if you don't listen, your life won't unfold that way." My grandfather grabbed me.

[6]   [But] I sort of squandered my life. That's due to this alcoholism. Now today there are so many drugs, so much marijuana. They had talked about [and predicted] this too. From where did they acquire their knowledge of all these things? I see it now.

[7]   Sometimes I'm scared about what I will do when I call upon the Spirit. So when I arrive here I see myself leaving [only after] I make an offering of the reflections he gave me. "Your fellow Indian people will address you in a good way." So too have I been taught to help them. So they follow my instructions in order for me to help them. They become smarter themselves and even correct me when I make a mistake speaking about something so that no bad thoughts will come of it.

[8]   That's it. This is where it is now. They must have known a lot about this earth. Maybe it is flying off its axis, I don't know. You see it snows in the south. It's cold. This never happened. It used to be cold only here. That's how it is now. You see it's also very warm [here] in the winter. After the warm season, it just doesn't get very cold. Yet it sure got cold over there in the south. That's it.

[9]   Namanj igo debwewaad ongow akiwenziiyag. Indinendam.
       Mii go ombibizowaad igo chimookomaanag igo gii-kagwe-
       gikendamowaad i'iw aaniindi. Giishpin a'aw manidoo
       gii-nandawenimaad onow bemaadizinijin gichi-aya'aan,
       odaa-gii-asaan iwidi, iwidi gii-tibendaagoziwaad. Gego
       babaamenimaakegon. Inashke dash o'ow maajiibideg i'iw.
       Obiindwekaminaan enigok baashkised o'ow ombibizod a'aw.
       Miish i'iw mashkawiziimagak o'ow babaamendamaan iko
       mikwendamaan akina o'ow gaa-mamigaadeg akiing.
       Mii i'iw naanganigwak. Miish wenji-onabiseg o'ow.
       Miish i'iw gii-noondawagwaa ko ingiw gichi-anishinaabeg
       dibaajimowaad. Inashke go awedi wayaabishkindibed
       noongom gaye wiin; mii go gaa-izhi-noondawag a'aw
       gii-nitaawigi'igooyaang.

[10]   "Maagizhaa," imbaapaagindibe'wig nimishoomis, "haa noozis,
       maagizhaa gaawiin niin igo indisaabandanziin." Miish
       noongom waabandamaan. Ingiiwitaa. Gaawiin wiikaa wii-
       noondawaasii ji-gaagiigidod wiin eta go imaa gaa-tazhi-
       gikinoo'amaadiing. Gaawiin indinendam. Miziwe ganabaj igo
       gichi-anishinaabe ogikendaan igo.

[11]   Miinawaa aabiding a'aw akiwenzii bezhig, ingoding dani-
       bimaadizing. Maagizhaa ongow gwiiwizensag, ongow
       abinoojiinyag gaawiin ingiw ogikendanziinaawaa.
       Namanj iidog. Bakiteshkamoogwaadog. Mii i'iw. Gaawiin
       bizindanziiwag. Mii i'iw bezhig wanitoowaad igo debwewin
       ji-ganawaabanji'iyaang. Owidi ishkweyaang mewinzha, namanj
       igo apii, mii imaa gii-maajii-izhi-noojichigaadeg o'ow
       gidinwewininaan miinawaa go gidanishinaabewiwininaan.
       Miish i'iw. Ingii-kiiwitaabii'aamin omaa noongom nawaj
       William Bobolink miinawaa gaye *George Goggleye*. Mii i'iw
       ishkweyaang gii-inendamaan.

[12]   Aaniin iidog apii gaa-wanitooyang i'iw
       gidanishinaabewiwininaan igo gaye inweyang?
       World War II. Mii imaa. Gaa-izhinaazhikaagooyaambaan
       iwidi gii-o-zhimaaganishiiwiyaan abinoojiinyag eta
       go zhaaganaashiimowag. Omaa dash gii-maajaayaan
       gii-ojibwemowag niibowa go abinoojiinyag, mii go akina.
       Noongom dash mii eta go zhaaganaashiimowaad. Miish i'iw
       imaa gii-miikamaan i'iw *World War II*, *1940s*. Mii imaa
       gii-wanising.

[9] These old men probably speak the truth. I think so. So the
white people fly up into space striving to know about
different places. If the Spirit wanted these people [or] other
beings over there, he would have placed them so, and they
would have belonged over there. Don't worry about them.
And you see this [space shuttle] starts off like that. He
enters a new realm when he blasts off and speeds up in the
sky like this. So my habitual worrying about this is very
sincere, as I remember how all of this was stripped from the
earth. So it's being hollowed out. So that's why its orbit is
altered like this. That's what I used to hear those elders say
about it. You see that one white hair himself now; so too did
I hear him when we were growing up.

[10] "Maybe," my grandfather tapped me on the head, "well
grandchild, maybe I won't live to see it." So today I see it all
around. Nobody is ever heard to say that. That teaching was
only given there. I think not. Maybe the elders know this
everywhere.

[11] And once that one old man, one time he lived a rich life.
Maybe these boys, these children, don't know about this.
I don't know. These things come back on them. That's it.
They don't listen. That's one truth they're losing, to observe
us. Over here in former times long ago, I don't know what
time, this language of ours and our Indian way of being were
starting to be under pressure. That's it. We used to sit in a
circle here more those days [with] William Bobolink and
also George Goggleye. That's what I thought formerly.

[12] When did we lose our Indian ways and our language? World
War II. Right there. At the time I was sent over there to be
a soldier the kids only spoke English. But here when I left
many of the children spoke Ojibwe, all of them. But now
they only speak English. I discovered that there in World
War II, 1940s. It was lost there.

[13] Gaawiin dash wiikaa ingii-wiikwajitoosiimin. Mii go bijiinag azhigwa maagizhaa endaso-niiyo-biboonagak aapiji go wiikwajitooyang wii-kagwe-gikinoo'amawindwaa ongow niniijaanisinaanig, noozhishenyinaanig ji-ojibwemowaad, ji-gikendamowaad awenen ayaawiwaad.

[14] Inashke go gaa-ikidoyaan awasonaago: ginwenzh ingii-tazhitaa i'iw gegaa gii-izhinaajii'igooyaan i'iw ishkodewaaboo. Mii a'aw maji-manidoo ayaang i'iw minikwewin. Mii eta go gaa-onji-anokiiyaan, gii-wiikwajitooyaan miinawaa go goshkoziyaan giziibiigiisaginige-giizhigak. Mii dash i'iw, da-gagwaadagizowag ongow giniijaanisinaanig da-gagwe-mikamowaad i'iw debwewin, debweng gichi-aya'aa. Gichi-weweni, gichi-weweni go niwiikwajitoo. Gaawiin gaye indoojaanimtaasiin igo. Gaawiin gegoo niwii-pishikoshkanziin. Akina go o'ow ingagwe-gikendaan. Gaawiin gabe-ayi'iin.

[15] Mii ko gaa-wanendamaan iko wii-kaganoonag a'aw manidoo. Hey, aaniindi ge-onji-bizindawid? Biinish ingii-pi-izhibaase imaa gaa-miikawag gii-wiidookawid iwidi niin izhi-ayaayaan weweni ge-izhi-ayaayaan. Miish ezhi-wenipaning i'iw gagiibaadiziyaan.

[16] Mii gaye noondawiyeg anooj igo indikidogwen omaa keyaa. Mii i'iw mekwendamaan iniw; nimishoomis weweni minawaanigwendang gegoo wii-ani-maazhendang bijiinag wiin i'iw. "Gidaa-dibendaan. Mii eta go i'iw gibimaadiziwin igo. Weweni, mii i'iw ge-bima'adooyan minawaanigoziwin. Gego babaa-maazhendangen. Mii imaa gii-kagwejichigeg. Ingoding da-ani-bimaadiziyan booch giga-nagishkawaag. Giga-nandawenimaag ingiw manidoog. Gego dabasenimaaken a'aw giijanishinaabe. Mii go dibishkoo gaye wiin ezhi-apiitendaagozid gaye wiin."

[17] Ahaaw. Mii i'iw minik. Haaw miigwech nimishoomis. Mii izhid iniw gibaakwa'amaan. Miigwech ge-bizindawid.

[13] And we never made an effort. This might be the first time now that we are making a sincere effort, endeavoring to teach these children of ours, our grandchildren, to speak Ojibwe, to know who they are.

[14] You see [it's like] I said the other day: I was there for a long time when I almost ruined my life with that alcohol. The devil owns that drinking. That's the only reason I worked, as I made that endeavor and got up on Saturdays. And that's it, these children of ours will suffer as they try to find the truth, the spoken truth of the elder. In the best way, in the best way possible, I try. And I'm not busy. I don't want to overlook anything. I try to learn about everything. Not all things.

[15] I used to forget about when I wanted to address the Spirit. Hey, why would he listen to me? Up until then I was in a [vicious] circle there when I found he helped me over there in my condition and I was well. It had been so easy for me to be foolish.

[16] And as you all listen to me I'm saying all kinds of things here. That's what I remember; my grandfather who was usually happy about things came to feel bad for the first time. [He said], "You should own it. This is your only life. In a good way, that's how you should carry that humor. Don't go around with a bad demeanor. That's what should be striven for there. Once in your lifetime you will certainly meet them. You will want those Spirits. Don't have a low estimation of your fellow Indian. And it's like he is held in the highest regard himself."

[17] All right. That's enough. Thank you grandfather. So he tells me when I bring something to a close. Thanks [to him] for listening to me.

PORKY WHITE

WALTER "PORKY" WHITE (b. 1919), whose Indian name is *Gegwe-dakamigishkang* (Prancing Horse), is, like his nephew Hartley, a prominent leader in recent efforts to revitalize the Ojibwe language and culture at Leech Lake. Even as an octogenarian and having endured a recent stroke, he travels tirelessly throughout the United States and Canada to teach, lead, and participate in traditional Ojibwe religious ceremonies, pow-wows, and educational forums.

Like most people of his generation at Sugar Point, Porky grew up immersed in the Ojibwe language and culture. Yet, even at a very young age he exhibited unique qualities that foreshadowed his current role as a spiritual leader among the Ojibwe. Porky constantly sought the company of his namesake—a Civil War veteran and widely respected elder. The fact that Porky is old enough to have known veterans of the Civil War is remarkable enough. However, the fact that even as boy he actively sought their company is even more impressive. His namesake was called *Gaag*, meaning Porcupine, and they spent so much time together that people called them "Old Man Porcupine" and "Little Porky."

Porky was fortunate in that he was able to attend day school at Sugar Point rather than boarding school, as did most of his peers. He certainly seemed to benefit both culturally and emotionally from the experience.

In addition to a great deal of serious learning, however, Porky knew how to have fun. He was an impressive pow-wow singer and frequently traveled to camp, sing, and dance.

Porky was eager to test his manhood in other ways as well. When America plunged into World War II, he enlisted in the United States army. For Porky and many of his contemporaries, military service was an extension of old warrior traditions and a subject of great pride.

Upon returning home, he continued to travel, sing, and dance. He began a more earnest effort to settle down and find work as well. He worked at a car wash and other odd jobs on the reservation and in Minneapolis, where he eventually settled for a good share of his adult life. In the late 1960s, the American Indian Movement began to fight for Indian-controlled education of Indian youth. The Red School House sprang up in Minneapolis, and Porky served there for twenty years as a teacher, advisor, and cultural coordinator.

In his retirement, Porky lives with his wife in Rosemount, Minnesota, and travels extensively to provide his services as an advisor and practitioner of Ojibwe religious ceremonies. He is a regular figure at Leech Lake pow-wows, language camps, and educational forums. The battle for Ojibwe language and culture continues to sustain him.

Gegwe-dakamigishkang Gaagiigido

[1]   Boozhoo. Gegwe-dakamigishkang indizhinikaaz. Maang
indoodem. Niiwing azhigwa nimidew. Gaa-
zagaskwaajiimekaag indoonjibaa. Imbaabaa, Baadwewidang,
gii-midewi. Gii-oshkaabewisiwi imaa midewing, gii-
wiidookawaad iniw akiwenziiyan midewing.
Gii-oshkaabewisiwi dibishkoo mii go gaye niin noongom
ezhi-anokiiyaan. Indooshkaabewisiw. Gabe-zhigwa
imbi-gikenimigoo ji-gikendamaan o'ow akeyaa midewiwin.
Aanishinaa, o'ow niibing, niibing azhigwa indizhichige o'ow isa
izhichigeyaan, wiidookawag sa niijanishinaabe gagwejimid
gegoo akeyaa waa-gikendang o'ow isa akeyaa midewiwin.

[2]   Inashke o'ow midewing gaawiin awiiya gidaa-bagidinaasii
ji-gikendang. Giimoodad. Gaawiin gaye awiiya, anooj
awiiya, gidaa-inaasii weweni eta go ji-bizindaman gegoo, ezhi-
gikenimigooyan weweni ji-gikendaman ezhi-atemagak o'ow
isa akeyaa, o'ow midewiwin.

[3]   Naa dewe'iganan ingii-miinigoog ingiw bwaanag. Naa a'aw
opwaagan, mii gii-miinigooyaan igaye. Naa opwaagan ingii-
miinigoo. Naa awiiya gwiiwizensiwi-dewe'igan imbimiwinaa.
Mii azhigwa ishwaaso-niibiñagak bimiwinag a'aw gwiiwizens.
A'aw opwaagan mii azhigwa ashi-niiyo-biboonagak
zhigwa bimiwinag indoopwaagan. Aa bwaan abezhig,
niijakiwenzii, ingii-miinig iniw opwaaganan. Mii gaa-
izhitwaad niijakiwenzii ji-miinaasig awiiya opwaaganan ji-
aabaji'aad giishpin misawendang gegoo biidinamawaad
ji-aabaji'aad. Mii gii-pi-ikidod niijakiwenzii. Gaawiin ingii-
adaawesii a'aw indoopwaagan. Ingii-pi-miinig niijakiwenzii
iniw opwaaganan.

[4]   A'aw niijakiwenzii ingii-pi-mawidisig ji-miizhid
gashkibidaagan. Mii sa gii-paakaakonamaan i'iw
gashkibidaagan, mii imaa waabamag a'aw opwaagan abid.
Mii imaa ezhi-ikidod a'aw akiwenzii, "Mii moozhag
eni-aabaji'ad a'aw gidoopwaagan, oon ji-inaakonigeyan,
mii i'iw wenji-miinigooyan." Mii gii-pi-igoowaad niizh
bwaanag, ininiwag wiijikiweg. Bezhig opwaaganan gaa-
miizhid, gii-nibo. *Amos Owen* gii-izhinikaazo a'aw inini
gii-miizhid iniw, iniw opwaaganan. Naa *Amos Crooks*
ani-bi-miinigoo iniw indoopwaaganan bemiwinagig,
moozhag gaye niin aabaji'ag. Indanama'etawaa ya'aw isa

Gegwe-dakamigishkang *Speaks*

[1] Hello. My name is *Gegwe-dakamigishkang*. I am of the Loon
Clan. I've been through the medicine dance four times.
I'm from Leech Lake. My father, *Baadwewidang*, was grand
medicine. He was [a] messenger there in the medicine dance,
helping those old men in the dance. He was a messenger
just like I am today in my work. I'm a messenger. All the
time now I have come to be known to know things about
the medicine dance. Well now, this summer, in the summer
I do this, doing things, helping my fellow Indian in what
he asks me of what he wants to know about the *mide* way
of doing things.

[2] And regarding the medicine dance, you can't let every
person know about it. It is secret. You can't tell people,
different people, the things you've heard there until you
are recognized as knowledgeable about what has been
put in the medicine dance.

[3] And the Sioux gave me a drum. And I was given a pipe too.
I was given that pipe. And I carry one of the Little Boy
Water Drums. It is eight summers now that I have been
carrying that Little Boy. And I've been carrying this pipe
for fourteen winters. This one Sioux guy, my fellow elder,
he gave me that pipe. My fellow elder believed that a pipe
shouldn't just be given to someone to use if he simply
wanted to be handed one to use. That's what that old man
said. I didn't buy that pipe. That pipe was given to me by
my fellow elder.

[4] That old man came to visit me to give me a pipe bag. When
I opened that bag up, I saw the pipe sitting right there.
Right there that old man said, "You will use this pipe all
the time to make [important] decisions, that's why it's
given to you." That's what those two Sioux guys were
told by their colleagues. The one who gave me the pipe
passed away. The one that gave me the pipe was named
Amos Owen. And Amos Crooks gave me the pipe I carry,
the one I always use myself. I pray for the Indian people
and deliberate on things. My pipe is strong. My pipe is
powerful. Sometimes at the hospitals I am spoken to, and

anishinaabe, inaakonigeyaan sa. Indoopwaagan zoongizi.
Indoopwaagan mashkawizii. Aangodinong aakoziiwigamigong
bi-gaganoonigooyaan, gaganoonag anishinaabe ayaakozid,
wenzaamined. Indaabaakawi'aa a'aw anishinaabe aakozid.
Bi-giiwe. Gaawiin geyaabi imaa aakoziiwigamigong ayaasii.

[5]   Mii ezhi-mashkawiziid indoopwaagan bi-gaganoonigooyaan
ji-gaganoondamawag niijanishinaabe. Mii go niso-giizhig,
maagizhaa gaye niiyo-giizhig, mii i'iw, mii bi-giiwed a'aw
anishinaabe gaa-chi-aakozid.

[6]   Mii sa i'iw ezhi-apiitenimag indoopwaagan. Gaawiin awiiya
bakaan indaa-awi-ayaasii aaniindi indoopwaaganan, mii ingoji
ezhi-ayaawaanen. Mii go moozhag bimiwinag indoopwaagan.
Gaawiin ingikendanziin apii waa-kaganoonigooyaan ji-
gaganoonag niijanishinaabe dibi go wenjibaagwen. Mii go
wii-wiidookawag niijanishinaabe moozhag.

[7]   Aanishinaa mii i'iw gaa-igooyaan, gaye niin sa eni-anokiiyaan
ji-wiidookawag sa niijanishinaabe gegoo wii-nanaandawi'ag.
Gaawiin mashkiki niin indayaanziin. Mii eta go indoopwaagan
haa aabaji'ag gaganoondamawag.

[8]   Aa niijanishinaabe gaye wiin sa aakozid maazhendang,
gaganoonag sa manidoo ji-wiidookawaad sa niijanishinaaben
ji-miinaad mashkawiziiwin ji-biinitood sa iniw
odinendamowinan, naa obimaadiziwin igaye. Mii gaye
niin noongom eni-anokiitawag sa niijanishinaabe
wiidookawag dibi go anoozhid ji-izhaayaan naadamawag,
wiidookawag. Mii go gaye wiidookawiwaad niijanishinaabeg
dibi go waa-izhichigewaanen, maagizhaa gaye wii-
madoodoowaad, maagizhaa gaye wii-wiidookawaawaad
sa iniw gwiiwizensidewe'iganan. Mii i'iw ezhi-onapinag
gwiiwizensidewe'igan niin sa naadamawag niijanishinaabe
dibi go wenjibaagwen.

[9]   Mii weweni go anishinaabe ge-baatayiinod mino-
anishinaabe-bimaadizid; bebakaan gidoonjibaamin,
bwaanag, maagizhaa gaye asinii-bwaan, maagizhaa gaye
midewanishinaabe, maagizhaa gaye omanoominii-
anishinaabe. Mii go moozhag waa-wiidookawagwaa
dibi go gaganoozhiwaagwen dibi ji-naadamawagwaa,
ji-wiidookawiwaad igaye ji-gikinawaabiwaad, booch ezhaayaan
akeyaa babaamaadiziyaan gaye niin sa ji-wiidookawag sa
niijanishinaabe. Namanj igo akeyaa waa-izhichigewaanen.

I talk to the Indian people who are sick or very ill. I revive the sick Indian. He goes home. He doesn't have to be in the hospital any more.

[5] That's how strong my pipe is when I'm asked to talk for my fellow Indian. In three or maybe four days, then the Indian that was so sick can go home.

[6] That's why I hold my pipe in such high regard. I can't be anywhere without my pipe, wherever I happen to be. So I carry my pipe with me all the time. I don't know when I might be asked to talk to my fellow Indian, wherever he's from. This is how I help the Indian people all the time.

[7] Well now, as I get called upon, working myself to help my fellow Indian in things, I do Indian doctoring. I don't use medicine myself. I only use my pipe and talk for [the people].

[8] When my fellow Indian is sick, bad off, I talk to the spirit to help my fellow Indian to give him strength to clean his thoughts, and his life too. Today I work for the Indian people, working to help him in whatever he commissions me, to go there to assist him, to help him. That's how the Indians help me in what I do as well, maybe when they have a sweat lodge ceremony, maybe when they want to help with the Little Boy Water Drum. When I tie down the Little Boy Water Drum myself, I help my fellow Indian, wherever he's from.

[9] The Indians leading the good life are numerous; we're from all different places, Sioux, and maybe Assiniboin, and maybe *mide* Indians, and maybe the Menomini Indians too. All the time I help all those who might ask me to help them, and for them to help me, learning through observation, as I really do travel around to help my fellow Indian. I don't even know where I might be doing things.

[10] Indizhichige akina gegoo akiwenziiyag izhichigewaad.
Aangodinong gaye niwiidigemaag. Naa gaye nimiinaag
odizhinikaazowiniwaan. Naa indabwezotawaag bi-
inigaaziwaad. Naa o'ow gaye nimaajaa'aag anishinaabeg,
gaa-nibojig. Niwiidookawaa ezhi-gagwejimid anishinaabe sa
akeyaa weweni ji-maajaanid odinawemaaganan gaa-nibonid.
Niwiindamawaa ojichaagwan sa akeyaa gaye ji-maada'adood sa
o'ow miikana gaye wiin sa ishkwaa-giizhichigaademagak sa
o'ow bimaadiziwin omaa akiing.

Gaagoons Indigoo

[1] Eh niyawe'e, Gaag-akiwenzii gaa-izhinikaazoban, gii-kete-
anishinaabew; a'aw akiwenzii, *Civil War* ogichidaa. Mii sa go
apane oodenaang gaa-izhaad. Mii gaa-izhaad oodenaang,
niyawe'e gaa-izhid, "Ambe baa-wiiji'ishin." Ingii-kwiiwizensiw
ow apii.
[2] Mii sa gaye anishinaabeg gaa-inaabinikaazowaad. Niyawe'e
Gaag-akiwenzii gii-kaaginaagozi, mii gaye niin sa gaa-
izhinaagoziyaan gaagoons, mii sa gaa-inendamowaad
ingiw bemaadizijig waabamiyangidwaa. Miinawaa sa gaye
chimookomaanag waabamiyangidwaa bimoseyaang ezhi-
ikidowaad, *"There goes Old Man Porcupine, and there goes Little
Porky."* Mii sa go wenji-maaji-izhinikaazoyaan *Porky*, maaji-
igooyaan Gaagoons. Mii iw.

Dibiki-giizisong

[1] Gii-pi-gwiiwizensiwiyaan, gaawiin aapiji odaabaanag gii-
ayaasiiwag. Mii eta go bebezhigooganzhiig, anishinaabe-
bebezhigooganzhiig, gii-ayaawaad. Aaniish sa aabiding
imbaabaayiban gaa-izhid, "Noongom igo bebezhigooganzhiig
niibowa ayaawag," ikido. "Naagaj," ikido, "niibowa odaabaanag
da-ayaawag, waasamoowidaabaanag da-ayaawag," ikido.
"Niibowa ingiw odaabaanag wii-taniwaad," ikido. "Igo gaye
ingiw ishkode-odaabaanag, mii sa go wii-pi-
dagoshinowaad," ikido. "Mii go gaye ji-baatayiinowaad
ingiw ishkodedaabaanag," gii-ikido. "Inashke mii gaye
ge-niibowagiziwaad iwidi akeyaa wenjibaayaan. Gaawiin
geyaabi mashkodedaabaan da-bimibizosii."

238

[10] I do everything elders do. Sometimes I perform marriage
ceremonies for people. And I give them Indian names. I
put them through [the] sweat lodge ceremony to acquire
humility. I also send off Indians, the ones who've passed
on. I help the Indian when he asks me this way, for his
departing relative to leave in a good way after he dies.
I tell his soul the way to follow this road and what will
happen when his life is finished here on earth.

I'm Called Porky

[1] Yes, my namesake, who was called Old Man Porcupine,
was a real old-timer; that old man was a Civil War veteran.
He was always going to town. When he went to town, my
namesake told me, "Come keep me company." I was a little
boy at this time.
[2] And the Indians stared. My namesake, Old Man Porcupine,
looked like a porcupine, and I looked like a little porcupine
myself, at least that's what those people thought when
they saw us. And the white people who saw us walking
said, "There goes Old Man Porcupine, and there goes Little
Porky." And that's how I got the name Porky and started
being called *Gaagoons*. That's it.

On the Moon

[1] When I was a little boy, there weren't many cars. There were
only horses, Indian ponies. Well one time my father told
me, "Toady there are a lot of horses," he says. "Later on," he
says, "there are going to be a lot of cars, a lot of gasoline
[-powered] automobiles," he says. "There's going to be a lot
of fancy cars," he says. "And those trains, they'll come here
too," he says. "And there will be a lot of those trains too," he
said. "There will really be a lot of them over there where I am
from. The ox carts won't be driven any more."

[2] "Igaye naa," gaa-izhid, "ani-ayaamagadoon bemisemagakin, niibowa gaye da-ani-ayaamagadoon niwii-ikido. Niibowa gaye da-aawadaasoowidaabaaniwiwag," ikido. "Maagizhaa gaawiin gidoodamendanziin," ikido. "Mii dash igaye babaamendamaan. Mii go gaye," gaa-ikidod a'aw akiwenziiwiban, "ingoding waa-izhi-onendamowaad wayaabishkiwejig," ikido, "ji-gagwe-izhaawaad iwidi dibiki-giizisong," ikido. Mii gaye izhiwebak i'iw: gii-izhaawaad sa go dibiki-giizisong. Gii-onwaachige indedeban; daa-waabandang i'iw isa waa-inagamigak niigaan akeyaa.

[3] Bagami-ayaamagad gaa-ikidod. Inashke izhiwebak sa noongom. Mii gaawiin geyaabi bebezhigooganzhiiyan sa odayaawaasiin anishinaabe sa go. Bangii eta go ayaawaad bebezhigooganzhiig. Niibowa odaabaanag ayaawag. Mii go gaye ingiw ishkodedaabaanag, mii i'iw niibowa gaye izhi-ayaawaad. Niibowa dash wiin bemisemagakin ayaamagadoon. Indedeban gaa-waabandang o'ow i'iw apii gaa-pimaadiziban.

Niibaa-giizhig

[1] Niibaa-giizhig, mii akiwenzii akina gegoo gikinoo'amawid, mii o'ow geyaabi aangodinong oon mawidisag, oon gagwe jimag weweni dinowa waa-kikendamaan, maagizhaa gaye gegoo booch igo moozhag gikinoo'amawid akiwenzii gegoo.

[2] Gaawiin aapiji baa-naazikaagesii a'aw akiwenzii. Nichi-apiitenimaa a'aw akiwenzii kina gegoo izhi-gikinoo'amawid. Mii go gaye noomaya gii-mawidisag iwidi aakoziwigamigong ji-gagwejimag ji-bi-wiidookawiyangid. "Haaw. Gidaa-wiidookoon," ingii-ig akiwenzii, Niibaa-giizhig.

[3] Mii sa gaa-inag, "Aaniish mii sa go aawiyan gichi-akiwenzii. Mii azhigwa zhaangasimidana ashi niizho-biboonagiziyan. Gidaa-anweb. Gego aapiji geyaabi izhichigeken o'ow anooj babaa-izhaayan moozhag giishpin gisinaamagak agwajiing. Mii wenji-aakoziyan, wakewajiyan, ge-dakamanji'oyan. Gidaa-kiizhooshin. Gidaa-anweb."

[2] "Also," he said, "I want to say that there will come to be a lot of airplanes. And there will be a lot of tractor-trailers too." he says. "Maybe you don't think about the consequences of this," he says. "But I worry about it. And also," that old man said, "sometime the white people are going to get it in their heads," he says, "to try to go to the moon," he says. And that's what happened: they went to the moon. My father had premonitions; he could see what was going to happen in the future.

[3] What he said has come to be. Look what's happening today. The Indian no longer has horses. There are only a few ponies. There are many automobiles. And the trains, well there really are a lot of them. There are also a lot of airplanes. My father saw all of this while he was still alive.

Niibaa-giizhig

[1] *Niibaa-giizhig*, that's the old man who taught me everything, and there are still times I visit him, to ask him properly about the things I want to know, and for sure that old man is always teaching me something.

[2] That old man can't get around much any more. And I hold him in such high regard for having taught everything to me. Recently I was visiting him at the hospital to ask him to come and help us. "All right. I'll help you," the old man told me, *Niibaa-giizhig*.

[3] I told him, "Well you are a big elder. You're already ninety-two years old. You should rest. You shouldn't go around doing all kinds of things if it's cold outside. That's why you're sick, why you can't take the cold and you get a chill. You should keep yourself warm. You should rest."

Ogii-izhinaazhishkawaan Bwaanan

[1] Inashke gaa-izhiwebak mewinzha, chi-mewinzha. Oon,
iwidi akeyaa waabanong gii-onjibaawaad ingiw anishinaabeg.
Mii iwidi akeyaa gaa-izhinaazhishkawaad bwaanan
ningaabi'anong.

[2] Niibowa gii-ayaawag omaa ingiw bwaanag. Aanish,
anishinaabeg iwidi gii-pi-izhaawaad Bawatigong akeyaa, mii
iwidi ishkwaa, ji-pi-gabeshiwaad Moningwanekaaning. Mii
iwidi gaa-inendamowaad ji-nandawaabandamowaad i'iw
wiisiniwin nibiikaang etemagak, mii manoomin. Manoomin
ogii-izhinikaadaanaawaa. Mii imaa gii-mikamowaad o'ow
manoomin. Mii sa omaa akeyaa, anooj igo omaa akeyaa
gii-pi-izhaawaad.

[3] Niibowa bwaanag omaa gii-taawag. Miish igo
gii-maajinizhikawaawaad iwidi mashkodeng. Mashkodeng
gii-izhinaazhikawaad iniw bwaanan, akina. Miish akina imaa
Minisooding gii-nagadamowaad mitigokaag, aanjigoziwaad.

[4] Mii sa naagaj, mii i'iw gaa-izhi-zagaswe'idiwaad ingiw bwaanag,
ingiw anishinaabeg igaye. Gaawiin geyaabi wii-miigaadisiiwag,
wiijikiwendiwaad.

Aabaji' Gidasemaa

[1] Chi-mewinzha gaawiin aapiji opwaaganag gii-ayaasiiwag.
Gaawiin igaye asemaa aapiji ogii-aabaji'aasiiwaawaan. Mii
eta go ko chi-anishinaabeg gaa-aabaji'aawaad asemaan.
Gii-kwiiwizensiwiyaan, mii gaawiin asemaan gii-
sagaswaanaasiiwaawaan anishinaabeg. Mii dibishkoo go
asabikeshiinyan gaa-tebibidawigod ingiw anishinaabeg. Mii
go gaye niibowa go anishinaabeg wenji-aakoziwaad. Mii iw
niibowa ingiw anishinaabeg wenji-nibowaad. Gaye naa, inashke
go naa gegaa gii-panaadenimigooyaang akina gegoo.

[2] Shke sa noongom baatayiino ya'aw asemaa zagaswaanigod. Mii
i'iw wenji-maaji-noojimod a'aw anishinaabe. Amanj igo dash
waa-inakamigak niigaan akeyaa. Mii go ayaamagak niibowa
bizhikinaagoowan, o'ow gebaabwegaadegin-wiisiniwin igaye.
Noongom ziinzibaakwadodaapineminzhigwan niibowa
ayaamagadoon, enh ishkodewaaboo gaye.

They Chased Off the Sioux

[1] Look at what happened in the past, a long time ago. The Indians came from over there toward the east. And they chased those Sioux out there to the west.

[2] There used to be a lot of Sioux here. Well, the Indians came toward Sault Ste. Marie, and, afterwards, they established villages at Madeline Island. Over there they were thinking of where to search for the food that was put in the water, that is [to say] the wild rice. They called it *manoomin*. And that's where they found this rice. So over this way, this is where they came.

[3] A lot of Sioux lived here. Then they chased them out to the prairies. They routed the Sioux out to the prairies, all of them. They [were forced] to move and abandon the forests there in Minnesota.

[4] But later on, they had a [pipe] ceremony, the Sioux and Chippewa too. They didn't fight any more, [and] made friends.

Use Your Tobacco

[1] Long ago there weren't too many pipes. And they didn't use tobacco much either. Only the elders used tobacco. When I was a boy, the Indians didn't smoke tobacco. It was just like a spider had caught the Indians. And that's why so many of the Indians were sick. And that's why so many of the Indians died. And we almost lost our faith in everything.

[2] Today a lot of this tobacco is smoked. That's why the Indian is starting to heal. I don't know what's going to happen in the future. There are lots of commodities and canned foods too. Today there's a lot of sugar diabetes, yes, and alcohol.

This glossary is intended to assist students of the Ojibwe language in their translation and comprehension of the stories presented here. The glossary, like the texts before it, employs the double vowel orthography, developed by C. E. Fiero in the 1950s, with additional writing conventions and refinements added by John Nichols and Earl Otchingwanigan (Nyholm) in the 1970s. Although some discussion of the format follows here, it is not comprehensive; students of the language are recommended to refer to a good double vowel Ojibwe dictionary for a more complete list of Ojibwe vocabulary and further discussion of the writing system. I recommend John D. Nichols and Earl Otchingwanigan (Nyholm), eds., *A Concise Dictionary of Minnesota Ojibwe* (Minneapolis: University of Minnesota Press, 1995).

This glossary is alphabetized according to the Ojibwe double vowel alphabet:

a aa b ch d e g h ' i ii j k m n o oo p s sh t w y z zh

Thus, *abi* comes before *aanakwad* because the double vowel *aa* is considered a single vowel, voiced by a single sound. Bear this in mind as you search for entries. The glossary follows the Ojibwe alphabet, not English. Also, many Ojibwe words take numerous conjugated forms, some of which differ significantly from the head word forms which are sequenced here. Therefore, it is necessary to uninflect the conjugated forms and use the word stems to look them up. This is a glossary, not a grammar book, and thus there is not sufficient space to provide a detailed grammatical analysis here. Students are recommended to refer to the *Oshkaabewis Native Journal*, Vol. 4.1, 121–38; Vol. 4.2, 61–108; and *Our Ojibwe Grammar* by Jim Clark and Rick Greszcyk for pedagogical double vowel grammar material.

The gloss format employed here follows the system devised by Nichols and Otchingwanigan (Nyholm). Entries begin with an Ojibwe head word. With the exception of preverbs and prenouns that attach to verbs, all head words are complete Ojibwe words. The head word is followed by a class code and abbreviation of the word class, identifying the type of word. The code is followed by the gloss that approximates as closely as possible the English equivalent of the head word. A basic entry looks like this:

```
omaa            pc            here
 |               |             |
(head word)   (class code)   (gloss)
```

Plural noun forms and alternate spellings of certain words are also provided with many of the entries. For example:

Manoominii	na	Menomini Indian;	pl **manoominiig**;	also **omanoominii**
(head word)	(class code)	(gloss)	(plural form)	(alternate reference)

Some of the verb entries also include a word stem immediately after the head word. This is done for the relatively small number of verbs for which the word stem is not a complete sentence or command. For example:

waabandiwag / **waabandi-**/	*vta*	they see one another	
(head word)	(word stem)	(class code)	(gloss)

The only head words presented here which are not complete words are preverbs and prenouns. Some *vta* entries use the *n* for certain conjugations and the letter *zh* for other inflections of that same word. Letters that fall in this pattern are written just how they are used in the texts (*n* or *zh*), but the glossary notes that letter in the word stem as *N*. For example:

miizh /miiN-/ vta give something to someone

All Ojibwe nouns and verbs are differentiated by gender as animate or inanimate. A list of class codes and Ojibwe word classes follows here:

Code	Word Class	Definition
na	animate noun	animate gendered noun
nad	dependent animate noun	animate gendered noun that must be possessed
na-pt	animate participle	animate gendered noun-like verb
ni	inanimate noun	inanimate gendered noun
nid	dependent inanimate noun	inanimate gendered noun that must be possessed
ni-pt	inanimate participle	inanimate gendered noun-like verb
nm	number	number
pc	particle	particle (can function as adverb, exclamation, or conjunction)
pn	prenoun	prefix attached to nouns (functions as adjective)
pr	pronoun	pronoun
pv	preverb	prefix attached to verbs (functions as adverb)
vai	animate intransitive verb	verb with no object and a subject of the animate gender
vai+o	animate intransitive verb plus object	verb with a subject of the animate gender and object (animate or inanimate) which inflects like a traditional *vai*
vii	inanimate intransitive verb	verb with no object and subject of the inanimate gender
vta	transitive animate verb	verb with a subject and object of the animate gender
vti	transitive inanimate verb	verb with a subject of the animate gender and object of the inanimate gender

The codes used here are consistent with those employed by Nichols and Otchingwanigan (Nyholm) in *A Concise Dictionary of Minnesota Ojibwe*. The codes for *pv*, *vti*, and *vai* are further divided into subclasses by Nichols and Otchingwanigan (Nyholm). There are some differences in conjugation patterns within class codes. The subclasses of these word types primarily denote further differentiations in inflection patterns, not class description. Those differences, while significant, are relatively minor. Thus, this glossary does not distinguish between them. Students of the language are encouraged to refer to the grammar references mentioned above for further analysis of inflection patterns.

Entries in this glossary have been carefully checked with the speakers who used these words. Mistakes in glossing and spelling words, however, are entirely mine. All original tape recordings, handwritten and typewritten texts, and notes are available in the Minnesota Historical Society's archives for those who seek to compare and improve upon the work presented here.

A

a'aw *pr* that one (animate)
abakway *ni* shingle; *pl* abakwayan
abanaabi *vai* peek behind
abi *vai* stay home, stay put, sit
abinoojiikaazo *vai* act like a child
abinoojiinh *na* child;
  pl abinoojiinyag
abinoojiinyiwi *vai* be a child
abiitan *vti* live in it, inhabit something
abwaadan *vti* roast something
abwaazh /abwaaN-/ *vta* roast someone
abwe *vai+o* roast things
abwezo *vai* sweat, take a sweat bath
abwi *ni* paddle; *pl* abwiin
adaawaage *vai* sell
adaawe *vai* buy
adikameg *na* whitefish;
  pl adikamegwag
adima' /adima'w-/ *vta* catch up to someone by boat
adite *vii* be ripe
agadendan *vti* feel bashful about something
agamiing *pc* on the shore, at the water, at the lake
agaasaa *vii* be small

agaasin *vii* be small (object)
agaasishkodeyaa *vii* be small fire
agaashiinyi *vai* be small
agidigamish *pc* on top of the lodge;
  also wagidigamish, ogidigamish
agiw *pr* those ones (animate)
ago /agw-/ *vta* haul someone in
agoo *vai+o* hang things
agoodoon *vti* hang something up
agoojin *vai* hang
agoozi *vai* be perched, sit overlooking something
agoozh /agooN-/ *vta* hang someone
agwajiing *pc* outside
agwanjitoon *vti* submerse something in liquid, soak something
agwazhe *vai* cover up, use blankets
akakojiish *na* woodchuck;
  pl akakojiishag
akamaw *vta* lie in wait for someone
akandoo *vai* wait in ambush, hunt game from a blind
akeyaa *pc* in a certain direction
aki *ni* earth; *pl* akiin
akik *na* kettle; *pl* akikoog
akina *pc* all
akiwenzii *na* old man;
  pl akiwenziiyag
ako- *pv* since

ako-bii'igad *vii* that is the extent of it, be so long

akoozi *vai* be a certain length

akwa'wewigamig *ni* fish house; *pl* akwa'wewigamigoon

akwaa *vii* be a certain length

akwaabi *vai* wait in watch

akwaandawe *vai* climb up

amanjidoowin *na* symbols, glyphs; *pl* amanjidoowinag

ambegish *pc* I wish; also apegish

ambeshke *pc* come on

amo /amw-/ *vta* eat someone

amoongi *vai* be consumed

anama'etaw *vta* pray for someone

anamewin *ni* prayer, religion; *pl* anamewinan

anami' *vta* pray for someone

anaakan *ni* mat; *pl* anaakanan

anaamakamig *pc* under ground

anaamibag *pc* under the leaves

anaamibiig *pc* under water

ani- *pv* coming up into time, getting along towards; also ni-

animikiikaa *vii* be thundering

animise *vai* fly away

animiwizh /animiwiN-/ *vta* take someone away, carry someone away

animosh *na* dog; *pl* animoshag

animoons *na* puppy; *pl* animoonsag

anishaa *pc* in vain, for nothing

anishinaabe *na* Indian; *pl* anishinaabeg

anishinaabemo *vai* speak Indian

anishinaabewin *ni* Indian custom; *pl* anishinaabewinan

anishinaabewinikaade *vii* it is named in Indian

anishinaabewinikaazh /anishinaabewinikaaN-/ *vta* call someone in Indian

anishinaabewitwaa *vai* follow an Indian religion

aniibiishaaboo *ni* tea

aniibiishaabooke *vai* make tea

aniibiishaabookewinini *na* Asian; *pl* aniibiishaabookewininiwag; also aniibiishikewinini

anokii *vai* work

anokiitaw *vta* work for someone

anokiiwinagad *vii* be work

anooj *pc* a variety of

anoozh /anooN-/ *vta* order someone, commission someone

anwebi *vai* rest

apagazom *vta* use someone in prayer, e.g., tobacco

apagidoon *vti* throw something

apagin *vta* throw someone

apa'iwe *vai* run away from people to a certain place

apakwaan *ni* roof; *pl* apakwaanan

apakweshkwe *na* birch bark roofing rolls; *pl* apakweshkweyag

apane *pc* always

apenimo *vai+o* rely on people, rely on things

apikan *ni* horse tackle; *pl* apikanan

apikweshimo *vai* use a pillow

apishimo *vai* lay a bed, use a mattress

apishimonike *vai* make bedding, make mats

apii *pc* time, at a certain time

apiichiikaw *vta* control someone to a certain extent

apiitad *vii* be a certain time, in the midst of a certain season, or be a certain height; also apiitaa

apiitaw *vta* make someone a certain height

apiitaanimizi *vai* be of a certain status, be important, be a certain height

apiitendaagwad *vii* be of great importance

apiitenim *vta* hold someone in high regard, feel about someone to a certain extent, be proud of someone

apiitizi *vai* be a certain age

asabaabisens *ni* thread; *pl* asabaabisensan

asabike *vai* make nets

aseke *vai* tan hides

asemaa *na* tobacco; *pl* asemaag

asemaake *vai* make a tobacco offering

asham *vta* feed someone

ashi /as-/ *vta* put someone in a certain place

ashigan *na* largemouth bass;
 pl ashiganag
asin *na* rock; *pl* asiniig
asinii-bwaan *na* Asiniboin Indian;
 pl asinii-bwaanag
atamaazo *vai+o* store things
ataadiwag /ataadi-/ *vai* they gamble
 with one another
atemagad *vii* put there
atoon *vti* put something somewhere
awanjish *pc* persistently, stubbornly,
 even though
awas *pc* go away
awashime *pc* more so, much more
awedi *pr* that one over there
awesiinh *na* wild animal;
 pl awesiinyag
awiiya *pc* someone
ayagwanan *vii* rest in a level position
ayaa *vai* be somewhere
ayaabita *pc* half way
ayaabojii *vai* forward one's
 understanding of something
ayaan *vti* have something
ayaangwaami'idizo *vai* take care one's
 self
ayaaw *vta* have someone
ayekozi *vai* tired
ayi'ii *pr* thing, something; *pl* ayi'iin
ayi'iing *pr* some place
ayikido *vai* speak, lecture
ayindanakamigizi *vai* something
 happens with someone
ayindi *vai* it is a certain way with
 someone
ayipidoon *vti* pull something a
 certain way repeatedly
azhe- *pv* backwards, returning
azheboye *vai* row
azheboye-jiimaan *ni* row boat;
 pl azheboye-jiimaanan
azhegiiwe *vai* returns
azhigwa *pc* now

AA
aabadad *vii* be used
aabaji' *vta* use someone
aabajitoon *vti* use something
aabawaa *vii* warm weather

aabaakawi' *vta* revive someone
aabiding *pc* once
aabita- *pn, pv* half
aabizhiishin *vai* perk up, come to,
 come back to life
aada' /aada'w-/ *vta* arrive before
 someone
aadamoobii *na* automobile;
 pl aadamoobiig
aadizookaan *na* main character
 of a traditional story, Wenabozho;
 pl aadizookaanag
aadizookaan *ni, na* traditional story;
 pl aadizookaanan; also
 aadizookaanag (for some dialects
 this word is animate, for others it is
 inanimate)
aagim *na* snowshoe; *pl* aagimag
aagonwetam *vai* disbelieve
aagonwetan *vti* disbelieve something
aagonwetaw *vta* disbelieve someone
aajigwaazh /aajigwaaN-/ *vta* hook
 someone, catch someone with a hook
aakoziwin *ni* sickness; *pl* aakoziwinan
aakoziinaagozi *vai* look sick
aakoziiwigamig *ni* hospital;
 pl aakoziiwigamigoon
Aanakwad *name* name of Lac Courte
 Oreilles elder Aanakwad
aanawi *pc* anyhow, despite, although,
 but
aanawitaw *vta* disbelieve someone
aangodinong *pc* sometimes
aanike- *pv* sequential, next in
 a sequence
aanind *pc* some
aanind dash *pc* the others
aanish *pc* well, well then
aanishinaa *pc* well then
aanizhiitam *vai* quit, finish, give up
aaniin *pc* how, why
aaniin danaa *pc* well why?, well how?,
 why not?
aaniindi *pc* where
aaniish *pc* well now
aanji-ayaa *vai* change one's condition
aanjibii'an *vti* re-transcribe, rewrite
aanjigozi *vai* change residence, move;
 also aanji-gozi

aano- *pv* in vain, to no avail, without result

aapiji *pc* very

aapijitaa *vai* to be about

aasamigaabawi' *vta* stand before someone

aasaakamig *ni* moss; *pl* **aasaakamigoon**

aatayaa *pc* exclamation (of male speech)

aate' *vta* extinguish him

aatebadoon *vti* turn off the light

aawadii *vai* haul things

aawadoon *vti* haul something

aawan *vii* be a certain thing

aawazh /aawaN-/ *vta* haul someone

aawi *vai* be

aazhawa'am *vai* go across by boat

aazhawaadagaa *vai* swim across

aazhawyayi'ii *pc* opposing bank of a body of water

aazhikwe *vai* scream

aazhogan *pc* across

Aazhoomog *place* Lake Lena, Minnesota

B

bababakite' /babakite'w-/ *vta* box someone, hit someone repeatedly

babagiwayaaneshkimod *ni* cloth bag; *pl* **babagiwayaaneshkimodan**; also **babagiwayaanimashkimod**

babaa- *pv* go about, here and there

babaamaadizi *vai* travel

babaamendan *vti* care about, pay attention to something

babaamenim *vai* care about, bother with someone

babaamibatoo *vai* run about

babaamibizo *vai* drive about

babaaminizha' /babaaminizha'w-/ *vta* chase someone about

babaamise *vai* fly about

babaamose *vai* walk about

babaamoode *vai* crawl about

babimise *vai* fly around

babimose *vai* walk around

babizindaw *vta* listen to someone repeatedly

babiinzikawaagan *ni* coat, jacket; *pl* **babiinzikawaaganan**; also **babiizikawaagan**

badakide *vii* be planted, be placed in the ground

bagaboodegozi *vai* move to a new residence by water

bagadoodegozi *vai* move here together (as a family)

bagamibizo *vai* drive up, arrive by motor

bagamise *vai* arrive by flight

bagamishkaw *vta* encounter someone upon arrival

bagandizi *vai* lazy, incompetent

bagaan *na* nut; *pl* **bagaanag**

bagaanibimide *ni* peanut butter

bagidanaamo *vai* breathe, exhale

bagidin *vta* offer someone, release someone

bagidinan *vti* set something down, release something, offer something

bagidinise *vai* stack wood, pile wood

bagijwebin *vta* release someone, let go of someone

bagijwebinan *vti* let go of something, release something

bagoneganaanjigaade *vii* have a hole shot through

bagosendan *vti* beg for something, hope for something

bakade *vai* hungry

bakadenaagozi *vai* look hungry

bakazhaawe *vai* clean fish

bakaan *pc* different

bakaaninakamisidoon *vti* make something different, change the condition of something

bake *vai* go off to the side

bakinaw *vta* beat someone in a contest

bakinaage *vai* win

bakite'an *vti* hit something, strike something

bakite'odiwag /bakite'odi-/ *vai* they hit one another

bakitejii'ige *vai* play baseball

bakobii *vai* go down into the water

bakobiigwaashkwani *vai* jump in the water

bakobiise *vai* fall into the water

bakwajindibezh /bakwajindibezhw-/ *vta* scalp someone

bami' *vta* support someone, take care of someone

bami'idizo *vta* be self sufficient

bamoozhe *vai* baby-sit

banaadizi *vai* be spoiled

banaajitoon *vti* spoil somthing, ruin something

bangii *pc* little bit, small amount

bangiiwagizi *vai* be a little bit, be few

banzo /banzw-/ *vta* singe someone

bapawaangeni *vai* flap wings, beat wings

batwaadan *vti* race after something

bawa'am *vai* knock rice

bawa'iganaandan *vti* knock rice

bawa'iminaan *vai* pin cherry; *pl* bawa'iminaanan

Bawatig *place* Sault Ste. Marie; also Bawating

bawaazh /bawaaN-/ *vta* dream about someone

bazakiteniwan *vii* built low to the ground

bazangwaabishim *vai* dance with eyes closed

bazigwii *vai* get up, stand up

bazhiba' /bazhiba'w-/ *vta* stab someone

bazhiba'odan *vti* it stabs someone (reflexive)

baabaabasaabiigad *vii* tighten up around something

baabige *pc* immediately

baabii' *vta* wait for someone

baakakaabi *vai* open eyes

baakaakonamaw *vta* open something (of wood) for someone

baakaakonan *vti* open something

baakibii'an *vii* ice clears off a body of water

baakinige *vai* lift (something) open

baakizige *vii* it is consumed in flames

baamaadagaa *vai* swim about

baamendan *vti* pay attention to something

baanimaa *pc* afterwards, later on

baapaagaakwa'an *vti* knock on something (of wood)

baapaagokozhiwewinini *na* barber; *pl* baapaagokozhiwewininiwag

baapaagokozhiwewininiiwi *vai* be a barber

baapaase *na* red headed woodpecker; *pl* baapaaseg

baapi *vai* laugh

baapinakamigizi *vai* good time with laughter involved

baasan *vti* dry something; also baasoon

baashkijiishkiw *vta* explode out of someone

baashkinede *vii* it steams, the breathing is visible

baashkiz /baashkizw-/ *vta* shoot at someone

baashkizigan *ni* gun; *pl* baashkizigan

baashkizige *vai* shoot

Baatawigamaag *place* Whitefish, Wisconsin

baatayiinad *vii* be numerous

baatayiinadoon *vti* have a lot of something, plenty

baatayiino *vai* plentiful, numerous; also baataniino

baate *vii* be parched, dry

baazagobizh /baazagobiN-/ *vta* scratch someone

bebakaan *pc* different

bebakaanad *vii* be different

bebakaanitaagod *vii* be talked about differently; also bebakaanitaagwad

bebakaanizi *vai* be different

bebezhig *pc* one at a time

bebezhigooganzhii *na* horse; *pl* bebezhigooganzhiig

bebezhigooganzhiiwigaan *ni* stable; *pl* bebezhigooganzhiiwigaanan

bebiboon *pc* each winter

bedose *vai* walk slowly

bekaa *pc* wait

bekish *pc* at the same time

bengo-bakwezhigan; *na* flour; also bibine-bakwezhigan

beshizh /beshizhw-/ *vta* cut someone

besho *pc* near

bezhig *nm* one

bezhig *pc* certain one; also **abezhig**

bezhigo *vai* be one, there is one, be alone

Bezhigoogaabaw *name* Bezhigoogaabaw (Stands Alone)

bi- *pv* coming

bi-naadin *vti* fetch it here, haul something inside

bi-naagozi *vai* appear, come forth

bi-naazikaw *vta* come to someone

bibine-bakwezhigan *na* flour; also **bengo-bakwezhigan**

biboon *vii* winter

biboonaginzo *vai* be so many years old

bigishkiga'ise *vai* chop wood into kindling

bijiinag *pc* after a while, recently, just now, for the first time

Bikoganaagan *place* Danbury, Wisconsin

bikwaakwad *ni* ball; *pl* **bikwaakwadoon**

bimagoke *vii* it rubs off onto something

bima'adoon *vti* follow it along

bimaadagaa *vai* swim by

bimaadizi *vai* lives, life goes by

bimaadizishi *vai* be alive

bimaadiziwin *ni* life

bimaadiziiwinagad *vii* lives

bimaaji' *vta* save someone's life

bimaazhagaame *vai* go along the shore

bimi-ayaa *vai* come by

bimibatoo *vai* run

bimibaagi *vai* it goes along (in its calling)

bimibide *vii* speed along, fly along, drive along

bimibizo *vai* drive by

bimishkaa *vai* paddle by

bimiwizh /bimiwiN-/ *vta* carry someone along, bring someone along

bimose *vai* walk

bimoom *vta* carry someone on one's back

bimoomigoo-apabiwin *ni* saddle; *pl* **bimoomigoo-apabiwinan**

bimoonda' *vta* carry something for someone

bimoondan *vti* carry something off on one's back

binaadizi *vai* pass away, die

binaan *vta* carry someone away

binaanoondan *vti* acquire knowledge of something

bine *na* partridge; *pl* **binewag**

binesi *na* thunderbird, eagle, large bird; *pl* **binesiyag**

bineshiinh *na* bird; *pl* **bineshiinyag**

bineshiinyiwi *vai* be a bird

bingwe'ombaasin *vii* cloud of dust is stirred up

binoobaan *vta* mark someone

biskaakonebidoon *vti* turn something on (appliance)

biskitenaagan *ni* birch bark sap bucket; *pl* **biskitenaaganan**

bizagaabiigizh /bizagaabiigiN-/ *vta* lead someone (horse or dog)

bizaani-bimaadizi *vai* live quietly

bizindaw *vta* listen to someone

biziigwebakiteshin *vai* spill things as a result of falling

bizhishig *pc* empty

bizhishigozi *vai* be single

bizhishigwaa *vii* be empty

bii *vii* be a certain amount of liquid

bii' *vta* wait for someone

biibaagiim *vta* call out for someone

biibii *na* baby; *pl* **biibiiyag**

biibiiwi *vai* be a baby

biidaboono *vai* float here, approach by water

biidaasamishkaa *vai* arrive by water

biidinamaw *vta* hand something over to someone

biidoon *vti* bring something

biidwewe *vai* be heard approaching

biidwewe *vii* sound approaches

biidwewebizo *vai* be heard approaching by motor

biikojii *vai* have a pot belly, be plump

biiminakwaan *ni* rope; *pl* **biiminikawaanan**

biinad *vii* be clean

biinashkina' /biinashkina'w-/ *vta*
load ammunition into someone

biindasaagan *ni* raft;
pl biindasaaganan

biindashkwaazh /biindashkwaaN-/
vta stuff someone

biindaakojige *vai* offer tobacco

biindaakoozh /biindaakooN-/ *vta*
offer someone tobacco

biindig *pc* inside

biindige *vai* go inside, enter

biindigebatoo *vai* run inside

biindigenaazhikaw *vta* chase
someone inside

biindigenisin *vii* wood is brought
inside

biindigewin *vta* bring someone inside

biindigeyaanimagad *vii* it enters
something

biindigeyoode *vai* crawl inside

biini' *vta* clean someone

biinish *pc* until, up to, including

biinitoon *vti* clean something

biinjayi'ii *pc* inside

biinji- *pn, pv* inside

bii'o *vai* wait

biizikan *vti* wear something

biizikiigan *ni* clothing;
pl biizikiiganan

booch *pc* certainly, for sure

boodawazo *vai* warm up by a fire

boodawaazh /boodawaaN-/ *vta* build a
fire for someone

boodawe *vai* build a fire

booni- *pv* quit an activity

booni' *vta* quit someone, leave
someone alone

boonitoon *vti* leave something alone,
quit something

boonii *vai* perch, come to rest from
flight

boono *vai* float, drift

boozi' *vta* give a ride to someone

boozhoo *pc* hello

bwaan *na* Dakota Indian;
pl bwaanag; also abwaanag

bwaana'owi *vai* feeble

Bwaanakiing *place* Sioux lands,
Dakota country

CH

chi- *pv, pn* large, big

chi-agaamiing *pc* across the ocean

Chi-agaamiing *place* Europe

chimookomaanikaazo *vai* be called
something in American (English)

D

dabasagidaaki *pc* knoll

dabasagoode *vii* hang low

dabazhiish *pc* at the bottom of a
lodge

dagon *vii* be located in a certain place

dagonan *vti* add something in, mix
something in

dagoshin *vai* arrive there

dagoshkaagozi *vai* it comes upon
someone

dagozi *vai+o* add things in, mix in

dakama'o *vai* ferry across

dakamanji'o *vai* feel chilly, feel cold

dakamaashi *vai* sail, cruise (by wind)

dakamii *vai* ferry

dakaasin *vii* frigid, cold wind

dakonan *vti* grasp something

dakoozi *vai* be short

dakwam *vta* bite someone, get a hold
of someone

dakwamidiwag /dakwamidi-/ *vai*
they bite one another

dakwange *vai* bite

danademo *vai* live in a particular place

danakii *vai* dwell, live, reside

danaapi *vai* laugh in a certain place

danaasag *pc* so to speak

danizi *vai* stay somewhere, belong
somewhere

danwewidam *vai* be heard speaking
in a certain place

dasing *pc* times, so many times

daso-giizhigon *vii* it is so many days

dash *pc* and, but

dashiwag /dashi-/ *vai* they are a
certain number, they are so many

dawaaj *pc* preferable, better to

dawegishkaa *vii* form a part, gap

dazhi- *pv* location

dazhim *vta* talk about someone

dazhindan *vti* talk about something

dazhinijigaade *vii* be talked about

dazhishin *vai* be buried in a certain place, lie in a certain place

dazhitaa *vai* spend time in a certain place

dazhiikan *vti* be involved with something, work on something

dazhiikaw *vta* work on someone, dress someone out (animal)

dazhiikodaadiwag /dazhiikodaadi-/ *vai* they are involved with one another

daa *vai* dwell

daangandan *vti* sample something by taste

daangigwanenige *vai+o* sign things

daanginan *vti* touch something

daangishkaw *vta* kick someone, kick someone along

de- *pv* sufficiently, enough

Debaasige *name* Debaasige (Light of the Sun)

debibido *vai+o* grapple over something, grab things

debibidoon *vti* catch something, grab something

debibizh /debibiN-/ *vta* catch someone

debinaak *pc* carelessly, any old way

debwenim *vta* believe someone, be convinced by someone

debwetan *vti* believe something, heed something, e.g., a warning or belief

debwetaw *vta* obey someone, believe someone

debweyendam *vai* become convinced, come to believe something

degitenim *vta* be impressed with someone

dewe'igan *na* drum; *pl* dewe'iganag

diba'igan *ni* hour; *pl* diba'iganan

diba'igebii'igaans *ni* receipt; *pl* diba'igebii'igaansan

dibaabandan *vti* inspect something, look something over

dibaadodan *vti* tell about something

dibaajim *vta* tell stories about someone

dibaajimo *vai* tell stories

dibaajimotaw *vta* tell someone stories

dibaajimowin *ni* story; *pl* dibaajimowinan

dibaakonigewinini *na* judge or lawyer; *pl* dibaakonigewininiwag

dibaakwa' *vta* charge someone with an offense, pass judgment on someone

dibaakwan *vta* indict someone

dibi *pc* wherever, I don't know where

dibidaabaan *ni* wagon, carriage; *pl* dibidaabaanan

dibiki-giizis *na* moon; *pl* dibiki-giizisoog

dibishkoo *pc* just like

dibishkookamig *pc* opposite, right across

dimii *vii* deep water

dino *pc* kind, type

dinowa *pc* kind, type

ditibiwebishkigan *ni* bicycle; *pl* ditibiwebishkiganan

ditibizo *vai* roll along, speed along by rolling

doodoon *vta* do something to someone

dooskaabam *vta* peek at someone

E

edino'o *pc* even, also

Eko-biising *place* Duxbury, Wisconsin

enda- *pv* just

endaso- *pv* every

endaso-dibik *pc* every night

endaso-giizhig *pc* every day; also endaso-giizhik

endazhi-ganawenimindwaa gichi-aya'aag *place* nursing home

endaawigam *ni* dwelling; *pl* endaawigamoon

enigok *pc* with effort, forcefully

enigoons *na* ant; *pl* enigoonsag; also enig

enigoowigamig *ni* ant hill; *pl* enigoowigamigoon

eniwek *pc* relatively

eshkam *pc* increasingly so

eta *pc* only
eta go gaawiin *pc* except
eya' *pc* yes; also enh

G

gabaa *vai* disembark, get out of
a vehicle or a boat
gabaashim *vta* boil someone
(in water)
gabe- *pv, pn* all, entire
gabe-zhigwa *pc* all the time now
gabeshi *vai* camp, set up camp
gabikaw *vta* catch up to someone
gadedan *vti* think something is funny,
think in a humorous way about
something
gaganoondamaw *vta* talk for
someone
gaganoonidiwag /gaganoonidi-/ *vai*
they talk to one another, converse
gaganoozh /gaganooN-/ *vta* converse
with someone
gagaanzitan *vti* act contrary to a
warning or belief
gagidagishin *vai* have spotted fur
gagiibaadad *vii* foolish
gagiibaadizi *vai* naughty, foolish
gagiibaakwan *vti* block something,
dam something
gagiibidwe *vai* be quiet for a time, be
heard periodically
gagiijiidiye *vai* be constipated
gagiikwewinini *na* preacher;
pl gagiikwewininiwag
gagwaadagitoo *vai* suffer
gagwaanisagendaagozi *vai* be
considered terrible, be considered
disgusting
gagwe- *pv* try
gagwejim *vta* ask someone
gagwejitoon *vti* try something; also:
gojitoon
gakaabikise *vai* fall down a hill, fall
off a cliff
ganawaabam *vta* look at someone
ganawaabanda'iyaa *vii* be revealed
ganawaabandan *vti* look at
something

ganawenim *vta* look after someone
ganoozh /ganooN-/ *vta* call to
someone, talk to someone
gashkapidoon *vti* bundle something
up
gashkendam *vai* sad
gashkibidaagan *na* tobacco, pipe or
bandolier bag; *pl* gashkibidaaganag
gashkigwaaso *vai* sew
gashki' *vta* earn someone
gashkimaa *pc* I'll show you, come on,
look
gashkinan *vti* do something to the
extent of one's ability
gashkitoon *vti* be able to do
something, be successful at
something
gawanaandam *vai* starve
gayaashk *na* seagull; *pl* gayaashkwag
gaye *pc* and
gayesh *pc* and also
Gaa-jiikajiwegamaag *place* Roy Lake,
Minnesota
Gaa-zagaskwaajimekaag *place* Leech
Lake, Minnesota
gaabawi *vai* stand
gaag *na* porcupine; *pl* gaagwag
gaaginaagozi *vai* look like a
porcupine
gaagiigido *vai* talk, give a speech
gaagiigidoo-biiwaabikoons *ni*
telephone; *pl* gaagiigidoo-
biiwaabikoonsan
gaagiijibidoon *vti* finish tying
something off
gaagiijitoon *vti* appease something
Gaakaabikaang *place* Minneapolis,
Minnesota
gaanda'igwaason *ni* thimble;
pl gaanda'igwaasonan
gaandakii'ige *vai* pole
gaanjweba'ige *vai* put logs through
a water shoot
gaashkiishkigijiibizh
/gaashkiishkigijiibiN-/ *vta* slice
somebody into pieces
gaawi'awiwi *vai+o* thwart people
gaawiin *pc* no

255

gaawiin ginwenzh *pc* not long

gaawiin ingod *pc* not a single thing

gaazootaw *vta* hide from someone

gaazhagens *na* cat; *pl* gaazhagensag

Gechi-miigaadiing *ni-pt* World War II

gegapii *pc* eventually

gegaa *pc* almost

geget *pc* truly, really

gego *pc* don't

gegoo *pc* something

gemaa gaye *pc* or

gete- *pn* old time, old fashioned

geyaabi *pc* still

gezikwendan *vti* vaguely remember something

gezikwenim *vta* vaguely remember someone

gibaakwa' *vta* lock someone up, imprison someone

Gibaakwa'igaansing *place* Bena, Minnesota

gibaakwe *vii* be blocked up, be dammed

giboodiyegwaazon *na* pants; *pl* giboodiyegwaazonag

gibwanaabaawe *vai* drown

gichi- *pn, pv* very, greatly

gichi-aya'aawi *vai* grown up; also gichaya'aawi

gichi-ginwaabikobaashkizigan, -an *ni* cannon

gichi-waaginogaan *ni* big domed lodge; *pl* gichi-waaginogaan

Gichi-ziibiing *place* St. Croix River

gichimookomaan *na* white man; *pl* gichimookomaanag; also chimookomaan

gidasige *vai* parch rice

gidimaagizi *vai* be poor, humble

gigizheb *pc* in the morning

gigizhebaa-wiisini *vai* eats breakfast

gigizhebaawagad *vii* be morning

gijiigibin *vta* snare someone

gikendan *vti* know something

gikendaasoowigamig *ni* college, university; *pl* gikendaasoowigamigoon

gikenim *vta* know someone

gikinawaabi *vai* learn by observing

gikinawaajitoon *vti* inscribe something, mark something (bark, rock)

gikinoo'amaadiwin *ni* teaching, instruction, lesson; *pl* gikinoo'amaadiwinan

gikinoo'amaagewigamig *ni* school; *pl* gikinoo'amaagewigamigoon

gikinoo'amaagozi *vai* be a student, go to school

gimoodin *vti* steal something

gina'amaw *vta* forbid someone

ginigawi' *vta* mix someone

ginigawisidoon *vti* mix something, integrate something

ginigawisin *vii* be mixed

Giniw-aanakwad *name* Giniw-aanakwad (Golden Eagle Cloud)

ginjiba' *vta* run away from someone

ginjiba'iwe *vai* escape by fleeing, run away

ginwaabamaawizo *vai* see one's self a certain way

ginwenzh *pc* long time

gisinaa *vii* cold

gitenim *vta* be impressed by someone, be proud of someone

gitige *vai* farm, plant

gitiwaakwaa'igaade *vii* it is made of logs, it is made of corduroy

gitiziim *na* parent, ancestor; *pl* gitiziimag

gizhaabikizan *vti* heat something

gizhaabikizigan *ni* stove; *pl* gizhaabikiziganan

gizhaagamezan *vti* heat something (liquid only)

gizhiibatoo *vai* run fast

gizhiibazhe *vai* be itchy

gizhiibizi *vai* itchy

gizhiibizo *vai* drive fast

giziibiiga'ige *vai* wash clothes

giigoonh *na* fish; *pl* giigoonyag

giigoonh-oodena *ni* fish camp; *pl* giigoonh-oodenawan

gii'igoshimo *vai* fast for a vision

giimii *vai* escape

giimoodad *vii* secret

giimoozikaw *vta* sneak up on someone

giin *pc* you, yourself
giishka'aakwe *vai* cut timber
giishkaabaagwe *vai* thirsty
giishkaabaagwenaagozi *vai* look
thirsty
giishkaabikaa *vii* there is a cliff
giishkiboojige *vai* saw wood
giishkigwebin *vta* twist someone's
head off, decapitate someone by
twisting his head
giishkitoon *vti* slice it
giishkizh /giishkizhw-/ *vta* cut
through someone
giishkizhan *vti* cut it through
giishkizhaa *vai* be cut through
giishkowe *vai* stop crying, stop
making a vocal noise
giishpin *pc* if
giiwanimo *vai* tell lies
giiwashkwe *vai* dizzy
giiwashkwebatoo *vai* run staggering
giiwashkwebii *vai* be drunk
giiwe *vai* go home
giiwebatoo *vai* run home
giiwegozi *vai* move home
giiwenh *pc* as the story goes
giiwewin *vta* take someone home
giiwizi *vai* be an orphan
giiwiziigamig *ni* orphanage;
pl giiwiziigamigoon
giiyose *vai* hunt
giizikan *vti* take an item of clothes off
the body
giiziz /giizizw-/ *vta* finish cooking
someone
giizizan *vti* cook something
giizizekwe *vai* cook
giizhaa *pc* beforehand, in advance
giizhendam *vai* decide, make a
resolution
giizhichigaademagad *vii* finished,
done
giizhig *na* day, sky
giizhigad *vii* be day
giizhige *vai* complete (building)
giizhitoon *vti* finish something
giizhiikan *vti* finish something
giizhiikaw *vta* finish someone, finish
working on someone

giizhiitaa *vai* ready
giizhooshim *vta* wrap, bundle
someone up warm-like
giizhoozi *vai* be warm
go *pc* (emphatic particle)
godaganaandam *vai* suffer miserably
from starvation
godagaagomin *ni* blackberry;
pl godagaagominan
godandaman *vti* taste something,
sample something
goji' *vta* try someone (tease)
gojitoon *vti* try something; also
gagwejitoon
gomaapii *pc* eventually, by and by
gonaadizi *vai* spend one's life, live in
a certain place
gonimaa *pc* possibly, perhaps, for
instance
gopii *vai* go inland
gosha *pc* (emphatic)
goshi /gos-/ *vta* fear someone
goshko' *vta* scare someone
gotan *vti* fear something
gozi *vai* move, change residence
gookooko'oo *na* owl;
pl gookooko'oog
gwanaajiwan *vii* beautiful
gwanaajiwi *vai* nice, beautiful,
glorious
gwashkozi *vai* wakes up
gwayako- *pv* correctly
gwayakose *vii* be correct, be right
gwayakotan *vti* hear something
correctly
gwaanabise *vai* capsize, flip over in a
boat
gwaashkwani *vai* jump
gwech *pc* so much, enough
gwek *pc* correctly, exactly, right
gwekigaabawi' *vta* turn someone
around while standing
gwiiwizensidewe'igan *na* little boy
drum
gwiiwizensiwi *vai* be a boy
Gwiiwizensiwi-zaaga'iganiing *place*
Boy Lake, Minnesota
Gwiiwizensiwi-ziibiing *place* Boy
River, Minnesota

H

hay' *pc* too bad; also: **hai'**

haaw *pc* all right, okay

I

i'iw *pr* that one (inanimate)

ikido *vai* say

iko *pc* as a habit, customarily

ikwa *na* louse; *pl* **ikwag**

ikwabi *vai* sit elsewhere

ikwanagweni *vai* roll up shirt sleeves

imaa *pc* there

imbaabaa *nad* my father;
   pl **imbaabaayag**

inademo *vai* cry a certain way

inagakeyaa *pc* towards that way there

inaginzo *vai* be a certain amount, be
   of a certain value

ina'am *vai* sing a certain way

ina'oozh /ina'ooN-/ *vta* gift someone
   in a certain way

inamanji'o *vai* be a certain condition

inandawenim *vta* want someone in a
   certain way

inanjige *vai* eat in a certain way, have a
   certain diet

inanokii *vai* work in a certain way

inapinazh /inapinaN-/ *vta* slice
   someone

inapine *vai* be ill in a certain way

inashke *pc* look, behold

inataadiwag /inataadi-/ *vai* they
   gamble, play games together in a
   certain way

inawemaagan *na* relative;
   pl **inawemaaganag**

inawiindamaage *vai* speak in a
   certain way

inaabi *vai* glance, peek

inaadagaa *vai* swim in a certain way

inaadamaw *vta* help someone in a
   certain way

inaadodan *vti* talk about something

inaajimo *vai* tell

inaakonige *vai* make a decree, law

Inaandagokaag *place* Balsam Lake,
   Wisconsin

inaanzo *vai* be colored a certain way

indaga *pc* please

indangishkaw *vta* kick someone in
   a certain way

indanitaawaadizookwe *vai* tell
   stories in a certain place

inday *nad* my dog; *pl* **indayag**

indede *nad* my father

indengway *nid* my face;
   pl **indengwayan**

indibaajimo *vai* tell things in a certain
   way

indiy *nid* my hind end

indoodem *nad* my clan;
   pl **indoodemag**

inendam *vai* think

inendamowin *ni* thought

inendaagozi *vai* be thought of in a
   certain way, have a certain destiny

inenim *vta* think of someone

ingichi-niigi'ig *nad* my grandparent;
   pl **ingichi-niigi'igoog**

ingiw *pr* them (animate)

ingo-diba'igan *pc* one mile or one
   hour

ingod *pc* singularly

ingoding *pc* one time

ingodoninj *pc* one inch

ingodwaasoninj *pc* six inches

ingodwewaan *pc* pair

ingoji *pc* somewhere, approximately,
   nearly

ingwana *pc* it turns out that, it was
   just so

ingwizis *nad* my son; *pl* **ingwizisag**;
   also **ningozis**

inigaatesidoon *vti* spread something
   out

inigaazi *vai* be poor, pitiful

iniginan *vti* ply something away

inigini *vai* be a certain size

inigokwadeyaa *vii* be a certain
   diameter

inikaw *vta* name someone

inikaa *vai* condition or life turn out a
   certain way

inime'odishi /inime'odis-/ *vta* host
   someone

ininan *vti* hand something down,
   present something

inini *na* man; *pl* **ininiwag**

ininigaade *vii* it is handled in a certain way

ininimaw *vta* hand something to someone

initaagwad *vii* sound a certain way

iniw *pr* those (inanimate)

inizh /inizhw-/ *vta* cut someone

iniibin *vta* line someone up in a certain way

iniibin *vti* line something up in a certain way

injichaag /-jichaag-/ *nad* my soul, my spirit; *pl* injichaagwag

inose *vai* walk a certain way, walk to a certain place

inwaade *vii* be a sacred place

inwe *vai* make a certain sound, speak a certain language, make a characteristic call (quack, bark)

inwemagad *vii* something sounds, something is spoken

inwewedam *vai* make a speech, lecture

inwewedan *vti* preach about something

inzhaga'ay /-zhaga'ay-/ *nad* my skin; *pl* inzhaga'ayag

ipidoon *vti* pull something in a certain way or direction

ipiskopoo *ni* Episcopal religion; *pl* ipiskopoon

ipitoo *vai* runs in a certain way

ipizo *vai* speeds, travels by motor in a certain way

iskigamizigan *ni* sugar bush; *pl* iskigamiziganiin

iskigamizige *vai* sugar off

ishkodewaaboo *ni* whiskey

ishkone *vai* survive

ishkonigan *ni* reservation; *pl* ishkoniganan

ishkwam *vta* place a corpse in a certain way

ishkwaa- *pv* after

ishkwaakamigad *vii* be over with

ishkwaane *vai* survive an epidemic

ishkweyaang *pc* behind, in the rear, in the past

ishpate *vii* there is deep snow

ishpaagonagaa *vii* be deep snow

ishpi- *pv* above

ishpiming *pc* up above, high, in heaven

itaming *loc* place, at a certain location

iwapii *pc* at that time

iye *pr* that one

izhaa *vai* goes there

izhaagowaataa *vai* climb onto a rock from the water

izhi /iN-/ *vta* say to someone, call someone

izhi- *pv* thus, thusly

izhi-ayaa *vai* to be of a certain condition

izhichigaazh /izhichigaaN-/ *vta* treat someone a certain way

izhichigaazo *vai* be treated a certain way

izhichige *vai* does so

izhichigewinagad *vii* be done (this way)

izhidaabaazh /izhidaabaaN-/ *vta* drag someone to a certain place

izhidaabii'iwe *vai* drive in a certain way

izhi' *vta* deal with someone a certain way, make someone a certain way

izhijiwan *vii* it flows

izhinaw *vta* think of someone a certain way, think of someone respectfully

izhinaagozi *vai* look like, be in the form of

izhinaagwad *vii* it looks a certain way

izhinaazhikaw *vta* chase someone to a certain place, send someone to a certain place; also **izhinaazhishkaw**

izhinikaadan *vti* name something, call something a certain name

izhinikaade *vii* be called

izhinikaazh /izhinikaaN-/ *vta* name someone a certain way

izhinikaazo *vai* he is called

izhinikaazowin *ni* name; *pl* izhinikaazowinan

izhinoo'an *vti* point at something

izhinoo'ige *vai* point

izhitoon *vti* prepare something

izhitwaa *vai* have a certain custom, belief or religion

izhitwaawin *ni* faith, religion; *pl* izhitwaawinan

izhiwe *vai* something happens to someone

izhiwebad *vii* it happens

izhiwebizi *vai* condition, behaves a certain way

izhiwidoon *vti* take something

izhiwijigaazo *vai* be carried or taken to a certain place

izhiwizh /izhiwiN-/ *vta* take someone somewhere

II

iizon *pc* as the story goes; also iizan

J

jaagide *vii* it burns up

jaaginan *vta* use somebody up, destroy someone

jaagizan *vti* burn something up

jaagizo *vai* burn up

jaagizodizo *vai* burn one's self

jejajiibaan *pc* various different locations

Jejaakwaag *place* Markville, Minnesota

ji- *pv* to, so that, in order to

jiibaakwaadan *vti* cook something

jiibaakwaazh /jiibaakwaaN-/ *vta* cook someone

jiigayi'ii *pc* adjacent

jiigeweyaazhagaame *vai* walk along the shore

jiigi- *pv, pn* near

jiigibiig *pc* along the shore, by the water

jiigishkode *pc* near the fire

K

konaas *ni* cloth, sheet; *pl* konaasan

M

madaabii *vai* go to the shore

madaabiiba' *vta* run away from someone to the shore

madaabiigozi *vai* move to the shore

madoodoo *vai* attend sweat lodge ceremony

madwe-ikido *vai* be heard to say, speak from a distance

madwe'oode *vai* be heard crawling

madwezige *vai* be heard shooting

maji-izhiwebizi *vai* misbehave

majiiwi *vai* be bad

makade-maanishtaanish *na* black sheep; *pl* makade-maanishtaanishag

makadewiiyaas *na* black man, African American; *pl* makadewiiyaasag

makakoonsike *vai* make baskets, make containers

makam *vta* take something away from someone by force

makizin *ni* shoe, moccasin; *pl* makizinan

makoons *na* little bear, bear cub; *pl* makoonsag

makwa *na* bear; *pl* makwag

makwan *vii* it is easy to peel (bark)

mamaazikaa *vai* agitate, move

mami /mam-/ *vta* pick someone up, take someone

mamikwendan *vti* recollect things

mamiskoshkiinzhigwe *vai* eyes turn red

mamoon *vti* take something, pick something up

manaajichigaade *vii* be respected

manaajichige *vai* be respectful

manepwaa *vai* crave a smoke

manezi *vai* to be in need

mangaanibii *vai* shovel snow

manidoo *na* spirit; *pl* manidoog

Manidoo-minisaabikong *place* Spirit Rock Island

manidookaadan *vti* consider something spiritual

manidoowendan *vti* consider something sacred

manoominike *vai* harvest rice

manoominike-giizis *na* September, the ricing moon

manoominii *na* Menomini Indian; *pl* manoominiig; also omanoominii

mashkawazhe *vai* have rough markings on the skins, e.g., scabs or severe rash mashkawisin *vii* be strong

mashkawizii *vai* be strong

mashkawiziiwin *ni* strength

mashkijiitad *ni* tendon;
pl **mashkijiitadoon**

mashkiki *ni* medicine

mashkikiiwigamig *ni* pharmacy,
hospital

mashkikiiwinini *na* doctor;
pl **mashkikiiwininiwag**

Mashkimodaang *place* Bagley,
Minnesota

Mashkii-ziibiing *place* Bad River,
Wisconsin

mashkode *ni* prairie; pl **mashkoden**

mashkodewanishinaabe *na* prairie
Indian; pl
mashkodewanishinaabeg

mashkosaagim *na* grass snowshoes;
pl **mashkosaagimag**

mawadishi /mawadis-/ *vta* visit
someone

mawadishiwe *vai* visit

mawi *vai* cry

mawim *vta* cry for someone

mawinazh /mawinaN-/ *vta* attack
someone, charge someone

mawinzo *vai* pick berries, go
blueberry picking

mawishki *vai* be a cry-baby, cry
constantly

mayagwe *vai* speak strangely, speak a
different language

mazinaatesijigan *ni* television;
pl **mazinaatesijiganan**

mazinaatesijiganimakak *ni* television
set; pl **mazinaatesijiganimakakoon**

mazinichigan *na* image, statue, doll;
pl **mazinichiganag**

mazinichigaazo *vai* be represented in
effigy, be represented as an image

mazitaagozi *vai* cry out

maada'adoon *vti* follow something
(trail, road)

maada'ookii *vai* share, share things,
distribute

maadakide *vii* it starts on fire

maadakizige'idim *vii* it bursts into
flames

maadanokii *vai* start working

maadaapine *vai* fall ill

maajaa *vai* leave

maajaa' *vta* send someone off,
conduct funeral services for
someone

maajiba'idiwag /maajiba'idi-/ *vai*
run away together, flee in a group

maajinizhikaw *vta* chase someone off

maajitoon *vti* start to make
something

maajii *vai* start an activity

maajii- *pv* start

maajiibadaabii *vai* start to come to
the shore

maajiidoon *vti* take something along

maajiigi *vai* grow up, start to grow

maajiigin *vii* start new condition, grow

maajiikam *vta* work on somone

maajiishkaa *vai* start, start one's life

maajiishkaamagad *vii* start to move

maajiizh /maajiiN-/ *vta* take
someone along

maakabi *vai* wound people

maamakaaj *pc* unbelievable, amazing,
awesome

maamawi *pc* all together

maamawookan *vti* do something
together, do something in
the company of others;
also **maama'ookan**

maamawootaa *vai* he is put together,
combined; also **maama'ootaa**

maamiginan *vti* collect something,
put something together

maanaadizi *vai* be ugly

maanendan *vti* feel bad about
something

maang *na* loon; pl **maangwag**

maanishtaanish *na* sheep;
pl **maanishtaanishag**

maanishtaanishibiiwiin *na* wool

maanzhi-ayaa *vai* be bad off

maazhendam *vai* feel out of balance,
sickly

maazhi-ayaa *vai* be bad off

maazhidoodaadizo *vai* cause self-
inflicted injury, injure one's self

maazhipogozi *vai* taste bad

maazhise *vai* have bad luck

megwaa *pc* while, in the midst of

megwaayaak *pc* in the woods
megwe- *pn, pv* in the midst of
 something, in the middle
megwekob *pc* in the bush
memaangishenh *na* mule;
 pl memaangishenyag
memwech *pc* exactly, just that, it is so
meshkwad *pc* instead
Metaawangaag *place* Hertel,
 Wisconsin
Metaawangaansing *place* Little Sand
 Lake, Wisconsin
mewinzha *pc* long ago
michisag *ni* floor; *pl* michisagoon
midaaswi *nm* ten
midewakiwenzii *na* mide priest;
 pl midewakiwenziiyag
midewanishinaabe *na* mide Indian;
 pl midewanishinaabeg
midewi *vai* be mide
midewiwin *ni* medicine dance,
 medicine lodge ceremony; also
 midewin
migi *vai* bark
migizi *na* bald eagle; *pl* migiziwag
migizi-giizis *na* February
migoshkaaji' *vta* pester someone,
 bother someone
migoshkaaji'iwi *vai* be a pest,
 annoying
migwandagoon *vii* grow
mikan *vti* find something
mikaw *vta* find someone
mikigaazo *vai* he is found somewhere
mikwamiwan *vii* hail
mikwendan *vti* remember something
mimigoshkam *vai* jig rice
mimigoshkaaji' *vta* tease someone
mindawe *vai* pout
mindido *vai* be big
mindimooyenh *na* old woman;
 pl mindimooyenyag; also
 mindimoowenh
minik *pc* amount, certain amount
minikwe *vai* drink
minikweshki *vai* drink chronically, be
 alcoholic
minis *ni* island; *pl* minisan
Minisooding *place* Minnesota

minji-niizh *pr* both
minjikaawan *na* glove, mitten;
 pl minjikaawanag
minjiminan *vti* hold something in
 place, steady something
minobii *vai* be pleasantly drunk, be
 tipsy
minochige *vai* do good
minogaamo *vai* be pleasingly plump
minopogozi *vai* tastes good
minotoon *vti* make something nice,
 good
minozogo *vai* he is well done
minwabi *vai* sit comfortably
minwaabandan *vti* look favorably
 upon something
minwendan *vti* like something
minwendaagwad *vii* be fun, likable
minwendaagwad *vii* be funny,
 humorous
minwenim *vta* like someone
misawendan *vti* want something,
 desire something
misaabe *na* giant; *pl* misaabeg
misaabooz *na* hare, jack rabbit;
 pl misaaboozoog
Misi-zaaga'iganiing *place* Mille Lacs,
 Minnesota
Misiiziibi *place* Mississippi River
miskomin *ni* raspberry;
 pl miskominan
miskwaabiminzh *na* red oshier, red
 willow; *pl* miskwaabiminzhiig
Miskwaagamiiwi-zaaga'iganiing *place*
 Red Lake, Minnesota
miskwaanzigan *ni* head roach;
 pl miskwaanziganan
miskwiiwi *vai* bleed, be bloody
miskwiiwinijiishin *vai* bleed on
 things, drip blood
mishiimin *na* apple;
 pl mishiiminag
mitaawigan *pc* bare back
mitig *na* tree; *pl* mitigoog
mitigokaa *vii* be a forest
mitigwaab *na* bow; *pl* mitigwaabiig
miziwe *pc* all over, everywhere
miziwezi *vai* intact
mii *pc* it is, there is

miigaadiwini-
  gikinoo'amaadiiwigamig *ni*
  military school; *pl* miigaadiwini-
  gikinoo'amaadiiwigamigoon
miigaazo *vai* fight
miigaazowin *ni* fight; *pl*
  miigaazowinan
miigaazh /miigaaN-/ *vta* fight
  someone
miigiwe *vai+o* give something away
miijin *vti* eat something
miijiin *vta* defecate on someone; also
  miiziin
miikana *ni* path, trail, road
miinawaa *pc* again
miinigoowaawiwag /miinigoowaawi-/
  vai they are given something as a
  group
miish *pc* and then
miishidaamikam *vai* have whiskers,
  mustache; also miishidaamikan,
  miishidaamikane
miishizinigon *vta* give someone a
  whisker rub
miiziin *vta* defecate on someone; also
  miijiin
miizh /miiN-/ *vta* give someone
moogishkaa *vai* rise up, surface
mookawaakii *vai* cry to go along
mookinan *vti* bring something out of
  storage
mookii *vai* rise to a surface, emerge
  from a surface
moonenimaazaw *vta* sense
  someone's presence
Mooningwanekaan *place* Madeline
  Island, Wisconsin
Mooniyaang *place* Montreal, Ontario
mooska'osi *na* shitepoke, swamp
  pump, American bittern;
  pl mooska'osiwag
mooshkin *pc* full
mooshkinatoon *vti* fill something up
  with solids
mooshkine *vai* be full
mooshkinebadoon *vti* fill something
  up with liquid
mooshkinebin *vta* fill someone with
  liquid

mooshkinebii *vai* full of water
moozhag *pc* always
moozhitoon *vti* feel something on or
  in one's body

N

nabanegaanens *ni* lean-to;
  pl nabanegaanensan
nagadan *vti* abandon something,
  leave something behind; also
  nagadoon
nagamo *vai* sing
nagamon *ni* song;
  pl nagamonan
nagamowin *ni* singing;
  pl nagamowinan
nagazh /nagaN-/ *vta* abandon
  someone, leave someone behind
nagishkodaadiwag /nagishkodaadi-/
  vai they meet one another
nagwaagan *ni* snare;
  pl nagwaaganan
nagwaaganeyaab *ni* snare wire;
  pl nagwaaganeyaabiin
nagwaan *vta* snare someone
na'enimo *vai* store things
nakom *vta* answer someone, reply to
  someone, promise someone
nakweshkaw *vta* meet someone
nakwetam *vai* answer
nakwetaw *vta* answer someone
namadabi *vai* sit
namanj *pc* I don't know (dubiative
  indicator)
name *na* sturgeon; *pl* namewag
namebin *na* sucker; *pl* namebinag
namebini-giizis *na* February
nanagim *vta* coax someone, convince
  someone
nanaa'ichige *vai* repair, fix
nanaa'idaabaane *vai* car repair
nanaa'idaabaanewinini *na* mechanic;
  pl nanaa'idaabaanewininiwag
nanaa'in *vta* organize someone
nanaa'itoon *vti* fix something
nanaandawi' *vta* doctor someone,
  heal someone
nanaandawi'idiwag /nanaandawi'idi-/
  vai they doctor one another

nanaandawi'idizo *vai* doctor one's self
nanaandawi'iwe *vai* doctor, heal
nanaandawi'iwewinini *na* medicine man, Indian doctor, healer;
  pl nanaandawi'iwewininiwag
nanaandawi'o *vai* doctor, heal
nanaandawi'owin *ni* doctoring, healing; *pl* nanaandawi'owinan
nanaandom *vta* make a request of someone
nanda- *pv* search
nandakwaandawe *vai* try to climb
nandam *vta* recruit someone, enlist someone for war
nandawaabam *vta* search for someone
nandawaabandan *vti* search for something, look for something
nandawaaboozwe *vai* hunt rabbits
nandawendan *vti* want something, desire something
nandawewem *vta* search for someone with sound, search for someone by calling out
nandobani *vai* search for the enemy, go to war
nandobaakinan *vti* search for something by uncovering and opening
nandom *vta* invite someone, request something of someone
nandomaakaw *vta* summon someone
nandomaandan *vti* smell something
nandone' /nandone'w-/ *vta* look for someone
nanisaanabi *vai* be in jeopardy
nawaj *pc* more so, more than
nawapwaan *ni* bag lunch, lunch taken along; *pl* nawapwaanan
nayenzh *pc* both
nazhike- *pv* alone
nazhikewi *vai* be alone
naa *pc* (emphatic)
naabisijigan *ni* tape recorder; *pl* naabisijiganan
naadamaw *vta* assist someone
naadin *vti* fetch something
naana'idaa *pc* by coincidence

naanaagadawendam *vai* reflect, ponder
naanaagadawendan *vti* reflect on something, consider something
naanaagadawenim *vta* think about someone
naanaakobinawinan *vti* make a path for something with one's fingers
naanaazikan *vti* pay attention to something
naangizi *vai* be light (weight)
naangizide *vai* be light footed (good tracker, good dancer)
naaningim *pc* often
naaniibawi *vai* stand around
naaniizaanendaagozi *vai* be dangerous
naawakwe-wiisini *vai* eats lunch
naawij *pc* middle of the lake
naazibii *vai* haul water, haul sap
naazikan *vti* approach something
naazikaw *vta* approach someone
naazikaage *vai* approach, go to people
naazh /naaN-/ *vta* fetch someone
naazhaabii'igan *ni* fiddle, violin; *pl* naazhaabii'iganan
naazhaabii'ige *vai* fiddle, play violin
negwaakwaan *ni* spile; *pl* newaakwaanan
Nenabozho *name* Nenabozho (Red Lake); also Wenabozho
Nenaandago-ziibiing *place* Tamarack River
Nesawegamaag *place* Shakopee Lake, Minnesota
Neweyaash *name* Neweyaash
neyaab *pc* as it was before
Neyaashiing *place* Nay-Ah-Shing, Minnesota
nibaa *vai* sleep
nibe' *vta* offer someone a place to sleep
nibi *ni* water
nibinaadin *vti* fetch water
nibiikaang *pc* in the water, on the waterways
nibo *vai* die
nibwaakaa *vai* be wise, intelligent

nibwaakaaminens *ni* smart berry, smart pill; *pl* **nibwaakaaminensan**

nichiiwad *vii* be a severe storm, catastrophe

nigig *na* otter; *pl* **nigigwag**

nigiigwadi *vii* it is frosted up

nimaamaa *nad* my mother; *pl* **nimaamaayag**

niminaaweshkaa *vai* paddle away from shore

nimisad *nid* my stomach

nimishoomis *nad* my grandfather; *pl* **nimishoomisag**

nindaanis *nad* my daughter; *pl* **nindaanisag**

ningaabii'an *vii* be west

ningwizis *nad* my son; *pl* **ningwizisag**; also **ningozis**

niningwanis *nad* my cross-nephew

niningwezhinaningodwewaanagizi *vai* be a member of a certain group or family

niniigi'ig *nad* my parent; *pl* **niniigi'igoog**

ninjaanzh *nid* my nose

ninzhishenh *nad* my uncle; **ninzhishenyag**

nipikwan *nid* my back; *pl* **nipikwanan**; also **nipikon**, **nimbikwan**

nisawa'ogaan *ni* lodge with a peaked roof; *pl* **nisawa'ogaanan**

nisayenh *nad* my older brother; *pl* **nisayenyag**

nisaabaawe *vai* get wet

nisidiwag /nisidi-/ *vai* they kill one another, kill each other

nisidotan *vti* understand something

nisidotaw *vta* understand someone

nising *nm* three times

niso-giizhig *pc* three days

nishi /nis-/ *vta* kill someone

nishimis *nad* my cross-niece

nishiwan *vti* do away with something

nishiwanaaji'aa *vai* be spared, saved from destruction or death

nishiimenh *nad* my younger sibling; *pl* **nishiimenyag**

nishkaadendam *vai* have angry thoughts

nishkaadizi *vai* angry

nishwaaso-diba'igan *pc* eight miles or eight hours

nishwaasoninj *pc* eight inches

nitam *pc* first time

nitaawichige *vai* be good at doing things

nitaawigi *vai* grow up

nitaawigi' *vta* raise someone; give birth to someone

nitaawizi *vai* be raised

niwiijaan *nad* my sibling unrelated by blood; *pl* **niwiijaanag**

niwiiw *nad* my wife

niyawe'enh *nad* my namesake; *pl* **niyawe'enyag**

niibawi *vai* stand

niibidan *nid* my tooth; *pl* **niibidanan**

niibin *vii* be summer

niibowa *pc* many; also **niibiyo**

niigaan *pc* in the future, forward

niigaanizi *vai* lead

niigi *vai* be born

niigi' *vta* give birth to someone

niigi'aawaso *vai* give birth

niigitaw *vta* bear for someone

niij- *pv* fellow

niijanishinaabe *nad* my fellow Indian; **niijanishinaabeg**

niijaya'aa *nad* my comrade, my companion; *pl* **niijaya'aag**

niijikiwenh *nad* my male friend; *pl* **niijikiwenyag**

niijii *nad* my friend (used by and in reference to males); *pl* **niijiiyag**

niijiikiwenz *nad* my fellow (between older men)

niikaanis *na* brother, brethren of a certain faith; *pl* **niikaanisag**

niikimo *vai* growl

niimi *vai* dance

niimi'idiiwag /niimi'idii-/ *vai* dance with one another

niimi'idiiwin *ni* pow-wow; *pl* **niimi'idiiwinan**

niin *pv* me, myself

niinizis *nid* my hair; *pl* niinizisan
niisaaki *pc* downhill
niisaandawe *vai* climb down
niisinan *vti* lower something
niishim *vta* place something with someone
niiwana' /niiwana'w-/ *vta* beat someone to death
niiwanaskindibe' /niiwanaskindibe'w-/ *vta* give someone a stunning blow to the head
niiwezh /niiweN-/ *vta* beat someone, defeat someone
niiwing *nm* four times
niiyaa *pc* exclamation (of woman's speech)
niiyoninj *pc* four inches
niiyoninjiiskaayaa *vii* be four inches in width
niizh *nm* two
niizho-diba'igan *pc* two miles or two hours
niizhobimaadizi *vai* lead a dual life, live in two worlds
niizhodens *na* twin; *pl* niizhodensag
noogigaabawi *vai* stop and stand in place
noogise *vai* stop flying
noogishkaa *vai* stop
noojigiigoonyiwe *vai* harvest fish
noojimo *vai* heal
nookomis *na* my grandmother; *pl* nookomisag
noonaan *vta* nurse someone, nourish someone
noondan *vti* hear something
noondaw *vta* hear someone
noondaagwad *vii* heard
noonde- *pv* need, want, crave
noongom *pc* today
nooni' *vta* nurse someone
noopiming *pc* in the woods
noopinadoon *vti* follow something (abstract)
noopinazh /noopinaN-/ *vta* follow someone
nooskwaada' /nooshkwaada'w-/ *vta* lick someone

O

o'ow *pr* this one (inanimate)
Obaashing *place* Ponemah, Minnesota
obi'ayaa *ni* narrows; *pl* obi'ayaan
obiigomakakii *na* toad; *pl* obiigomakakiig
odamino *vai* play
odaminotaw *vta* play with someone
odayi *vai* be a horse or dog owner
odaabaan *na* car; *pl* odaabaanag
odaake *vai* direct, steer affairs
odaapin *vta* accept someone, take someone
odaapinan *vti* accept something
odaapinaa *vai* take
Odaawaa-zaaga'iganiing *place* Lac Courte Oreilles, Wisconsin; also Odaawaa-zaaga'eganiing
odikwami *vai* have head or body lice
ogichidaa *na* warrior; *pl* ogichidaag
ogichidaawi *vai* be a warrior
ogidakamig *pc* on top of the ground, on the bare ground
ogimaa *na* chief, boss; *pl* ogimaag
ogimaakwe *na* head woman; *pl* ogimaakweg
ojibwe *na* Ojibwe Indian; *pl* ojibweg
ojiitaad *ni* sinew; *pl* ojiitaadoon
okaadakik *na* kettle with legs, tripod kettle; *pl* okaadakikoog
omakakii *na* frog; *pl* omakakiig
omanoominii-anishinaabe *na* Menomini Indian; *pl* omanoominii-anishinaabeg; also manoominii-anishinaabe
omaa *pc* here
ombi-ayaa *vai* come to the surface, rise up, have one's spirit lifted
ombigiyaawaso *vai* raise a family
ombiigizi *vai* be loud
omigii *vai* scab up
omigii *vii* it is scabby
omin *vta* furnish oats to someone (animal)
onapidoon *vti* tie something
onapizh /onapiN-/ *vta* harness someone, tie someone
onashkinadoon *vti* load something

onaagoshi-wiisini *vai* eats supper

onaagoshin *vii* be evening

onda'ibii *vai* get water from somewhere

ondakaanezi *vai* be from somewhere, be raised somewhere

ondamitaa *vai* be busy

ondaadizi *vai* be born, come from a certain place

ondaadiziike *vai* give birth

ondemagad *vii* boil

ondin *vta* get someone

ondinamaw *vta* furnish someone with something

ondinan *vti* get something from somewhere

onganawisin *vii* meant to be a certain way, be divined or watched over

ongow *pc* these ones (animate)

oningwiigan *nid* his wing; *pl* oningwiiganan

oninj *nid* his finger; *pl* oninjiin

onishkaa *vai* get up (from a lying position)

onizhishin *vii* be nice, good

oniijaanisi *vai* has a child

onji- *pv* reason for

onjibaa *vai* be from somewhere

onjigaa *vii* leak from somewhere

onji'idim *vai* be prohibited from doing something, be restricted

onjishkaawaaniwe *vai* be challenged, be up against certain things (in life)

onjii *vai* be from somewhere

onjiikogaa *vai* come from a remote area

onow *pr* these ones (inanimate)

onwaachige *vai* be psychic, have premonitions

onzan *vti* boil something

onzaabam *vta* see someone from somewhere, see someone from a certain vantage point

onzaam *pc* overly, too much, extremely

onzaamibii *vai* drink too much

onzaamine *vai* deathly ill, extremely sick

onzibii *vai* get water from somewhere

opime- *pv, pn* side

opime-ayi'ii *pc* on the side of something

opime-miikana *ni* side trail; *pl* miikanan

opwaagan *na* pipe; *pl* opwaaganag

opwaaganebi *vai* pipe is offered

osidaagishkaw *vta* affect someone's condition, afflict someone with something

oshaakaw *vta* scare someone away

oshkaabewis *na* messenger, official, helper; *pl* oshkaabewisag

oshkaabewisiwi *vai* be messenger

oshkiniigikwe *na* young woman; *pl* oshkiniigikweg

oshtiwagidigamig *pc* on the roof top

owaakaa'igani *vai* has a house

owiiyawe'enyi *vai* be a namesake

Ozaawaa-zaaga'iganiing *place* Yellow Lake, Wisconsin

ozaawizi *vai* he is brown

ozhaawashkobiigizi *vai* have blue welts

ozhaawashkwaabaawe *vai* have blue marks on one's body

ozhichigaade *vii* be built

ozhiga'ige *vai* tap trees

ozhigaw *vta* build a house for someone

ozhige *vai* build lodges

ozhimo *vai* flee

ozhimobatoo *vai* run in flight

ozhisinaagane *vai* sets the table

ozhishenyi *vai* have an uncle

ozhitoon *vti* make something

ozhiitaa *vai* prepare

OO

oodena *ni* village; *pl* oodenawan

oonh *pc* oh, well (emphatic)

S

sa *pc* (emphatic)

SH

shaanh *pc* come on now, oh please

shke *pc* (emphatic)

T

tayaa *pc* good golly

W

wa'aw *pr* this one (animate)

wagidigamig *pc* on the roof

wajebaadizi *vai* spry, peppy

wajiw *ni* mountain; *pl* wajiwan

wakewaji *vai* get cold easily, unable to withstand cold temperatures

wanagek *na* tree bark;
 pl wanagekwag

wanagekogamig *ni* bark lodge;
 pl wanagekogamigoon

wanaa'itoon *vti* fix something wrong

wani' *vta* lose someone

wanisin *vii* be lost

wanishin *vai* be lost

wanitoon *vti* lose something

wawanendan *vti* forget something from time to time

wawaabijiizi *vai* have dapple-colored fur

wawaanendan *vti* have no understanding of something

wawaasese *vii* be lightening

wawenabi *vai* be seated, sit down

wawiiziigiminag *ni* dried berry;
 pl wawiiziigiminagoon

wayaabishkiiwed *na-pt* white man;
 pl wayaabishkiiwejig

wayeshkad *pc* beginning of a time sequence

wayiiba *pc* soon

Wazhashkoonsing *place* Wisconsin

waabam *vta* see someone

waabamoojichaagwaan *ni* mirror;
 pl waabamoojichaagwaanan

waaban *ni* east

waabanda' *vta* show someone

waabandan *vti* see something

waabashkiki *ni* swamp;
 pl waabashkikiin

waabishkaa *vii* be white

waabishkaagoonikaa *vii* there is a white blanket of snow; also waabishkaagonagaa

waabishkiiwe *vai* be white

waabiingwe *vai* be pale faced

waaboowayaan *ni* blanket;
 pl waaboowayaanan

waabooyaan *ni* blanket;
 pl waabooyaanan

waabooz *na* rabbit, cottontail;
 pl waaboozoog

waaboozoo-miikanens *ni* rabbit trail;
 pl waaboozoo-miikanensan

waagaakwad *ni* ax;
 pl waagaakwadoon

waagaashkan *vti* bend something to a certain shape

waagaawi *vai* be bent, hunched over

Waagoshens *name* Little Fox

waakaa'igan *ni* house;
 pl waakaa'iganan

waakaa'igaanzhish *ni* shack;
 pl waakaa'igaanzhishan

waakoon *na* fungus; *pl* waakoonag

waasa *pc* far

waasamoo-makakoons *ni* battery;
 pl waasamoo-makakoonsan; also ishkode-makak

waasamoobimide-zhooshkodaabaan *na* snowmobile;
 pl waasamoobimide-zhooshkoodaabaanag; also waasiganibimide-zhooshkoodaabaan

waasawad *vii* it extends, it goes far

waaswaa *vai+o* shine things

Waaswaaganing *place* Lac du Flambeau, Wisconsin

waawanoo *vai* lay eggs, nest

waawaabiganoojiinh *na* mouse;
 pl waawaabiganoojiinyag

waawaabishkimoose *na* grub worm;
 pl waawaabishkimooseg

waawaashkeshi *na* deer;
 pl waawaashkeshiwag

Waawiyegamaag *place* Big Round Lake, Wisconsin

waawiyeyaakwad *vii* be round (something of wood)

waawiyezi *vai* be round

waawiiji'iye *vai* be in someone's company, assist

webin *vta* throw someone away, part with someone

webinan *vti* throw something away

wegodogwen *pc* whatever

wegonen *pr* what, what is it

wegwaagi *pc* behold

wemitigoozhii *na* Frenchman;
pl **wemitigoozhiiwag**

wenabi' *vta* place someone in a sitting
position

Wenabozho *name* Wenabozho; also
Nenabozho (Red Lake)

wendaabang *vii* east; *conjunct* of
ondaaban

wenipan *pc* easily

wenipanad *vii* be easy, be simple

wenipanendan *vti* think something is
easy

wenjida *pc* on purpose, for a
particular reason; also **onjida**

wewebinan *vti* shake something

weweni *pc* properly, easily, in a good
way

wewiib *pc* hurry, fast

wiidabim *vta* sit with someone

wiidigem *vta* marry someone

wiidigendiwag /wiidigendi-/ *vai* they
are married to one another, be
married

wiidookaw *vta* help someone

wiigiwaam *ni* bark lodge, dance
arbor; *pl* **wiigiwaaman**

wiigiwaamike *vai* make wigwam

Wiigoobiiziibiing *place* Grantsburg,
Minnesota

wiigwaasimakak *ni* birch bark basket;
pl **wiigwaasimakakoon**

wiiji- *pv* together, with

wiiji' *vta* go with someone,
accompany someone

wiiji'iindiimagad *vii* be worked
together, be woven together

wiijiwaawendiwag /wiijiwaawendi-/
vai they are partners

wiijii'iwe *vai* accompany people

wiijiikiwendiwag /wiijiikiwendi-/ *vai*
they are friends, be friendly to one
another

wiijiiw *vta* go with someone

wiikaa *pc* ever

wiikobidoon *vti* pull something

Wiikonamindaawangaag *place*
Hertel, Wisconsin

Wiikonamindaawangaansing *place*
Maple Plain, Wisconsin

wiikwaji' *vta* try someone, try to
escape from someone, or enable
someone

wiikwajitoo *vai* endeavor

wiikwajitoon *vti* try to do something

wiin *pc* by contrast

wiin *pr* him, himself

wiin *vta* name someone

wiindamaw *vta* tell someone

wiinde *vii* be called

wiindigoo *na* windigo, cannibal,
winter monster; *pl* **wiindigoog**

wiineta *pr* only him, only her

wiinibiigoo *na* Winnebago Indian;
pl **wiinibiigoog**

wiinzo *vai* have a certain name

wiinzowin *ni* name; *pl* **wiinzowinan**

wiipemaawaso *vai* sleep with a child
protectively

wiisagendam *vai* be in pain, be sore,
suffer

wiisini *vai* eat

wiisiniwin *ni* food

wiisookaw *vta* spend time with
someone

wiiyaas *ni* meat; *pl* **wiiyaasan**

Z

zagaswaa *vai* smoke

zagaswaadan *vti* smoke it

zagaswe' *vta* offer smoke to
someone

zagaswe'idiwag /zagaswe'idi-/ *vai*
they smoke together, share a smoke,
have a ceremony or meeting

zagaswem *vta* offer smoke to
someone in prayer

zaka' /zaka'w-/ *vta* light someone,
smoke someone, e.g., a pipe

zaka'on *ni* cane; *pl* **zaka'onan**

zakwane *vii* burst into flames

zaziikizi *vai* be the oldest, be older
than others

zaaga'am *vai* go outside, exit, go to
outhouse

zaaga'igan *ni* lake; *pl* zaaga'iganiin; also zaaga'egan (Wisconsin)

zaagajiwe *vai* come out over a hill

zaagajibatoo *vai* run around a hill

zaagakii *vii* sprout

zaagi' *vta* love someone

zaagiziba'idiwag /zaagiziba'idi-/ *vai* they run out together

zaagizibatoo *vai* run out of someplace

zaasaakwe *vai* give a war whoop

zegi' *vta* scare someone

zegizi *vai* scared, fearful

zezikaa *pc* right away, immediately

zipokaani *vii* it closes

ziibi *ni* river; *pl* ziibiwan

ziibiins *ni* creek; *pl* ziibiinsan; also zhiiwoobishenh (archaic)

ziiga'andaw *vta* baptize someone, pour water on someone

ziiga'anjigaazo *vai* be baptized

ziiginan *vti* pour something

ziigobiigin *vii* be poured

ziigwan *vii* be spring

ziikaapidan *vti* gulp something down

ziinzibaakwad *ni* sugar; *pl* ziinzibaakwadoon

zoogipon *vii* be snowing

zoongide'e *vai* be brave

zoongizi *vai* strong, solid

ZH

zhashagi *na* great blue heron; *pl* zhashagiwag

zhawenim *vta* pity someone, bless someone, love someone

zhayiigwa *pc* now already

zhazhiibitam *vai* stubborn

zhaabwii *vai* survive

zhaaganaashiimo *vai* speak English

zhaaganaashiimotaadiwag /zhaaganaashiimotaadi-/ *vai* they speak English to one another

zhaaganaashiiwinikaadan *vti* name something in English

zhaagode'e *vai* be cowardly

zhaashaaginizide *vai* be barefoot

zhimaaganish *na* soldier; *pl* zhimaaganishag

zhingaatesidoon *vti* spread something out to dry

zhingibiz *na* helldiver (grebe); *pl* zhingibizag

zhingishin *vai* lie down

zhingobikaadan *vti* line something with evergreen boughs

zhishigagowe *vai* puke, vomit

zhiiigonan *vti* empty something, pour something out

zhiishiib *na* duck; *pl* zhiishiibag

zhiishiigi *vai* urinate

zhiiwaagamizigan *ni* maple syrup

zhodaawinini *na* Jew; zhodaawininiwag

zhooshkodaabaan *ni* sleigh; *pl* zhooshkodaabaanan

zhooshkodiyebizo *vai* slide quickly on one's hind end

Some of the speakers whose stories appear in this book have published versions of the same stories and other tellings in the *Oshkaabewis Native Journal* or in the monolingual Ojibwe anthology *Omaa Akiing*. In addition, some of the contributors have published their own books about Ojibwe grammar and syntax, while others have had articles published about them and their remarkable accomplishments. To assist readers interested in researching the lives and language contributions of the storytellers, an abbreviated list (excluding the numerous articles from the *Oshkaabewis Native Journal*) follows.

Abrahamzon, Bernice. "Nebageshig, Grandson of Mosay, the Caterpillar." *News From Indian Country*, mid-September 1996, 7A.

———. "The Mosay Chiefs." *News From Indian Country*, mid-September 1996, 6A.

———. "The Mosay Chiefs." *The Polk County Leader*, August 7, 1996, 10.

Associated Press. "Archie Mosay, Spiritual Leader of Ojibwe Indians." *Chicago Tribune*, July 31, 1996.

Clark, James and Rick Gresczyk. *Our Ojibwe Grammar*. St. Paul: Eagle Works, 1998.

———. *Traveling With Ojibwe*. St. Paul: Eagle Works, 1992.

DeMain, Paul. "Neebageshig Passes On." *News From Indian Country*, mid-August 1996, 1B.

Gardner, Bill. "Ojibway Spiritual Leader Archie Mosay Dies at 94." *St. Paul Pioneer Press*, July 30, 1996, 1B, 3B.

Hanners, David. "Spirit World Now Beckons to Legendary Tribal Leader: Hundreds Attend Funeral of Preserver of Ojibway Customs." *St. Paul Pioneer Press*, July 30, 1996, 1B, 3B.

Hustvet, Julie. "Legacy Survives Death of Spiritual Leader Mosay." *Spooner Advocate*. 96.33 (August 8, 1996): 1, 12.

Knoche, Eldon. "St. Croix Band Chief Was Spiritual Advisor." *(Milwaukee) Journal Sentinel*, August 1, 1996.

Losure, Mary. "American Indian Language Revival" (radio broadcast). Washington, D.C.: *National Public Radio*, December 26, 1996.

Mosay, Archie. "Ojibwewi-gaagiigidowin" (radio interview). Reserve, Wisconsin: WOJB 88.9FM, April 10, 1996.

SUGGESTIONS FOR FURTHER READING

Olson, Kathy. "Balancing the World: Archie Mosay, Chief of the St. Croix." *Wisconsin West,* November 1992, 8–11, 26.

Treuer, Anton. "Revitalizing Ojibwe Language and Culture" (radio interview). Reserve, Wisconsin: WOJB 88.9FM, March 8, 1997.

———. *Omaa Akiing.* Princeton, New Jersey: Western Americana Press, 2000.

Woods, Amy. "Indian Spiritual Leader Archie Mosay Dies at 94." *(Minneapolis) Star Tribune,* July 31, 1996.

272

Living Our Language was designed and set in type by Will Powers at the Minnesota Historical Society Press. The typeface is Legacy Serif, designed by Ron Arnholm. This book was printed by Malloy Lithographing, Ann Arbor.